9. 06

D0564017

The
Early
Fidel

Roots of
Castro's
Communism

The
Early
Fidel

Roots of Castro's Communism

by

LIONEL MARTIN

Lyle Stuart Inc.   Secaucus, N. J.

Library of Congress Cataloging in Publication Data
Martin, Lionel.
  The early Fidel.
  Includes index.
  1. Castro, Fidel, 1927-   2. Heads of
state—Cuba—Biography. I. Title.
F1788.22.C3M27   972.91′064′0924[B]   77-12245
ISBN 0-8184-0254-7

To Jean, Julie and Curtis

Contents

Introduction

During the last sixteen years, I've trekked along behind
Fidel Castro on visits to farms, schools, and the mountain
locales of his guerrilla exploits. I watched him as he inter-
rogated the prisoners after the Bay of Pigs invasion, and
I sat in a small television studio–theater as he painfully told
the Cuban people of Che's death in Bolivia. I've seen and
listened to him in hotel lobbies, at diplomatic receptions,
at the inaugurations of new towns, and before the multitude in Revolution Square. I've stood on the edge of the
tarmac at José Martí airport dozens of times as Fidel welcomed important world leaders. I've participated in I don't
know how many impromptu news conferences with him.
I've written about him for newspapers and fed voice reports
about him to ABC and CBC.

For more than a decade and a half, I've talked about the
Revolution and Fidel with dozens of journalists, scholars,
technicians, and tourists. One question inevitably arises—
"When did Fidel Castro become a socialist, a Marxist-Leninist, a Communist?" That is what my book is about.

Early one morning, a month after my arrival in Cuba,
the pounding of antiaircraft guns and several distant bomb
blasts startled me awake. I rushed out into the ninth-story

corridor of Hotel ICAP.[1] Its louvered-glass windows, facing south, gave a panoramic view of Havana.

In the sky several miles away, two airplanes were circling. From the ground came the rapid fire of defense batteries. Suddenly, one of the planes veered sideways, like a seagull floating on an air current, and headed down for a run on its target. As it pulled its nose up, rising and heading north, I saw a ball of fire shoot up and seconds later heard the reverberating boom of explosions. The date was April 15, 1961.

That afternoon foreign journalists were taken to the target of the Havana raid, the principal base of Cuba's tiny air force. The headquarters building was pockmarked by machine-gun bullets. Its windows had been blown out, and two gaping holes gave evidence of direct rocket hits.

In one office was a large pool of blood—that of a young militiaman mortally wounded in the attack.[2] Before he died, he had written a single word on the cream-colored door with his own blood—"Fidel."

On the night of the bombing, thousands of people filed past the row of the bomb victim's coffins at the university. Revolutionary music blared deafeningly through loudspeakers. For an hour I sat on a stone bench near the coffins with Leo Huberman and J. P. Morray, who was a visiting professor of international relations at the University of Havana.[3] We talked about the day's events and agreed that the bombing was the prelude to an invasion.

The following day, tens of thousands of soldiers, militiapeople, and women and men, old and young, followed behind the trucks carrying the coffins in a death-cadence march to the cemetery. After the burial, Fidel Castro spoke from a jerry-built wooden platform in front of Colon Cemetery's ornate entrance.

Fidel's speech was as angry as the sun was hot that day.

He recalled how the counterrevolution had set fire to the sugar-cane fields, had blown up the French munition ship *Coubre* in Havana Harbor, and had now bombed three Cuban airfields. The people shouted for vengeance over and over again: "Paredón . . . paredón . . . paredón!" (To the wall!)

Fidel was defiant: "What the imperialists cannot pardon us for is the dignity, heroism, revolutionary ideology, and spirit of sacrifice of the people of Cuba. They cannot forgive us for making a socialist revolution in the very nostrils of the United States."

". . . A socialist revolution." For the first time since Batista's panicky flight two years before, the word *socialist* was officially used to describe the Cuban Revolution.

•

Two days later came the Bay of Pigs invasion and, seventy-two hours after that, victory for Fidel Castro's revolutionary forces. While mopping-up operations were still in progress I was taken on a tour of the fighting front with other foreign newspeople.

Our first stop was Jaguey Grande, a town near the battle area. We were led to the small, rustic funeral parlor where many of the war dead had been taken. Bodies lay on tables and on the floor. Blood covered the cement like grease on a garage floor. Boots and blood-stained clothing were piled in a heap. Flies swarmed over the bodies, and the fetid stink of death hung heavy. In an adjoining room, a man was cutting boards on a circular saw.

On leaving, we had to step around the body of a young black militiaman lying on a stretcher. One of our guides paused to look down at the dead man and said earnestly, "Another *compañero* who died for our socialist revolution." A week before, he would not have used the word *socialist*.

We went on to what had been the beachheads of the invasion, Playa Larga and Playa Giron. We passed the debris of war, a burned-out truck, a shot-up tank, an artillery piece out of action. There was occasional gunfire. Along the way some veterans of the three-day war saluted as we went by—a new salute for Cuban revolutionaries, the raised, clenched fist.

The revolution had taken on a new hue, *red*. Red neckerchieves, red bandannas, red flags became as plentiful as the hibiscus. Statuettes of Lenin and Soviet-star pins with hammer and sickle miraculously appeared on the street stands in downtown Havana. Posters and banners proclaimed: "Viva la primera republica socialista de América." The *Internacional* shot up to number one on the Cuban hit parade. People sang it at public meetings, with interlocked arms and swaying bodies. It was even played, five times or more, at the nightly dances of the Cristina Naranjo social club near my hotel.

A titillating little ditty caught on and was being chanted all over town and at the most unexpected moments:

> *Somos socialistas,*
> *P'alante, P'alante,*
> *Al que no le guste*
> *Que tome purgante.*

> We are socialists,
> Forward, Forward,
> And whoever doesn't like it
> Can take a laxative.

•

On May 1, Fidel Castro again spoke to the nation, this time in front of a million people gathered in Havana's Revolution Square. His speech was preceded by a ten-hour parade, a true test of revolutionary fortitude for the marchers and the Cubans on the reviewing stand. It seemed as if most of Cuba marched by that day—the men's and women's militia; units of the revolutionary army, tiny navy, and tinier air force; workers; farmers; students; professionals, and tens of thousands of literacy-campaign volunteers with Chinese-made "Coleman" lanterns in their hands and aluminum cups hanging from their shoulder straps.

Night fell, and the powerful floodlights were turned on. Fidel began his speech. "I'm going to be brief," he announced, and went on to speak for more than three hours!

Around midnight, with Fidel's voice booming over the loudspeakers as vibrant as ever, I left my privileged seat in the reviewing stand to take a stroll around the square. The surrealistic effect of the scene was heightened by the varying intensity of light in different parts of the square. Most of the public were now sitting down or stretched out on the black asphalt, exhausted physically and emotionally by the long day's events. The majority, it seemed, had their eyes closed or stared ahead somnolently. But for the voice of Fidel and its echo, absolute silence reigned.

The ambience was that of delicate calm, like the magic quietude one experiences between early twilight and dusk in the countryside. One felt, in the ethereal magic of the moment, that there was absolute communion between Fidel and the people. I remember wondering, was this Rousseau's idea of *volonté générale?* Inexplicably, a line of Yeats flitted through my mind: "And knitted mesh to mesh, we grow immortal."

•

Not long after May Day, Raúl Castro, Fidel's younger brother, said that when Fidel proclaimed the socialist character of the Revolution, "he didn't do any more than give a name to a child already born." [4] A few months later, Osvaldo Dorticós, the able president of Cuba, repeated the same idea with more detail:

> We nationalized the principal industries; We nationalized the banks; we established a state monopoly over foreign commerce. That is to say, we socialized the main part of our industrial economy and overseas trade. The people applauded those transformations of our economy.
>
> And one fine day, they discovered that what they were applauding . . . was a socialist revolution. [5]

The French philosopher Jean Paul Sartre rightfully noted months before the Bay of Pigs invasion "that the originality of this Revolution consists precisely in doing what needs to be done without attempting to define it by means of a previous ideology." [6] Huberman and Sweezy, basing their premise on "the objective characteristics of the social order which was emerging," had already concluded that "the new Cuba is a socialist Cuba." [7]

Cold warriors, too, picked up strange vibrations on their political seismographs. Already in 1959, when revolutionary leaders parried anti-Communists' attacks by insisting that the Revolution was "as green as the palms," right wingers would comment wryly, "Yes, like a watermelon—green outside and red inside."

With each new revolutionary law, the accusations of Communism by a small minority became shriller. But the vast majority of the Cuban people were "Fidelistas."

In October 1960, when Fidel announced the nationalization of foreign-owned industry in Cuba, a new song, with profound ideological implications, caught the people's fancy. The song was "Cuba, Sí; *Yanqui*, No." One of its stanzas went:

Si las cosas de Fidel
Son cosas de comunistas,
Que me ponga en la lista;
Estoy de acuerdo con él.

If the things of Fidel
Are communist things,
Then put me on the list;
I'm in agreement with him.

The song's popularity heralded changing ideas. It was the first self-conscious expression of a people crossing forbidden ideological frontiers. Their guide, Fidel, however, moved with surprising sureness of foot. For him, at least, it seemed that the territory beyond the new frontier was not *terra incognita*.

Fidel Castro has said over and over again that by the time he left the university (nine years before the victory of the Cuban Revolution and twelve years before he announced that Cuba would strike out on the socialist road), he was already a convinced Marxist-Leninist, already dreaming of a socialist Cuba. He said this in a speech in December 1961. He said the same to Lee Lockwood in the mid-sixties, and he repeated it to me, with additional facts, on several occasions in 1974 and 1975.

Yet Fidel's version of his own ideological development is met with across-the-board skepticism by many. These doubters scoff at Castro's version, while others benignly admit to his precocious revolutionary vocation but are convinced that he did not *consciously* guide the Cuban revolutionary process towards a Jacobinic overthrow of the capitalist system and an alliance with the socialist camp.

The skeptics seem to have strong arguments in their favor. The strongest is that there is no evidence generally available that before 1961 Castro publicly embraced Marxist-Leninist doctrine. On the other hand, there is an important body of evidence showing that Castro was a radical, but in the bourgeois-democratic tradition of populism. Skeptics also point out that Castro himself, on a few occasions before and after the Cuban Revolution, made declarations that seemingly disassociated him from Communism. His contention that he was a precocious Marxist-Leninist was retrospective, affirmed only after the Revolution opted for the socialist road, and is therefore suspect.

To assess Fidel's ideological development prior to the Revolution presents a writer with perplexing problems, in light of this apparent contradiction. Where, then, were we to find the entrance into the labyrinth of Castro's thinking during his formative period as a revolutionary?

One obvious point of attack was Castro's associations with Marxist ideas and with those who subscribed to them. On this front, even the most serious studies of Castro show a distressing dearth of data. In my own study, I have ferreted out new facts about Castro's relationships with Marxists dating back to his university years—facts both surprising and portentous.

These revelations undoubtedly shed new light on Castro's growth as a socialist. If they have substance, the skeptical attitude toward Castro's explanation of his own development will have to be rectified.

Information on Castro's contacts with Marxism and Marxists is hard to come by, a mitigating circumstance for writers who have ignored or underestimated this line of inquiry. However, Castro's pre-Revolution speeches, letters, manifestos, and articles have been generally accessible, so the superficiality with which they have been treated is inexplicable. Writers have learned to scrutinize every affirmation and inference of Plato, Hobbes, or young Marx. Why have they skipped so facilely over Castro's earlier works, quoting him here and there but seldom analyzing his arguments and thinking processes? The reason would seem to lie in their *a priori* refusal to accept Castro's assertion that he was Marxist-Leninist when he composed these letters or manifestos. I found that analysis of these materials was highly rewarding, that behind the reformist appearance lurked a revolutionary essence.

I.

University
Days

I was the Don Quixote of the university, always under the guns and bullets. What I suffered at the university has more merit than the Sierra Maestra.

Fidel Castro, Havana, January 13, 1959.

Cited in *Diario de la Marina* the following day.

1.

Rough School for Beginners

Alfredo Guevara, who became the founder of Cuba's revolutionary film industry, entered the University of Havana in September 1945. He was already a veteran of high school politics, an active member of the National Anti-Fascist Front, and a convinced communist. At the university he lost no time sizing up the political situation. Who were the potential allies and enemies? One of his fellow freshmen, Fidel Castro, commanded his attention from the start.

Castro was tall and good-looking, athletic and articulate. He was from a wealthy landowning family, and he was a graduate of Havana's exclusive Belén parochial school, where he had been a star athlete. He almost always wore a suit, adding, in Guevara's eyes, to his patrician appearance.

Guevara described to me how he sized up Fidel Castro:

> I was in a panic. Here was this Castro dressed up fit to kill in his black party suit, handsome, self-assured, aggressive, and obviously a leader. He had come out of Belén parochial school, and I saw him as a political threat. Here was the specter of clericalism threatening the campus, and I believed that Castro would be its instrument.[1]

21 ·

Castro seemed to have all the necessary qualities that make an Establishment politician on campus—wealth, physical presence, a private-school education under the Jesuits, a quick mind, and a strong personality. But he was neither the patrician nor the conservative that Guevara imagined.

Guevara did not know that Fidel Castro's upbringing had not followed the typical course of a member of his social class. He was unaware that Fidel had spent his first dozen years on a farm in rural Oriente, Cuba's easternmost province, a region of large plantations, poor farmers, and poorer laborers.

Fidel's father, Angel Castro, had come from Spain before the turn of the century. By the time Fidel was growing up, Angel had become the owner of a large cattle and sugar farm near Nipe Bay, an area studded with some of Cuba's biggest sugar mills. The elder Castro was a practical man with little formal education who spent his days managing the farm. Fidel's mother, Angel's second wife, had come from a poor Cuban family. She devoted her days to household chores.

Fidel once observed that his formative years would have been different if his father had been a second-generation landowner.[2] In that case, the family would have lived in a wealthy section of some large city, perhaps even Havana, and Fidel would not have been that university freshman so profoundly aware of Cuba's social predicaments. As it was, Fidel and his brother Ramón were brought up as country boys.

Fidel's playmates were the children of the poor families of the area. He attended the local primary school with them, an experience he recounted with singular poignancy years later in a letter from prison.

> My classmates, sons of humble peasants, generally came to school barefoot and miserably clad. They

were very poor. They learned their ABCs very badly
and soon dropped out of school, though they were
endowed with more than enough intelligence. They
then foundered in a bottomless, hopeless sea of
ignorance and penury without one of them ever
escaping the shipwreck. Today, their children will
follow in their footsteps, crushed under the burden of
social fatalism.[3]

Fidel was separated from his schoolmates when his father
sent him off to parochial school in the city, but he never
forgot them. His experiences with them undoubtedly helped
to sensitize him to injustice and played an important role
in shaping his political outlook. It also gave him a rapport
with the rural folk, a profound understanding of the *guajiro*
mentality,[4] so decisive during his guerrilla war in Oriente
province. Some of these schoolmates and many like them
joined his rebel army. After the victory their children were
given new opportunities for education and self-development.
The burden of social fatalism had been lifted.

According to his brother Ramón, when Fidel was sent
from public school in Marcané to a Jesuit school, the birthdate on his records was pushed back one year, to 1926, to
make him eligible for enrollment. The question of Castro's
year of birth has led to confusion on the part of biographers.[5]

Fidel's religious development was complex. A Chilean
priest once asked him when he had experienced his "religous
crisis." He answered, "The fact is that I didn't have a crisis;
my religious education was superficial. . . ." In answer to
the question of another priest he replied, "A religious sense?
I didn't have even ten percent." [6]

Despite his lack of piety, Castro's rural experiences made
him susceptible to certain elements of Christianity. Although
rejecting supernatural content, he found it easy to accept
the social essense of primitive Christianity—its sense of

justice and its identity with the humble and disinherited. His religious training, Castro affirmed many years later, instilled in him "ethical imperatives" through whose prism he evaluated the world around him.[7]

•

A few weeks after the 1945 university term began, the Federation of University Students (FEU) held its elections. Baudilio Castellanos, a friend of Fidel's, ran for student-body president of the law school.[8] He urged Fidel to run for class representative. Mario García Ichaústegui, another friend of Castellanos, ran for vice-president.[9] All three were independents free of any ties to the powerful machine backed by off-campus forces interested in tightening their hold on the FEU. Their election was, in effect, a victory for an independent student government. All three later became part of a vociferous group of anti-Establishment students that carried on vigorous campaigns against corruption, U.S. influence in Cuba, and higher bus fares.

Fidel soon discovered that the campus was very much part and parcel of life around it, despite its much-vaunted tradition of autonomy. Governmental corruption, the rule rather than the exception in Cuba, seeped like an overflowing cesspool into the university. The unholy trinity of politicians, cops, and gangsters operating in symbiotic fraternity did not stop at the wide Escalinata steps or the stone walls that divided the university from the rest of the city. Extortion, payoffs, and sinecures all found expression on campus— the selling of diplomas, payroll padding, plunder of educational funds, and embezzlement.

Atop the heap sat the president of Cuba, Ramón Grau San Martín. Cubans who believed in his promises and voted for him in 1944 expected a reform government. Instead, they got graft and corruption. Grau gave out sinecures and padded the payrolls with the magnanimity of an emperor and allowed his ministers to do the same. Funds destined for public works illegally found their way into private pockets. Vast sums of money kicked back by the gambling, prostitution and drug-running enterprises were divvied up among high government and police officials and their underlings.

Grau diabolically distributed leading police posts around the capital to rival racketeering factions. The chiefs of the secret police, Havana police, the National Police Academy, and other "law-enforcement agencies" staked out their own domains and often came into conflict over the division of the spoils.[10]

Government subsidies through payroll padding were handed out to the gangs of gunmen (*pistoleros*) that abounded in Havana. These *pistoleros* liked to think of themselves as lineal descendents of the revolutionary-action groups that arose after the fall of the Machado dictatorship in the early thirties and during the bloody repression of the incipient revolutionary movement. However, by the end of the thirties, these original groups had virtually ceased to exist. Following the election of Grau to the presidency in 1944, the new "action groups" were organized to wreak vengeance on those who had repressed the post-Machado revolutionary movement, especially the followers of Fulgencio Batista.[11]

The action groups gave themselves revolutionary-sounding names such as Insurrectional Revolutionary Movement (UIR) and Socialist Revolutionary Movement (MSR), but there was nothing revolutionary about them. It wasn't long before Grau and other politicians had them on their payroll as hired guns. For the average Cuban they were simply *pistoleros*.

Grau created an equilibrium of mutual threat and slaughter upon which his regime neatly perched. During his four-year administration, about 120 gangland-style assassinations took place in Havana.[12]

This was the atmosphere when Fidel Castro entered college. By the end of his freshman year, Castro was conscious of the general depravity of Cuban political life. He had discovered that powerful interest groups operating through government controlled the destiny of the nation. He came to hate Ramón Grau San Martín as the personification of the evil that corrupted the nation. He was on his way to becoming a rebel.

•

It was natural that Fidel would be attracted by the flamboyant Eduardo Chibás, a middle-aged congressman of Grau's own Authentic party, was Cuba's number-one muckraker. Each of his widely listened-to radio programs brought new disclosures of graft and corruption in high places. Often imprudent, always impetuous, he lashed out without seeming to care where the chips fell. More and more, he had begun to level his verbal blasts at Grau himself. As he became more polemical, his notoriety grew, and so did the size of his bodyguard.[13]

Shortly after Fidel returned to the university for his sophomore year, Rubén de León, an Authentic-party congressman, made a vitriolic radio attack on Chibás in response to Chibás's attacks on the Grau administration. A few days later, when de León began to speak at an outdoor rally, Fidel Castro was among the students who hooted him off the stage.[14] As far as I know, this marked Fidel's debut as a political activist.

Fidel had already begun to make his mark as a campus leader. For that reason the powerful machine that had controlled university politics would have preferred him as an ally, rather than an enemy. Manolo Castro (no relation), the president of the Federation of University Students (FEU), made an attempt to co-opt him. Manolo had slowly been drawn into the web of corrupt practices and, as a reward for services rendered, had been offered the post of National Sports Director.[15] He encouraged rumors that Fidel might be his hand-picked successor. It was a baited hook. Fidel's acquiescence would have required him to revamp his opposition politics. His "ethical imperatives," however, stood in the way of a deal. It became apparent that Fidel Castro could not be bought.[16] In a defiant mood, he affixed his signature to a militantly worded petition that declared, "We pledge to fight against the reelection of Grau 'though the price of the struggle be our blood.'"[17]

Fidel's stubbornness brought him face to face with Mario Salabarría, the feared chief of Cuba's secret police, who in Castro's own words was "the master of the capital."[18] Salabarría, who controlled some of the most lucrative rackets in town, viewed the campus as his private domain. Fidel was beginning to become a thorn in his side. When it proved impossible to co-opt Castro, Salabarría resorted to threats. He told Castro menacingly either to tone down his opposition politics or to get off the campus for good.

Fidel has told how he went to a beach near Havana and sat on the sand mulling over Salabarría's ultimatum. Salabarría and his *pistoleros* did not play games. If Castro defied the ultimatum, his life would be in constant danger. He made his decision. "I decided to go back, and I went back."[19]

It is said, but not by Castro, that when he returned to the campus, he was armed. This would not be surprising considering the dangers that stalked anyone militantly involved in campus politics.

His enemies have accused Castro of having been a member of one of the *pistolero* groups, the Unión Insurreccional Revolucionaria (UIR). As far as I have been able to discover, he did have certain contacts with the UIR that could easily be misconstrued. These contacts were based on the UIR's deadly enmity with Mario Salabarría and with the *pistolero* group Movimiento Socialista Revolucionario (MSR), which had close connections with Salabarría. The MSR was lead by Rolando Masferrer, an ex-Communist who was already on the way to becoming Fidel's mortal enemy.[20]

Common hatred for Salabarría and Masferrer was the main link between Fidel and the UIR.[21] Fidel did not join the UIR, however, or benefit from the sinecures and subsidies its members received from the Grau machine. Nor did he follow its political orientation. In fact, one former leader of the UIR, now in exile, complains that Fidel Castro "used us for his own political battles within the university," a clear reference to Castro's independent line.[22]

•

In answer to a question I once put to him about the development of his thought, Fidel replied that "even before I had contact with socialist literature, I studied political economy and came to some definite personal conclusions— I became something akin to a utopian socialist." This was after he had read an "intolerably boring" political-economy textbook that led him to question the rationality of the capitalist system.

The book had spoken about the crisis of overproduction and unemployment as "inexorable and immutable laws of society," a conception Fidel intuitively rejected. He could not understand why in England—an example given in the book—unemployed workers froze, although there was an abundance of coal in the ground. His questioning was derived, he has suggested, from a notion of "justice and injustice and a certain spirit of rebelliousness against oppression." [23]

This idealism led him to greet enthusiastically Eduardo Chibás's announcement that he was going to form a new political party. The call, made public on May 11, 1947, listed the party's watchwords: "nationalism, anti-imperialism, socialism, economic independence, political liberty, and social justice." [24] A few days later, Fidel attended the founding assembly of the party, the Party of the Cuban People (Orthodox).[25] He remained affiliated to the Orthodox party for eight years, and it was the only political party to which he belonged prior to the revolutionary victory.

After Manolo Castro left the university to take his new job as National Director of Sports, the anticorruption movement on campus developed greater intensity. The dynamic movement focused its main activities on convening a student constitutional assembly aimed at reorganizing the FEU along more democratic and progressive lines. Fidel devoted a great deal of his energy organizing the assembly, which was held after final exams, in mid-July 1947. He was among those nominated to be secretary of the assembly, but Alfredo Guevara won the coveted position with the backing of the well-organized Young Communists, together with some tactical allies.[26] Guevara, of course, no longer viewed Fidel as the instrument of clericalism, and at the assembly they found themselves in agreement on most important matters. They left the assembly as personal and political friends.[27]

At the inaugural meeting Fidel made a speech as a representative of the law-school student body. In my research in Havana, I discovered a published portion of that speech— the earliest Castro speech that exists in verbatim form.[28] It has historical importance because it offers us an insight into the thinking of Fidel Castro—who had not yet turned twenty-one, according to his official records.

Castro began his speech by invoking the names of two heroes of progressive university students. One was Julio Antonio Mella, the handsome founder of the FEU in 1923 and a founder of the Cuban Communist party in 1925. Mella was assassinated on a Mexico City street in 1929 at the age of twenty-seven.[29] The other was Ramiro Valdés Daussa, a politically progressive professor of architecture who had been assassinated in 1941 during a campaign to force the delinquent El Bonche off the campus.[30]

Fidel declared:

> This constitutional assembly has been the greatest aspiration of the students since 1923, when it was suggested by Mella, and it has continued to be so throughout the years of struggle that had their culmination in the death of Ramiro Valdés Daussa.
>
> Now this fervent aspiration has been crystallized. It presents us with the opportunity of writing a brilliant page in the history of the university. This assembly must not be another cause for disillusionment.
>
> We must stop the university from being a place where ideas are handled as if they were merchandise, where ideals are manipulated and mocked.
>
> Optimism must be infused into the student environment; apathy must be ended. We cannot allow ourselves to become the victims of pessimism because of the two false leaders of recent years and the groups who use the reason of force and not the force of reason, in a shameful atmosphere of collective cowardice.[31]

Castro urged the students to "unmask the merchants who profit by the blood of martyrs" and stigmatized the Grau administration as "a tyranny that hovers over the country."

In this first Castro speech available to us, certain essentials of his personality and thinking are as discernible as the arches, loops, and whorls of a fingerprint. His courage and inner conviction are evident. He challenges the power elite, the *pistoleros,* and the government, who "use the reason of force." Young Castro blasts indifference and timidity and demands optimism and audacity. Already some of the inspiration and authority of the latter-day Castro is present. In short, Fidel begins to display his qualities of leadership.

•

While the constitutional assembly was going on, exciting news whipped through the campus—an invasion of the Dominican Republic was being planned in Havana. A group of Dominican exiles and Cubans had a scheme to bring down the government of dictator Rafael Leonidas Trujillo, and recruits were being sought. The plan was supposed to be a secret, but everyone in Havana, including, of course, the embassies, knew about it.[32]

It was an enterprise calculated to attract young action-minded idealists like those who had taken part in the assembly but could look forward, for the most part, only to a lazy and unproductive summer. Trujillo's name alone was sufficient to set the adrenalin flowing in any Latin American democrat. Since 1930, the megalomaniacal and theatrical Trujillo had ruled Cuba's Caribbean sister with an iron hand that mercilessly crushed opponents on the island and reached out to murder exiled Dominican democrats beyond its borders. The archetypal Latin American despot, he personally enriched himself while allowing the rape of his country by foreign—primarily U.S.—economic interests.[33]

The idea of striking a blow for freedom with gun in hand was alluring to Fidel. A pent-up fury had been slowly building up within him, borne of frustration with the corruption of traditional politics and the blunted spirit of those around him, "the shameful atmosphere of collective cowardice." Then, too, he was a *martiano,* an intellectual follower like many young Cuban idealists, of José Martí, who had taught that "our America," meaning Latin America, was indivisible and had to struggle against "the other America," that is, the United States.[34] Fidel had the *need* to express his heady passions in some heroic and preferably insurgent form like a Latin American war for liberation. He was drawn like a moth toward light, although he was conscious that participation entailed greater danger for him than for other recruits.

The Cuban backers of the venture were the same calculating and corrupt elements whom Castro had come to despise and who, in turn, recognized him as an enemy. The Minister of Education, Alemán, whom Castro had publicly attacked for misuse of state funds, helped to channel money into the invasion project. The chief of the armed forces, General Genovevo Pérez Dámera, gave his blessings to the undertaking. Rolando Masferrer was given a key role in the military aspects of the invasion, while his MSR *pistoleros* and Salabarría's secret-service gunmen were to participate as soldiers. Castro knew that many of them would gladly murder him, and to minimize his risks, he decided to separate himself as far as possible from the men of Masferrer and Salabarría by joining the Dominican exile contingent.

More than one thousand men, an amalgam of idealists, delinquents, and adventurers, were recruited for the invasion. It had been estimated that the Cuban government underwrote the plan with one million dollars.[35] Altruism can be ruled out as a motivation for government backing. General Pérez Dámera possibly saw in the expedition an opportunity to enhance the power of the army. It has been said that Alemán might have seen it as a means of channeling money into his own pocket. Others saw the spoils of war as their reward.

At the end of the July, after superficial military training in Oriente, not far from his family home, Fidel was sent to the tiny, virtually barren Key Confite off the Cuban north coast, the staging area for the expedition. The more than a thousand men began a period of nerve-shattering, seemingly interminable waiting—one week, two, four, five. The atmosphere was tense, and discord became rife.[36]

Alfredo Guevara, in Havana, frequently visited the "general-staff headquarters" at the Hotel Sevilla on the Prado. Bizarre Caribbean-comic-opera images are still imprinted on his mind—a Dominican leader running around the hotel in a white cork explorer's hat and a dresser drawer filled with neat stacks of American money.[37]

The planned invasion received international publicity when Trujillo accused Ernest Hemingway of being a propagandist for the undertaking.[38]

Six weeks after they arrived, the men at Key Confite received news that destroyed what little morale remained. Mario Salabarría's agents had gunned down Emilio Tro after a two-hour battle in the Havana suburb of Marianao.[39] During the street battle President Grau San Martín had refused to intervene to bring about a truce.[40] After Tro's death, the army stepped in and arrested Salabarría, who had 10 one-thousand-dollar bills in his shoe.[41]

General Pérez Dámera had ordered the Cuban navy to Key Confite to arrest the men there. He also sent troops to a farm near Havana, belonging to the minister of education, where they "discovered" an enormous cache of arms, including aerial bombs and depth charges.[42] Michael McDermott, the U.S. State Department spokesman, on hearing the news from Cuba, said he was pleased that the threat to peace had been eliminated.[43]

Fidel was among those who escaped from the key before the navy arrived. He left on a small boat, the *Fantasma*, along with many followers of Salabarría and Masferrer.

Fearing vendetta death at their hands, he slipped away from the boat on a small raft with his weapons during the night and got ashore safely. Some say that he left the sinking raft and swam ashore through shark-infested waters.

The newspaper *Información*, in a front-page editorial, asked but did not answer: "Why did the army allow the Dominican invasion plans to proceed for so long? . . . Why did it now swoop down on the operation in such a sensational way?" [44] Chibás accused President Grau of having planned to use the Dominican-invasion scheme as a rationale for suspending elections. Alfredo Guevara alleged in a speech that General Pérez Dámera had received orders from Washington to crack down on the invasion and to step up military intervention in the nation's political life.[45]

The Dominican experience had a galvanizing effect on Fidel. He came back to his junior year at the university convinced that Grau had to be removed from office by revolutionary means—exactly how this was to be done, he did not know.

2.

Under Clubs
and Bullets

"Down with Grau! . . . Down with Grau!" chanted several thousand enraged students, as they marched past the stately Presidential Palace. In the vanguard, a group of them carried a casket draped with the Cuban flag. Fidel was in the front ranks of the turbulent demonstration. One student, it was reported, glowered at an upper-story window of the palace, shook his clenched fist, and shouted, "Grau, come out and see your handiwork!" [1]

The casket carried the body of a Havana High School student who had been killed only hours before.[2] The student had been part of another demonstration, which had taken to the streets to protest a political rally for the Minister of Education, Alemán. Alemán had become the target of anti-Grau forces. He was considered one of the principal culprits in the miscarriage of the Key Confite expedition. He had been flayed for his flagrant misuse of educational funds, his sponsorship of *pistoleros,* and his generous policy of sinecures to his camp followers. Opposition parties in the senate had proposed a resolution of nonconfidence, in which they accused him of "causing harm to education and gravely affecting the civic peace of the nation." [3]

Alemán had organized the pro-Alemán "confidence rally" himself to undercut the attacks on him. It had been advertised in the newspapers, on radio, and on wall posters.

The student had been shot in cold blood by an Alemán follower before the "confidence rally" began. Alemán thoughtlessly insisted that the rally go on, and after it ended, he led his retinue of political hacks and *pistoleros* on a march to the Presidential Palace in a parody of popular acclaim. There, Grau, from a balcony, bestowed his blessings on Alemán.[4]

Later, the student marchers carrying the coffin continued their derisive shouting as they paraded from the Presidential Palace, up the streets of a crowded working-class district, toward the university, a mile away. Thousands, including children, joined the procession of rebellious students. At the Escalinata, the broad steps leading onto the campus, the marchers halted and a mass rally was quickly organized. An indignant Fidel Castro spoke to the protesters. He lashed out at the *pistoleros* and held the Cuban president personally responsible "for these tears and this pain."[5]

Rumblings continued in Havana and spread to other parts of Cuba. A nationwide forty-eight-hour student strike was declared, and indignant activists from the interior headed for Havana. Trade unions passed resolutions condemning the government. Another march on the palace took place— one of the largest of its kind Cuba had ever seen. A new slogan was chanted over and over as students and workers filed past the palace: "King Kong, que se vaya, Ramón" (King Kong, get out, Ramón). It is said the Grau watched the demonstrators surreptitiously from behind a curtain.[6]

Fidel was active throughout these tumultuous days. His improvised diatribes, wrathful, impetuous, and righteous, attracted many students—but only a minority. Most students, fearing the *pistoleros* or simply "apolitical," avoided involvement in campus politics and skirted the edges of political controversy. One woman, recalling her apolitical student stance of that time, told me how impressive and forceful Fidel was in haranguing the students. She had viewed him then as a wild-eyed agitator.

Castro was a man with a cause, and his enemies knew it. When he observed years later that "what I suffered at the university has more merit than the Sierra Maestra," [7] that is, the war against Batista, he was thinking about the dangers he confronted on campus and the fact that he survived.

In his junior year, Fidel Castro was elected vice-president of the Association of Students at the law school. He was identified on campus with a minuscule group of fervent activitists who challenged most of the political shibboleths of Cuban society. They were harsh critics of government corruption and racism, of economic inequality, and of the cold war, which had only recently begun, with its concommitant McCarthy-style red baiting. They all considered themselves "anti-imperialists" and shared a disdainful view of U.S. influence in Cuba. Fidel was a member of the FEU's Puerto Rican–independence committee.

Two major political alignments characterized the majority of members of the group. There were the Young Communists and Orthodox Youth—like Fidel Castro—the followers of Eduardo Chibás. In terms of political outlook, they had their American counterpart in young progressive groups organized on many U.S. campuses to support the presidential candidacy of Henry Wallace in 1948.

There was something anomalous about the convergence of these two currents, because Eduardo Chibás would have nothing to do with the Communists. Fidel, however, was part of the left wing of the Orthodox Youth and counted Young Communists among his friends and political partners. Among them was Alfredo Guevara, whom Fidel knew to be a Communist, although his membership in the Young Communists was supposed to be a secret. Fidel developed a close working relationship with Lionel Soto, a Young Communist who came to the university from Havana High School in 1946. He also had periodic conversations with Flavio Bravo, the national head of the Young Communists, and with Luis Más Martín, the general secretary of its Havana branch. These relationships were of a continuing nature and tended to become closer during Fidel's last years at the university.[8]

It would be illogical to think that Fidel's close association with the Communists were limited strictly to joint undertakings on and around the campus. In his daily contact with these friends, in their planning sessions and conversations, he must have absorbed something of their Marxist-Leninist view of society.[9] The very fact that he did associate and cooperate with them is definitive proof of his own fierce independence in the face of strong anti-Communism, even within the Orthodox Party.

Castro, however, does not attribute his conversion to Marxism to his having had Communist friends. He has said that Marx's and Engels's *Communist Manifesto,* published a century earlier, had an almost apocalyptic influence on his thinking. "For me it was a revelation. . . . It was so persuasive that I was absolutely amazed. I was converted to those ideas." [10]

Years later Castro recalled having been impressed by Marx's affirmation that 10 percent of capitalist society lives on the backs of the other 90 percent.[11] He could relate this to his own experience and the massive poverty he saw next to the sumptuous living of the few. There was a nine-month "dead season" between harvests, with 600,000 unemployed from a work force of 1.5 million. There was the dollar or two a day in wages for ten hours of inhuman work in the cane fields and an income that seldom surpassed five hundred dollars a year. He had seen how the poor families had existed on cornmeal and *guarapo,* the juice of sugar cane, for months on end. His readings on Cuba had given him an even deeper understanding. He knew from statistics that only one-quarter of those who worked the land in Cuba owned it. The rest were sharecroppers, cash renters, and agricultural workers. Less than 0.1 percent of Cuban landowners owned 20 percent of the land and 8 percent of them owned 70 percent. On the bottom rung, 70 percent of the landowning farmers possessed only 11 percent of the land.[12]

Marx had also hit a responsive chord in his mind when he declared that capitalism "left remaining no other nexus between man and man than naked self-interest, than callous 'cash payment.' It has drowned the most heavenly ecstasies of religious fervor, of chivalrous enthusiasm, of philistine sentimentalism, in the icy water of egotistical calculation." [13]

The great revelation, however, was Castro's discovery of the Marxist tenet that history has its laws of development, that the motive force of that history is the class struggle, and that socialism is the inevitable outcome of that struggle. He found in the proselytizing pamphlet the fallacies of his own utopian socialism, which viewed progress as the result of a rational struggle between good and evil, rather than a struggle between social classes.

There is little doubt that Fidel Castro, the son of a wealthy landowner, welcomed the *Manifesto*'s observation that a small section of the ruling class "cuts itself adrift and joins the revolutionary class." Castro proved to be a prime example of it.[14]

•

Fidel spotted Alfredo Guevara from the street and burst into the cafeteria. Within seconds he was pouring out the details of a wild scheme. The first step was to go to Manzanillo, in Oriente province, and bring back the Bell of La Demajagua, the historical bell whose tolling had signaled the beginning of Cuba's war for independence against Spain in 1868. It was like planning to move the Liberty Bell from Philadelphia to Chicago. Guevara's astonishment became even more pronounced as Fidel expounded his plan.

The eyes of the nation would be on the venerable bell. When it arrived in Havana, a mass meeting would be called. Tens of thousands would attend, and the bell would be rung, just as it had eighty years before. As the sound reverberated through the narrow streets of the capital, the people would be called on to march to the Presidential Palace, and Ramón Grau San Martín would be asked to step down from the presidency.[15]

The idea of bringing the bell to Havana had been proposed by the government a few weeks before. Grau had wanted to use it as the centerpiece for the official celebration of October 10, the anniversary of the beginning of Cuba's war against Spain. The city council of Manzanillo had angrily turned down the loan request and almost declared Grau's emissary *persona non grata*.[16]

Fidel was convinced he could succeed where the *políticos* had failed. Manzanillo was a radical working-class city and would welcome the opportunity to embarrass Grau.

With the backing of the FEU, Fidel and his Communist friend Lionel Soto were off to Manzanillo, the city known for sugar, shoemaking, fishing, and the first Communist mayor ever elected in Cuba.[17] Soto and Fidel persuasively argued their case. Before long the two were back on the train, this time heading west, with the bell and two chaperons for it from Manzanillo.[18]

Havanans knew the bell was coming before the train pulled into the station on November 3, 1947. Student representatives were waiting there with a big convertible. Fidel,

Soto and the three-hundred-pound bell wended their way to the university in a triumphant tour that took two and a half hours for a normal twenty-minute ride. Once on campus, it was carried to the rector's office, where university police were assigned to guard it.[19]

While the bell sat in the rector's office for the next few days, it became the center of a well-publicized controversy. Grau followers attacked its use for partisan political purposes. The anti-Grau camp differed sharply on how the bell should be used. A meeting on campus argued through the night to decide what kind of rally should be held.

While the meeting was going on, about one hundred *pistoleros* showed up and stood around menacingly. They were followers of Masferrer and Salabarría, now in prison. Word went around that "somebody would get hurt" if the students approved the plan for a militantly anti-Grau meeting. Later, the press reported that Fidel Castro was the leader of "the most violently antigovernment position—that which wanted to call for Grau's resignation to the ringing of the bell." [20]

This was another demonstration of Fidel's death-defying attitude. He had already earned the enmity of Salabarría and Masferrer. By leading the fight to organize a movement to force Grau's resignation, he added the UIR to his list of antagonists. The UIR came out with a public attack on Fidel's proposals. "We believe that the call to force the resignation of President Grau will provoke anarchy. . . ." Its statement appealed for an all-out struggle against the "intrigues of Creole Stalinism," [21] a thrust aimed at Fidel and his left-wing allies.

The morning of the rally, when the doors of the rector's office were opened, it was discovered that the bell had disappeared. The campus policemen denied any knowledge of the theft.

Fidel showed up on campus at midmorning, not long

after news of the bell's disappearance had spread like a sugar-cane fire through the campus. Within minutes he was haranguing a crowd of students who had gathered around him. He angrily berated Grau, the politicians, the *pistoleros,* and the police. When he had whipped his listeners up to fever pitch, he pushed through the circle that enclosed him and shouted, "The rats stay here. We're going to report the theft." [22] He led a sizable group of irate students off the campus and down the streets to the nearest police station. The throng barged its way into the station aggressively, with Fidel leading the way.

Major Manuel Cruz listened passively to the torrent of accustations Fidel unleashed. Castro told how *pistoleros* had threatened students the evening before, and then he boldly named Rolando Masferrer, Manolo Castro, Eufemio Fernández, and the followers of Mario Salabarría as the men behind the threats and the conspiracy to sabotage the rally. On leaving the station, Fidel repeated the same charges to newsmen. [23]

The bell could not have been carried from the rector's office without the collusion of the campus police. It was no secret that most of the force had been appointed during Manolo Castro's reign as czar of the campus, and many were still loyal to him. The rector sought to mollify the agitated students by suspending the guards who had been on duty when the bell disappeared.

When the rally began that night, the bell's whereabouts was still a mystery. Fidel Castro was one of the speakers, and his speech contains significant clues to his political acumen almost six years before the attack on the Moncada Barracks. [24]

Castro zeroed in on President Grau:

> Wasn't it that professor [Grau] who spoke of national
> dignity, of the abandoned peasant, of hungry

children? Wasn't it he who spoke of the recovery of national dignity, of crystal-pure honesty, and who inspired the students to the point of sacrifice and even death?

Today all that has crumbled, and the coming years presage misery. People have lost faith, but woe to those who have killed that faith when the people become angry.

We, for whom the deception was most terrible, ought to proclaim that the youth will never say, 'We surrender.' Those who think that the present generation of students are not capable of emulating those of past generations are wrong. . . .

Grau is estranged from the people of Cuba because he has deceived them, just as he has deceived the university students and just as he has deceived all those who honestly believe the pronouncements he made before becoming president of the republic.

He promised land reform to the peasants, schools for the children who didn't have them, advanced social legislation for the workers and the millionth to the teacher.[25] None of these pledges has been fulfilled.

The merchant marine still doesn't exist, the children without schools are still without them, civilian power has not been rescued, the national bank has not been established,[26] the law for the establishment of a fiscal-overseer court has been vetoed.[27] This is not what Grau promised.

The revolution of which he spoke when he was a candidate has been betrayed. Nationalism has received a severe blow. The peasants are still without land and the teachers without their millionth. The riches of the country are in foreign hands. That is the nationalism of Grau.

Since the government of President Grau assumed power, an outlay of some 256 million pesos has been voted. Public works have been alloted 112 million

pesos; defense, 116; public health, 14! It is not hard
to see why Cuba is so backward in matters of public
health. . . .

In 1940 Grau noted that the cost of living had
skyrocketed 300 percent and declared that the higher
echelons were responsible for the corruption and the
encouragement of the black market. The situation
today is very much the same; it is now Grau who
protects the black market.[28]

Fidel spoke about the tensions that had cropped up between the army (Camp Colombia) and the executive
branch (Presidential Palace).

There are differences between Colombia and the
Palace. The Palace does harm to Colombia, and Columbia does harm to the Palace. But in reality the
only ones harmed are the people of Cuba, harmed
by both the Palace and Colombia.

Fidel spoke of the growing power of the military and the
threat of militarism.

Young Castro made a survey of the men around Grau,
characterizing them as "robbers of the public coffers." He
referred to the murder of Emilio Tro and singled out Salabarría for condemnation. He claimed that Grau was fully
aware of the criminal activities of Salabarría. He blamed
Salabarría for the death of law student Hugo Dupotey and
for the disappearance of Havana High student Andrés
Noroña. He charged him with stealing university funds,
"the most perverse of his crimes," since the university offered refuge to revolutionaries when they were persecuted
and therefore ought to be inviolate.

In spite of Salabarría's previous history, Dr. Grau
kept him in his high office and gave him his back-

ing. What a sad state of affairs for the citizens to have an archcriminal as the defender of order and their liberties.

Castro audaciously accused the president, Fabio Ruíz; the Havana police chief; and Cossío del Pino, the Minister of Interior, of having tried to seize the filmed evidence of the massacre during which Emiliio Tro died.[29] He said that this had all "culminated in friction with the army and signaled the abandonment of the great cause of Santo Domingo."

Castro said that the students should be militant and that their attitude

> should be that of independent opposition because we cannot allow ourselves to be confused with the followers of Machado or Batista. . . .
>
> With regards to the university, we must seek the greatest possible link between students and professors through reform of the *alma mater*. With regards to the national scene, we must strive to bring about cooperation among different social groupings, creating the fighting unity of the people, so that they can win their true independence, their economic liberation, and their political freedom. The definitive emancipation of our nation is the fundamental aim of the unversity.

The speech is unquestionable proof of Fidel Castro's growing maturity as a political thinker. It is a coherent attack on the *status quo* from a left point of view. It is instructive to compare Castro's words of that night with those of Justo Fuentes, a leader of the FEU and member of the UIR. Fuentes also criticized Grau but, in keeping with the general anti-Communist atmosphere of the times, found it necessary to conjure up the specter of the "red hordes." [30] It is significant that Fidel Castro avoided all such concessions to the Cuban brand of McCarthyism that had become an important element of political life on the island. This avoidance was not fortuitous. It is an important clue to Castro's growing familiarity with Marxism and with members of the Communist party.

A few days after the rally, unnamed followers of Grau handed the stolen bell over to the president through an intermediary. It was later returned to Oriente province. [31]

Through bringing the Bell of La Demajagua to Havana, Fidel had dreamed of sparking a massive movement against Grau, one that would shake the government to its foundations. From the first, however, forces infinitely more powerful than those he could muster dampened the effects of the gimmicky operation. Grau had the support of the Authentic-party machine and much of the press, as well as the intimidating weapon of the *pistoleros* and the police. Even on campus, the rebellious elements of which Fidel was a leader represented a small minority of the student community.

A smoldering anger fumed within Fidel. Politics, action-oriented politics, had become his one consuming preoccupation. He dispatched his studies with a minimum expenditure of time. His extraordinary memory and keen mind permitted him the luxury of cramming for tests and passing most of his courses with honors. He spent most of his days in new protests and reading widely, with special emphasis on the social sciences. He read Marxist literature and studied the voluminous writings of José Martí. Like other Cuban leftists, he saw no contradiction between the two. Martí's frustrated dream of a just society in Cuba, free of foreign domination, racism, and the power of monied interests, converged in Fidel's mind with the socioeconomic teachings of Marxism.

Castro's sympathetic attitude toward the working class and its honest leaders was demonstrated in his attitude toward the murder of a black Communist trade-union leader and congressman, Jesus Menéndez.[32]

Menéndez, an incorruptible labor leader, had been shot on a railroad platform near Manzanillo by an army captain, Casillas Lumpuy. Many Cubans alleged that it had been a political assassination ordered in cold blood by the army chief of staff, General Pérez Dámera and that the murder was in direct reprisal for the sugar workers' strike that Menéndez had called just as the harvest was getting under way. In a more profound sense, it was a continuation of the attack launched in 1947 against Communist and progressive influence in the Cuban trade-union movement,[33] the imposition on the movement of Authentic-party labor leaders. At that time the minister of labor, Prio, had ordered the police to dislodge the legally elected trade unions from their halls and to protect the takeover of the unions by government-backed rump groups.[34] Resistance to the government move had led to the arrest of one thousand trade unionists on October 15, 1947, among them, Jesus Menéndez.[35]

The sugar workers, from whose ranks Jesus Menéndez had come, refused to accepted the imposition of the government-sponsored leaders. They continued to support Menéndez, and his prestige was unchallenged among them. He was a symbol of the struggle for the "advanced social legislation for the workers" about which Fidel had spoken during his Bell of La Demajagua speech.

Menéndez had been warned that his death warrant had been signed. The head of a military post at the Hormiguero mill in Las Villas had tipped off his followers, and the story was confirmed as he traveled from mill to mill.[36] Captain Casillas Lumpuy had been waiting on the railroad platform for him. He told Menéndez that he was under arrest, and Menéndez invoked his parilamentary immunity. A friend of Menéndez later recalled the conversation:

CAPTAIN: If I violate the Constitution, I'll assume the responsibility. But I'm taking you in, dead or alive.

MENÉNDEZ: Captain, the problem is not that of killing me. It is a simple matter of law. I am a congressman, and you cannot arrest me.[37]

Menéndez turned and began to walk away. The captain took out his .45 and shot him in the back.

On hearing of the incident, General Pérez Dámera announced, "We are very pleased with the conduct of Captain Casillas Lumpuy, who was forced to make use of his weapon. It was a correct, dignified, and manly act that serves as a stimulus to the army that in similar cases, others may act in an identical way." [38]

Tens of thousands of Cubans filed past Menéndez's bier as his body lay in state at the *Capitolio* in Havana. The funeral procession was one of the largest ever seen in Cuba. Fidel was among those at the cemetery. He listened to Blas Roca, the Communist leader who twenty-eight years later would become the president of the Cuban revolution's first National Assembly. The well-known Cuban reporter Kuchilán was standing next to Fidel. He remembers how Fidel, brimming with anger and impetuousness, turned to him and said, "What would you think if I got up on a tomb and called on the people to march on the presidential palace?" [39]

A few weeks later, Fidel got the chance to vent some of his pent-up fury. For his efforts he received a lesson in civic virtue from the business end of a policeman's nightstick. It all began as just another student protest against police brutality—this time in solidarity with brethren in Guantánamo, in Oriente province. The University of Havana activists left the traditional sanctuary of the campus and went on a rampage, during which a streetcar was virtually wrecked.

A police charge sent the students scrambling back up the long steps of the Escalinata. Major Carames, the police chief in the university district, rushed up the Escalinata with a pistol in hand, just behind the students, thus violating the sanctuary rule of campus antonomy. Carames caught one student, a cripple, and pistol whipped him as Carames's own men, with greater *sangfroid,* urged him to retreat from the campus grounds.[40] Some students had guns, and an invasion of the university might have ended in a pitched battle.

Fidel called for a peaceful demonstration for the following day. The line of the march would once again be down the Escalinata, but a high premium was to be put on the non-violent aspect of the parade. However, the terror tactics of the police had intimidated many students, and only about one hundred showed up.

Fidel and another student marched in the vanguard carrying a big Cuban flag between them. Just behind them was a row of students covering the width of the street with a banner reading, WE PROTEST THE VIOLATION OF UNIVERSITY AUTONOMY.[41] Hotter heads among the students were prepared for action in case of another police invasion of the campus. Posted in the pharmacy and social-sciences buildings flanking the Escalinata were armed students. There was even an old .50-caliber machine gun, a prize that had survived the abortive Dominican-invasion venture.[42]

The small band of marchers walked down San Lázaro Street toward Infanta, the usual route for such parades. As they approached a police barricade ahead, they sang the

Cuban national anthem—"To die for your homeland is to live. . . ."

When they were twenty yards or so from the policemen, they broke off singing and began shouting, "Out with Carames; down with Grau; murderers!" The police moved in with flailing clubs. Fidel was the first to be hit, although miraculously he escaped serious injury.[43]

The student protest brought results. The canny Grau, in a move to defuse the situation, transferred Major Carames out of the university district.[44] A year later, the same Carames, then the national police chief with the rank of colonel, would lock horns with Fidel in still another demonstration.

Before February was out, Fidel was defending himself against charges that he had taken part in the murder of Manolo Castro. Manolo, after becoming National Sports Director in the Grau regime, had been sucked more and more into the vortex of corruption. He had become inextricably linked to the government power structure. His close ties with Masferrer's MSR, with the Salabarría gunmen, and with crooked politicians had become notorious.

Manolo had received death threats and taken them seriously. The day before his murder he expressed fears to Flavio Bravo and Más Martín, the two leaders of the Communist Youth organization, whom he met casually on the street.[45] In his earliest days at the university, Manolo had maintained relations with the left-wing students. He had attended the World Youth Congress in London in 1945 with Flavio Bravo [46] and had among his advisors two Young Communists, Pedro Valdés Vivó and Manolo Corrales. But his growing ties with the corrupt regime made him part of the enemy camp.

Manolo hoped that Bravo could use his influence to remove him from the list of marked men. He was panic stricken and contrite. He had lost his way, he said. Bravo and Más Martín listened to his cry for help with sympathy. Although they viewed Manolo as a political enemy, their organziation opposed on principle the murder and violence of the *pistoleros*. However, they had no power to change the course of events.

The following day, Manolo was gunned down in front of Cine Resumen, of which he was part owner. A known UIR member was captured a few blocks away with the smell of gunpowder still sharp in the barrel of his pistol. He was the only one eventually tried for the crime.

Radio Bemba, Havana's efficient mouth-to-ear communications system, soon had it that the police were seeking Fidel Castro and several other university activists in connection with Manolo's murder. The next morning's newspapers wrote that the captured man was part of a group at the university "captained" by Fidel Castro. Two other students were mentioned, both alleged to be members of the UIR.[47] Fidel's early defensive alliance with the UIR had left its stigma on him. By this time, however, Fidel and the UIR had long parted ways. Fidel was an independent on campus, a member of Chibás's Orthodox Youth organization, and, like the Communists, an opponent of political assassinations. He was a believer, as his activities showed, in organizing movements and striking political blows against the power structure.

Although miles apart on most matters, Fidel and the UIR continued to have a common antipathy toward Rolando Masferrer, a politician and editor of the magazine *Tiempo en Cuba*. Masferrer had been a leftist in his early days, had joined the Communist party, and had fought in Spain. On his return he had worked for a time with the CP newspaper, *Hoy*, and then, over supposed doctrinal disputes, had left the party to devote the rest of his days fighting it. He swung to the other end of the spectrum, ending up as a staunch defender of the *status quo* and operating under the aegis of dictator Fulgencio Batista. His feared private army, "The Tigers of Masferrer," were used to torture and murder rebellious workers, farmers, and revolutionaries.

Only two weeks before Manolo's murder, Masferrer's *Tiempo en Cuba* had aimed its propaganda guns at Fidel, linking him to the *pistoleros* at the university.[48] Following the murder, Masferrer was one of those who charged Fidel with complicity in Manolo's death. No warrant was ever issued for Fidel's arrest. For those who were privy to the gangland style of Cuban politics, it was clear that allegations of Fidel's involvement marked him for retribution at the hands of his enemies' hired guns.

In his declaration to the police a few days after Manolo Castro's murder, Fidel told how, on the evening of the murder, he had gone to the El Dorado café with two friends, whom he named, and then spent the night at the Hotel Plaza. The next morning, after seeing his name included among the suspects in a newspaper article, he immediately went to the third-precinct police station but was turned away by the officer in charge, inasmuch as no warrant had been issued for his arrest.[49]

Fidel logically concluded that he was now fair game for Masferrer's *pistoleros*, a conclusion confirmed by his contacts. He called Alfredo Guevara by telephone. Guevara agreed that Castro's life was in danger, and they made an appointment to meet at the house of Lidia Castro, Fidel's sister. Over the next few days, Lidia, Guevara, and Mario Incháustegui helped to hide him.[50]

Three days after the shooting, Fidel, accompanied by the other two university students mentioned in the press, walked up to a police patrol car and asked to be taken to the third-precinct station. The three made statements to the police in which they denied involvement in Manolo's murder and gave their alibis. Paraffin tests were taken of their hands. They gave negative results, and since there was no evidence against them, they were released on "provisional liberty." [51]

Before leaving the station, Fidel spoke to police reporters:

> We presented ourselves although there was no warrant out for our arrest. . . . Accusations have been made against us, principally by Masferrer, whose activities are well known. Masferrer is interested in only one thing—to take over the leadership of the university students for his own personal interests. We've prevented this despite the coercion and violence he has employed against us for a long period, dating back to the time when Mario Salabarría and his henchmen were still at liberty.[52]

Over the next few weeks, Fidel lived a semi-clandestine life. He knew that his enemies were gunning for him and made sure to keep out of their line of sight. When an opportunity arose for him to leave Cuba on a mission for the Federation of University Students, he accepted it.[53] On March 19 he went to Rancho Boyeros airport to board a plane for Caracas. Police at the airport spotted him and took him into custody. He was taken before a judge, charged with attempting to violate the terms of his "provisional liberty." Fidel answered:

> It is stupid to think that I am trying to run away. . . . My detention is the result of dastardly accusations made by those who are trying to obstruct my student activities, to confuse things in order to create for me a disfavorable situation before public opinion.[54]

He told the Judge that he was being sent on a mission by

the FEU to "strengthen the ties of friendship" with Latin American students. Fidel also declared that he wanted it to be put on record that there was a group of individuals in Havana who were out to kill him.[55]

A police reporter for one of the big Havana dailies said in his article the following day, "Since there did not exist concrete charges against the student, nor is there any evidence that he participated in the events under investigation, the judge freed him." [56] He reported that they kept Castro's passport and some of his documents. The following day, Fidel was allowed to pick them up, free to leave the country.

Hugh Thomas's succinct description of Fidel's alleged involvement in the murder of Manolo Castro is misleading. He writes:

> Manolo Castro . . . was lured out of a cinema . . . and shot down. Fidel Castro was accused of being implicated in this assassination. He was arrested at the airport, appeared before a judge, and had his passport removed.[57]

What Thomas fails to make clear is that no warrant was ever issued for Castro's arrest, that he gave himself up to police three days after the shooting, and that in the absence of evidence, he was released. From Thomas's account one cannot know that the airport incident occurred more than three weeks after the murder and only then was his passport taken away, for a single day.

3.

'Twixt the Tropics of Cancer and Capricorn

With his passport restored, Fidel immediately left Cuba on his FEU mission. His initial assignment was to make contact with the student movements in Venezuela and Panama and then fly on to Bogotá, Colombia, to attend the preparatory sessions for the Latin American Student Congress.

The youth congress in Bogotá had been scheduled to coincide with the Ninth Inter-American Conference, one of whose main aims was to establish a cold-war-era Latin American regional organization—the Organization of American States (OAS). General Juan Perón's nationalist-minded Argentine regime, although not opposed to the anti-Communist thrusts of the inter-American conference, was interested in bringing to the fore the question of British control of the Falkland Islands [1] and in winning a hegemonic position among Latin American states. In the hope that university students would support its aims, the Argentinian government became one of the prime movers of the Latin American Student Congress.[2]

Senator Diego Luis Molinary, the president of the foreign-relations committee of the Argentine senate, had gone to Cuba to gain backing for the congress and the Argentine cause. He had stayed at the Hotel Nacional in Havana, invited student leaders to dine with him, expounded the Argentine view, and offered to defray the expenses of Cuban delegates to the youth congress. Progressives at the university whom Molinary approached had mixed feelings about Perón. On the one hand, his nationalist stance had a certain anti-imperialist content. On the other, his regime was notorious for suppressing leftist activities. One Communist Youth leader who dined with Molinary asked him pointedly to describe how the Argentine police used electric cattle prods against militant trade unionists.[3]

The Young Communists and leftist independents on campus, the contingent that Fidel later called "the small group of anti-imperialists," saw the possibility of converting the congress into a forum for attacking U.S. Latin American policy under the general slogan of anticolonialism.[4]

Following Manolo Castro's death, Fidel had refused to heed the advice of his friends to leave the country temporarily, lest his departure be mistaken for cowardice or a sign of guilt. The congress, however, offered a legitimate reason for him to get out of the country until things cooled off. Castro was interested in the anticolonial struggle, and his FEU friends gave him the important task of coordinating plans with the Venezuelan and Panamanian student delegations before going on to Bogotá. Prior to his departure from Cuba, Castro noted that the student congress would be held simultaneously with the Inter-American Conference and would thus be able "to support the demands against colonialism that will be put forth by several Latin American nations." He called on the students to "unleash a wave of protests" to support these anticolonial demands. The aim, he said, was to "initiate a movement of greater proportions that will gather support in all of Latin America, especially among university students, united under the banner of the anti-imperialist struggle."[5]

The strategy was to raise questions at the congress far more radical than those proposed by the Peronists. Among these were the issues of independence for Puerto Rico, the return of the Canal Zone to Panama, and condemnation of the Trujillo dictatorship in the Dominican Republic. It was hoped that the congress would go so far as to denounce the proposed Organization of American States, which was seen as an instrument to prevent needed radical changes in Latin America. During his visits to Venezuela and Panama, Castro met with student leaders to ensure a common anti-imperialist front at the congress. In Panama he visited the Canal Zone, made a fighting anti-Yankee speech to students,[6] and wrote a letter to his friend Mario Incháustegui about the need for a revolutionary upsurge in Latin America on a Bolivarian scale.[7]

In Bogotá Fidel and Alfredo Guevara, the secretary of the FEU, who was also a delegate to the student congress, met with youth leaders and had plans to converse with Jorge Eliecer Gaitán, the incorruptible and highly popular leader of the Colombian Liberal party. Gaitán had organized a powerful opposition movement, which was clashing head-on with the reactionary government. In the weeks preceding the inter-American conference, Liberal party and Communist activists were victims of terrorist activities by the ultraright Conservative party led by Laureano Gómez.

On the afternoon of April 9, while Guevara and Fidel were walking toward the Hotel Granada, the meeting place for both the Gaitán and Peronist delegations, pandemonium suddenly broke loose around them. People rushed past the two students shouting hysterically, "Gaitán has been murdered!" Minutes later, the body of a man said to be Gaitán's murderer was being pulled through a Bogotá street, followed by an enormous crowd shouting for vengeance against the government.[8]

Within hours, the city was the scene of a veritable war.

Street fighting was taking place, and certain units of the police had sided with the Gaitán followers against the government. The fighting spread to other cities and in the coastal town of Barranquilla, the Gaitán forces and leftists took over the governor's mansion. Students seized the radio stations and called the people to arms.

Fidel's activities during the *bogotazo* have been the subject of much speculation over the years. Sir Norman Smith's assertion that Castro arrived at his hotel during the fighting with a "load of arms" [9] tells us little of his actual participation in the events, although it is suggestive. The American diplomat William Pauley's recollection, a decade later, that he heard a voice on the radio shouting, "This is Fidel Castro from Cuba. This is a communist revolution," [10] must be chalked up to a vivid, self-serving imagination triggered in part by the trauma of seeing his holdings in Cuban airlines and transport recently nationalized by the Castro government.[11]

Alfredo Guevara recalled that upon hearing of Gaitán's assassination, he and Fidel decided to go to the university. Guevara told me, significantly, "Fidel disappeared from sight near a spot where police were handing out weapons to the pro-Gaitán forces." [12] This is credible, since the chief of police and many on his force were loyal followers of the Liberal party.

According to one account, Castro participated in the frustrated attempt to take the Presidential Palace.[13] The multitude wandered the streets in bands with little leadership, and it is said that Castro went to Liberal-party headquarters hoping to find some semblance of a centralized command. Finding none there, he went to one of Bogotá's large police stations that was in the hands of the pro-Gaitán forces. Police were milling around, and Fidel tried to convince them that they should leave the station and go into action.[14]

The next morning, the Liberals and the government of President Ospina agreed to a cease fire. It was a clearcut government victory. The final toll was some thirty-six hundred dead in the brief civil war, most of them Gaitán followers and leftists. A photo published in *Bohemia* shows Castro in a rubble-strewn street of Bogotá, wearing a leather jacket with a shirt and tie.[15] At the time the photo was snapped, some government officials were claiming that the Cuban delegation at the youth congress were Communists and had played a role in the street fighting the previous day. Facing the possibility of arrest, Fidel took refuge in the Cuban embassy and was later taken out of Colombia on a plane carrying bulls to Cuba.

Although details of his activities during the *bogotazo* are hazy, it is certain that Fidel Castro was impelled to join antigovernment forces. For him, the issue was clear. The Ospina government represented an antipopular and reactionary force—the power of the Colombian oligarchy and United States imperialism. There is no doubt that he agreed with his friend Alfredo Guevara, who said in an interview upon returning to Cuba that they had witnessed "the fervor of a people fighting for its liberation and against injustice and misery." [16]

The Bogotá events could not have helped but make a profound impression on Castro. He had witnessed a Latin American people in arms, crushed by an oppressive government. He had seen how most of the representatives at the inter-American conference had labeled the pro-Gaitán forces "Communist inspired." The experience certainly contributed to Castro's undying hatred for the Organization of American States, whose principal purpose, as he must have understood it, was to put down popular revolutions in Latin America.[17]

One can speculate that events in Bogotá gave Castro a

practical lesson in the divisive force of anti-Communism. It was clear from what had happened that any attempts to upset the *status quo* and bring about needed transformations in Latin American society would be stigmatized as Communist. This would block the unity of the people and justify repression and foreign intervention. These lessons undoubtedly helped to shape Castro's tactics and strategy for the future.

Fidel returned to the university for his junior year just as Eduardo Chibás's election campaign for the presidency was moving into high gear. He immediately threw himself into the campaign with the conviction that Chibás could trigger the development of a massive popular movement, win the election, and thus create the preconditions for revolutionary change. Chibás's combative speeches and his slogan, "Pit honor against money," had fired the imagination of millions of Cubans. His campaign had taken on hallmarks of a chiliastic crusade against corruption. It represented, said the editorialists of the serious newspaper *El Mundo,* "the moral forces of the nation."[18]

The Bogotá experience had heightened Castro's hatred for U.S. imperialism. But his sense of the historical moment, his seemingly intuitive grasp of tactics and strategy, told him that anti-imperialism in itself was not yet a concept that could move the Cuban people into action. He once explained to me that because pro–U.S. propaganda was omnipotent in Cuba, most Cubans had not yet developed an anti-imperialist consciousness.

> The conclusion that I came to was that the people attributed the social malaise to the corrupt governments, to politicians who robbed, to politicking, to all that. But they had not yet seen the true essence of the social problems.[19]

The Communist party forcefully raised the concept of anti-imperialism, but Fidel has said, "because of the McCarthyist campaign and the incessant bombardments in the press, they were very isolated." [20] He believed then that "non-Communist popular movements could advance toward the left." Chibás's Orthodox party, to his mind, was that sort of movement. It explains why Fidel threw himself so wholeheartedly into Chibás's presidential campaign.

Carlos Prio, the labor minister who had engineered the conservative takeover of the trade-union movement, was running for president on the Authentic-Republican alliance ticket. In mid-May he began a tour of Oriente province, the birthplace of both Chibás and Fidel. Chibás decided to follow on Prio's heels. Fidel, already recognized as one of the most attractive Orthodox Youth leaders, became a member of Chibás's entourage, one of the handful of speakers that preceded Chibás at each political rally.

In Holguín, not far from his father's farm, Fidel lashed out against the widespread practice of families' selling their votes to politicians in exchange for favor.[21] That was the price corrupt politicians charged for their beneficence in recommending a family member for treatment at a "public" hospital, a scholarship to a vocational school, or a job. Along with the ballot forgeries, dead-person votes, and the use of outright terror, vote selling was one of the many practices that made "representative democracy" in Cuba a mockery.

On May 23, 1948, Chibás received a tumultuous home-town welcome in Santiago de Cuba. As usual, Fidel preceded him to the microphone.[22] That day, however, Fidel said something with overtones of a warning to Chibás. He declared that the students would support Chibás, but if he betrayed the faith placed in him by the Cuban people, they would withdraw that support and combat him. Luis Conte Agüero, another student representative, who followed Fidel to the speaker's rostrum, challenged Fidel's allusion and insisted that Chibás would never betray the Cuban people. When Chibás spoke, he also took note of the warning: "No, *compañero* Fidel Castro, you needn't have any doubts." The day he felt he was losing the people's confidence, he said, he would put a bullet through his own heart.[23]

•

Castro's unexpected departure from the usual adulatory language of campaign rallies was an expression of his free-wheeling outlook. It proves that he did not have the mentality of a blind follower or a political hack. In effect, he was saying that loyalty to a cause is more important than blind loyalty to a leader or a party.

Young Fidel was not beloved by the upper echelons of the Orthodox party. He was too free-spirited and impetuous to gain the confidence of the politicians. A follower who would dare to admonish the party leaders could not be counted on to toe the political line. Fidel never attempted to ingratiate himself with the leaders. On the contrary, he often battled them within party ranks.

What attracted Fidel to the Orthodox party was its potential for galvanizing the people to action. He most enjoyed the moments of the campaign when he was among the people. One newsreel film of the period shows him next to Chibás amid an ecstatically enthusiastic multitude. Although he was being jostled by the throng, there was a broad smile on his face that unquestionably radiated inner satisfaction.[24]

Fidel had strong reservations about some of the politicians and millionaires whom Chibás had brought into the Orthodox party. Among them were "Fico" Fernández, the multimillionaire sugar baron from Oriente province; Gerardo Vázquez, the cattle king from Camagüey province; and Nazario Sargent of Las Villas province. Each had a powerful position within the party, and Fidel did not disguise his opposition to them. He told me that Chibás had no need to bring these monied elements into the party. "There was no real necessity for that, because it was a mass movement built around his own personality, and he could have pushed new personalities to the fore." [25] Castro never reconciled himself to being a party bedmate with these representatives of the Cuban oligarchy.[26] To his mind they were the ones who kept the party from becoming an instrument for deep-seated change. This point of conflict conditioned Castro's loyalty to the Orthodox party. It explains how Castro could hold Marxist ideas and still be an activist in the party.

Although Chibás made concessions to the tycoon politicians, he had refused to accept any accord with the Communists. In April 1948, when a sector within the Orthodox party proposed a limited alliance with the Communist PSP (People's Socialist Party) around some senatorial races, Chibás angrily vetoed the idea.[27] A few days later he refused a pact on common objectives proferred by Blas Roca, the PSP general secretary. In fact, Chibás was a diehard anti-Communist and seldom missed the opportunity to launch scathing attacks on the PSP.

On this issue Fidel parted ways with Chibás. Neither in public meetings nor on his weekly COCO radio program, which began during the election campaign, did he ever lash out against the PSP or "international Communism" as Chibás did.[28] In fact, whereas Chibás disdained PSP support, Castro seemed to welcome it and on one occasion was quoted in the press as declaring approvingly that "the PSP preferred Chibás over the other presidential candidates." [29]

After returning from Bogotá, Castro "seems to have dropped what little feeling for Marxism he may have had," [30] writes the author of a voluminous book on Cuba. This is a serious misinterpretation, one that adds still another element of confusion to the saga of Fidel's ideological development. In fact, it was precisely in the period following the *bogotazo* that Fidel began studying Marxism in earnest. He had come back from the Bogotá experience more restlessly radical than ever, impelled to learn more about the realities of historical development, the roots of imperialism, and the tactics and strategy of making a revolution. This is attested to by his regular attendance at a Marxist study group organized by the Communist party in 1949.[31]

Fidel had already read Marx's and Engel's *Communist Manifesto.* Now he was to discover "two superphenomenal books," Lenin's *The State and Revolution* and *Imperialism, the Highest Stage of Capitalism.*[32] During a visit to the United States in the winter of 1948, he bought the first volume of Marx's *Capital,* a striking proof of his interest in Marxism inasmuch as he bought it during his honeymoon.[33]

These four works that Castro read are considered to contain the essence of Marxist-Leninist doctrines: the theories of class struggle, of surplus value, of the state and revolution, and of capitalism in its imperialist stage. Yet in speaking of Castro's claim that he was essentially a Marxist-Leninist when he led the attack on the Moncada Barracks, *five years after his return from Bogotá,* Hugh Thomas comments superciliously: "All this surely was to say at some length that at the University Castro was influenced in a modest and superficial way by Marxism and nationalism . . . he perhaps meant no more than that he heard for the first time the theory that society is divided into antagonistic classes." [34]

After Bogotá, even though Communists were anathema to the leadership of the Orthodox party, Fidel Castro continued his friendly relationships with Flavio Bravo, Luis Más Martín, Alfredo Guevara, Lionel Soto, and other Communists. He often had long discussions with Flavio Bravo, and he was a regular client of the Communist bookshop.[35] Carlos Rafael Rodríguez, who is now one of the key figures of the Cuban revolutionary government and was at that time a leader of the PSP, received periodic reports from the party youth groups. He considered Fidel "perhaps the most important personality among the small group of anti-imperialists and progressives at the university." [36]

When one understands young Fidel's serious approach to Marxism-Leninism and his fraternal attitude toward the Communists, his future ideological development ceases to be an enigma. Admittedly, however, Castro's early development in the realm of ideas has been enveloped in a nebulousness *of his own making.* He never mentioned *Marx, Lenin, Communism,* or, for that matter, even the less prejudicial word *socialism* in any of the speeches or writings that have come down to us. Furthermore, he is recognized as having been a bona-fide activist of Chibás's Orthodox party and never of the Communist party.

In a review of his early political development, Castro has asserted that the Communists "still hadn't recruited me; I recruited myself and began to fight." [37] This must be interpreted to mean that Castro became a *Marxist,* but one who kept his ideology and final aims to himself, while throwing himself into the practical political work of supporting a progressive mass movement that he hoped would attract the Cuban people and lead them toward revolutionary goals.

Shortly after summer vacations began in 1948, Fidel was accused of being among those who gunned down a University police sergeant, Oscar Fernández Caral, in front of his own house.

Castro first read about his alleged involvement in the newspapers. He immediately went into hiding, and the FEU officially protested the inclusion of his name on the list of suspects. From his hideout, Fidel sent a letter to Judge

Riera Medina, who was hearing the case. He gathered, he said, by the newspaper accounts, that he was expected to turn himself in to the police. "Why should I?" he asked. The only witness who had identified him from photos as a participant in the murder had later recanted his testimony "in the press and categorically, civilly, and valiantly before Judge Riera Medina, despite the threat of reprisal and the offer of bribes by the police." Inasmuch as there was no substantiation to the charges against him, Castro asked the judge to quash the order for his arrest and to bring those who threatened and tried to bribe the witness to trial.

Castro had gone underground because he suspected that the charge brought against him by his enemies was a prelude to *pistolero* vengeance. He announced to Judge Riera that he would not turn himself in:

> Who would be responsible, Dr. Riera Medina, if, because of a warrant for my arrest, obviously without motive and unjust, some "police agents" in the service of bastard interests that I have combatted take advantage of the situation to assassinate me? [38]

Castro's plea convinced the judge, and his name was stricken from the list of the accused.

On returning to the university for his senior year, Fidel immediately became involved in the heated battle against an increase in bus fares. The increase had been authorized by the Council of Ministers on September 8, 1948, one of the last giveaways of the lame-duck Grau administration. A month later the new president, Carlos Prio, took office.

Omnibus Aliados, a self-styled cooperative, had become the target of consumers' ire. The enterprise claimed that it was losing money, but statistics published by its opponents showed that it had made a five-million-dollar profit in 1947.[39]

When the company raised its fares in January, there was a violent reaction, which included several bus burnings. The Communists played a big role in condemning the fare hike, and at a mass rally in Havana's Central Park, Communist trade-union leader Lázaro Peña and Young Communist leader Más Martín called on the people to fight the increase.[40]

The most dramatic reply to the fare hike came from University students. Students began hijacking buses and driving them onto the grounds of the university, where city police, by tradition, were forbidden to enter. The first war prize was adorned with Cuban and FEU banners. By the end of the day there were eight hijacked buses on campus. FEU issued a proclamation: "In solidarity with the people's demands, we will keep the buses as a symbolic gesture".[41]

The evening of the hijackings, shots were heard around the campus. The Communist-party newspaper, *Hoy*, speculated that "the police are preparing conditions of terror in order to invade the university campus." The article went on to say that "the student leaders faithful to the struggle, Fidel Castro, Lionel Soto, Guevara, and others, have adopted the decision to take even more drastic measures if the police dare to violate University autonomy." [42] Here again is Castro fighting shoulder to shoulder with his two Communist friends, documentary proof of his ideal of unity, which years later would evolve into overt socialist goals.

Justo Fuentes, president of the FEU and a member of the UIR, opposed the hijack action, blaming it on "outside elements that have filtered into the student masses." [43] He was probably referring to Más Martín, the Young Communist leader who had worked closely with Fidel and the other student leaders in organizing the protest movement.

The students left their banner-bedecked buses on campus overnight. The next morning, they were gone. When Más Martín heard the news, he rushed to Fidel's apartment.

Castro was studying for an exam. Más told Fidel about the buses and added, "They say Justo Fuentes sold out for money, and the worst of it is, if you don't get your ass out there, some people might say you were in on the deal." With that Fidel flung his book across the room, let loose with some expletives, and rushed off to the university.[44]

On campus, Castro soon became the center of an impromptu meeting. He accused Justo Fuentes and a small group around him of having sold out to the bus company. Later, at an FEU meeting, he took the floor and began by citing rumors "that some leaders of the FEU, without its knowledge or consent, held interviews in the Vista Alegra cafeteria with Mr. Saud Juelle, manager of bus lines 21 and 22, and accepted $2,500 each to stop the fight against the rise in bus fares." [45] Before he could go on, he was ruled out of order. A half year later, following Justo Fuentes's murder, *Bohemia* recalled the hijack incident and commented, "At that time, Castro accused Justo Fuentes and others of having sold out to Omnibus Aliados." [46]

Not long after the triumph of the Cuban revolution, the American eagle that perched atop the monument to those killed when the U.S.S. *Maine* was sunk off Havana Harbor in 1898 was pulled down. The removal of the eagle was charged with symbolism, and for many Cubans it served as just retribution for an incident that occurred more than a decade before and involved another monument and Fidel Castro.

The incident took place in March 1949. Several American sailors, in a drunken or simply thoughtless prank, climbed up the statue of the revered José Martí in Havana's Central Park. One of them urinated on its base, an unspeakable affront to the Cubans who had gathered to watch. A photograph, now famous in Cuba, shows one of the sailors sitting astride Martí's head. Cubans take their patriotism seriously, and only police intervention saved the sailors from an angry crowd. They were taken to a local police station, where irate Cubans gathered shouting anti-Yankee epithets. Later, the U.S. naval attaché arrived and spirited the frightened sailors back to their ship.[47]

When news got back to the university community, Fidel was one of those who organized a guard of honor to take its place beside Martí's statue during the night. A call was sent out for a protest demonstration to be held in front of the U.S. embassy the following morning.

Fidel, Alfredo Guevara, Lionel Soto, and Baudilio Castellanos were among the demonstrators. Some shouted anti-American slogans, and rocks were thrown at the embassy. There was also a plan to pull down the American flag to hold as symbolic hostage until the guilty sailors were handed over to Cuban courts.[48]

U.S. Ambassador Robert Butler made an appearance and spoke in conciliatory tones to the demonstrators. While he was speaking, a police contingent led by the new police chief, Colonel Carames, waded into the group of demonstrators with swinging clubs. One year earlier, police under Carames's command had attacked a demonstration and injured Castro. This time, again, Castro was struck by a police club.

Ambassador Butler seemed disconcerted by the police brutality. He got into his car and set off for the Cuban foreign ministry. Some of the FEU activists followed him there. Butler met with Cuban Foreign Minister Hevia and drafted a short speech on the spot. He then read his apology to the students. When he affirmed that the United States had helped Cuba win its independence, Alfredo Guevara interrupted: "Yes, you helped us to be free so that you could impose the Platt Amendment on us." [49] Butler later left the ministry and drove off to Central Park, where he laid a wreath on the Martí statue.

Meanwhile, Fidel, Alfredo Guevara, and Lionel Soto,

among others, began making the rounds of newspaper offices
to hand in a declaration protesting the police brutality. "It
is a disgrace," the declaration said, "that Cuba has a police
chief who devotes his efforts to attacking those who go out
in defense of honor instead of preventing Yankee sailors
from profaning Martí." [50]

There is a footnote to the statue incident. On the same
day that he laid the wreath at the statue of José Martí,
Ambassador Butler made a newsreel film. Following the
revolutionary victory, the several discarded "takes" of the
Butler apology were discovered. In the first, Butler delivered
several lines and then: ". . . the statue of . . . uh, uh . . ."
A sheepish grin spread over his face as he waved at the
cameraman and shouted, "Cut!" He had forgotten the name
of José Martí.[51]

Fidel, like other stalwarts of the Martí-monument protest,
had not slept on the night of the desecration or during the
entire following morning. One can imagine that the tension
of prolonged activities had left him exhausted. It would have
been normal for him to cancel his dates for the rest of the
day, to sleep. Instead, however, he went to a meeting on
campus of the University Committee to Fight Racial Discrimination, of which he was an executive-board member.
"Fidel had promised to attend," recalled one of the black
leaders of the committee, "and he did attend, with blood-
shot eyes." [52]

When I first heard this story, it seemed to me perfectly
natural that Fidel would have strong feelings about racial
discrimination. Only later, however, when I read Hugh
Thomas's allegation that before 1953 Fidel Castro "never
had anything yet to say on the problem of the Negro in
Cuba," [53] did I realize the importance of the factual evidence
I had unearthed about his attendance at this meeting.
Although it is only one incident, it does prove that Castro

was an active opponent of racism, that he did have something to say on "the problem of the Negro in Cuba."

I have found other proofs of Castro's deep concern for the problems of racism. One of the most revealing was the testimony of newspaperman Felix Olivera, a black whose encyclopedic knowledge of Cuban prerevolutionary politics is almost legendary among his fellow journalists in Cuba. Olivera says that Fidel was well known around the campus and within the Orthodox party as a hater of racial discrimination. "On his radio programs on COCO, between 1948 and 1950," Olivera recalls, "Fidel lashed out against white chauvinism dozens of times."

Olivera recalls three specific occasions.[54] The first was when the Hotel Nacional refused to give a room to the famed black singer Josephine Baker. The second was when Colonel Carames punched singer Pepe Reyes at the Tropicana while Reyes, a black, was showing Puerto Rican actress Diosa Costillo how to dance the mambo. (Carames had shouted, "Who the hell gave you permission to dance, nigger?") The third involved the hiring of "token" blacks by the El Encanto department store and Woolworths.

Castro's attitude toward racial discrimination was perfectly consistent with his general political outlook. It should be noted that he was also a member of the FEU's committee for Puerto Rican independence.

When one reviews Fidel's university years, it is obvious that he had accumulated a vast array of political experience. He had suffered the deception of the Grau regime and the Dominican-invasion fiasco. He had visited Panama and Venezuela and had been a participant in a popular uprising and a witness to sanguinary repression in Bogotá. He had participated, often as a propulsive force, in dozens of rallies and demonstrations. He had been an active member of a mass political party, and he had been threatened, calumniated, and attacked in word and deed. In these years of activism he had discovered a doctrine that was to guide him.

Knowing all this, I had no reason to doubt Fidel when he told me, "When I had finished at the university, I already had a Marxist political formation." [55] In fact, one can speculate humorously that Fidel's law-school grades for the spring semester of 1949, his senior year, presaged his life's course. He received an *outstanding* (*sobresaliente*) in labor legislation but only a simple *pass* (*aprovechado*) in property and real estate, grades befitting a convinced socialist.[56]

Fidel Castro Ruz, now Doctor of Laws, joined a small firm that had its offices near the Old Havana docks.[57] To the disappointment of the well-connected Díaz-Balart family, into which he had married and had "given" a son,[58] he showed no interest in becoming a successful lawyer on their terms. Little could have prevented him from achieving monetary success had he so desired. He was brilliant, persuasive, and from an acceptable social class. But money was not his guiding star, and he was satisfied with a clientele of workers, poor widows, and such, whom he charged very little.

Nor did he throw himself entirely into his law business. He enrolled under a plan at the university that allowed him to pass courses by examination, and in his first year after graduation he passed *dozens* of subjects. His Orthodox-party activities also absorbed much of his time. He attended meetings of grass-roots Orthodox clubs in the working-class sections of Havana and was known as a spokesman of the radical wing of the party.

Castro's professional status did not domesticate him, and his enemies knew it. Masferrer once again accused him of attempted murder—the victim being Masferrer himself. The assault had taken place on the Capitol steps, with a toll of one dead and three wounded. Masferrer had miraculously escaped unharmed. A woman associated with the UIR had been arrested near the scene, and Masferrer had immediately named other UIR members as his assailants.[59] Two days after his original accusations, he added his old enemy Fidel Castro to the list. Fidel successfully appealed to Judge Hevia to quash a warrant for his arrest.[60]

Six years later, when he was in Mexico preparing his invasion of Cuba, Fidel was obliged to defend himself against a charge that he had been one of the "trigger happy" elements at the university.

> Every time my adversaries tried the vile and selfish procedure of involving me with gangsterism, I stood resolutely against the slander, I appealed to the courts, and honest judges (there are only a few) like Hevia or Riera Medina can certify my innocence.
>
> Thousands of students, who are professionals today, saw my actions in the university for five years. I always had their support (because I have always fought with the weapon of public denunciation, going to the masses). It was with their cooperation that I organized large meetings and protests against the existing corruption. They can testify to my conduct. . . .
>
> At a time when corruption was unprecedented, when many youth leaders could get dozens of government positions and so many were corrupted, it is worthy of some merit to have led student protests against that regime for a number of years without ever having appeared on any government payroll.[61]

II.

Ballots

to

Bullets

In politics I had to be a guerrilla also.

Fidel Castro to author, July 29, 1974.

[Batista] . . . you are a faithful dog of imperialism.

Fidel Castro, under the pseudonym Alejandro, August 1952.

Only a Marxist could have written the Moncada Manifesto.

Armando Hart, member of the political bureau of the Cuban Communist party, to author, January 9, 1975.

4.

J'accuse

In Bonachea and Valdés, *Selected Works of Fidel Castro,* there is only a single entry for the years 1950 and 1951, a letter dated December 1951 in which Fidel quotes his mentor, José Martí: "For a suffering country, there is no New Year other than that of the defeat of its enemies." [1] The period is given equally short shrift in other books on Castro. Yet important clues to his political predilections at that time are available to the assiduous researcher. One discovers them, significantly, in *Mella,* the national magazine of the Cuban Communist Youth, and in *SAETA,* a thin underground newspaper put out by the Communists and their sympathizers on the University of Havana campus.

The first mention of Fidel in these publications links him with the Stockholm Peace Appeal, which received international notoriety at that time, issued at Stockholm by the World Committee in Defense of Peace in March 1950. The World Committee and the ad-hoc national committees, set up to gather signatures on the petition, were inevitably labeled by the non-Communist Western press as "Communist fronts" and the petition itself, "Moscow inspired."

The wording of the appeal seemed innocuous enough to one who is not familiar with the international political atmosphere of the period. It was simply a demand to outlaw atomic weapons "as instruments of intimidation and mass murder of peoples" and to treat "any government that first uses atomic weapons against any other country whatsoever . . . as a war criminal." The Soviet Union and Communist parties throughout the world backed the appeal enthusiastically, while United States policy makers viewed it as a Trojan horse, an insidious propaganda threat emanating from the ranks of "world Communism."

Opposition to the appeal was based on the fact that the United States had, or believed it had, a monopoly on an operative A-bomb. This monopoly formed the basis of Secretary of State John Foster Dulles's brink-of-war and massive-retaliation gamesmanship. The United States spearheaded a world campaign to expose the sinister meaning of the Stockholm Peace Appeal, and U.S. organizations, from the American Legion to the United Auto Workers, warned Americans to beware of the petition.

Cold-war propaganda in Cuba was as pervasive as in the United States. Even the head of Fidel's own Orthodox party, Eduardo Chibás, seldom lost an opportunity to tongue lash the domestic Communists and the Soviet Union.[2] When the war broke out in Korea in June 1950, he supported the position of the United States. Chibás recognized that "the conduct of the U.S. government in Latin America . . . has frequently deserved the imperialist tag" but then added, "despite these discrepancies, we, the democracies of America, are faced with a much greater danger, the threat of the totalitarian Communist imperialism of Moscow."[3] In view of his general world outlook, it was inconceivable that Chibás would lend his name to anything so questionable as the Stockholm Peace Appeal.

The facile characterization of Fidel by most writers as a "follower of Chibás" tends to obscure the differences in their outlook. Unlike Chibás, Fidel at this time was disposed to lend his name and reputation to a cause that had been stigmatized as Moscow inspired and which actually was sponsored by people he knew to be Communists. Shortly after the outbreak of the Korean War, Fidel signed the Cuban Youth Committee for Peace version of the Stockholm Peace Appeal.[4] His name, "Fidel Castro, University Leader and Member of the National Committee of the Party of the Cuban People—Orthodox," was printed among the appeal's backers in *Mella*. A photograph in the following issue of *Mella* shows two Communist friends of Fidel, Luis Más Martín presenting filled petitions to Lionel Soto.[5]

Castro's support for the Stockholm Appeal did not mean he was a Communist, any more than was Abbe Boulier, the French Catholic leader, who also signed it. It did indicate, however, that he refused to accept the premises of the cold war and the coercive pressures of the anti-red hysteria. Search as one may, one cannot discover any indications that Fidel Castro identified himself with Chibás's cold-war view on domestic and international policy.

Two months after Chibás's statement on "the threat of the totalitarian Communist imperialism of Moscow," the Communist-influenced underground newspaper, *SAETA*, came out with a condemnation of the Korean War written by one of its editorial-board members, Raúl Castro, Fidel's younger brother.[6] Raúl had only recently entered the University of Havana and had already become identified with the left-wing forces who opposed U.S. cold-war policy. Significantly, Fidel Castro had given Raúl his first Marxist literature[7] and was thus partially responsible for having introduced him to radical politics. In the same issue of *SAETA* in which Raúl's opposition to Cuban involvement in the Korean war appears, there is a declaration under which Fidel Castro's name appears sponsored by the University Committee for Democratic Rights and Liberties. The declaration attacked the Prio regime's "repression of students . . . violations of freedom of the press and . . . the right of assembly." [8] Enemies of the committee also labeled it Communist inspired.

Another issue of *SAETA* featured an article by Fidel on its front page, which also contained a picture of Julio Antonio Mella, the founder of the FEU in 1923 and of the Communist party in 1925. Castro's article attacked those who called for student apoliticism. He wrote:

> University students should remain firmly united and demand adoption of a program that includes the long-sought-after university reform. It is not possible for students to be divorced from national problems. It is necessary for them to define themselves in favor of what is just and revolutionary. . . . The students . . . must chase out the demagogues who weigh everything like merchandise or hide behind false "equidistances" in order to castrate the revolutionary spirit of the students.[9]

The same issue of *SAETA* also published a program of university reform as envisioned by progressives at the university. In view of Castro's lead article, one can presume that it was the kind of "just and revolutionary" program Fidel suggested. It included planks on political repression, student participation in university government, international peace, access to the university by the poor, eradication of racial discrimination at the university, elimination of racist content in textbooks, and the struggle against gangsterism.[10]

It is evident that Castro's radicalism went far beyond that of Eduardo Chibás. Castro, however, continued within the ranks of the Orthodox party because he saw it as a vehicle for a massive progressive upsurge among the Cuban people. Eduardo Chibás, then, was a catalyst, rather than an ideological mentor, for Fidel and many of his latter-day followers. He was a spark that awakened them, that helped them throw off defeatism bred of frustration. He taught them the secrets of the mass movement, publicity, and propaganda. Once in action, the self-generating experiences based on revolutionary activity carried Fidel far beyond the ideological horizons of Chibás.

Since he was a populist, influenced profoundly by Martí and Marx, Fidel's deepest sympathies were reserved for the sharecroppers, landless farmers, and workers—the largest, poorest, and most abused segments of Cuban society. His sensitivity to the plight of these social classes is reflected in the kind of clientele he undertook to defend. Stymied by the law's partiality toward those of moneyed power, he sought to air his cases before public opinion. His goal was to awaken people politically and move them into action against the conservative Establishment.

In the spring of 1951, Fidel co-authored a letter that appeared in the newspaper *Alerta* and explicitly expressed his partisanship for the rights of the poor. The letter tells how the owner of a large fruit cannery had fired nine hundred employees seven months before and replaced them with lower-paid workers without eliciting a single objection from the Ministry of Labor. It also exposes a big landowner who arbitrarily forced small farmers off the land. The letter ends with a cry that elevates the case from the specific to the general: "We raise our voice responsibly and ask only one thing: justice for Cuban workers and farmers." [11]

Fidel's own consecration to lofty ideals was doubtless reinforced by the shock of Eduardo Chibás's dramatic suicide. On Sunday, August 5, Chibás had taken his place before the microphone of CMQ for his weekly nationwide program. He had ended his program by shouting in his strident voice: "Members of the Orthodox Cuban party, Forward! For economic independence, political liberty, and social justice. People of Cuba: rise up and walk! This is the last call to your conscience!" [12] And with that, Eddy Chibás took a .38-caliber Star pistol out of his belt, pointed it into his belly, and fired.

Chibás had been distraught and depressed. Only days before, he had filed suit against the Minister of Education, Aureliano Sánchez, charging him with embezzlement and misuse of education funds, accusations he had already made on the Senate floor and on a previous radio broadcast. Fidel Castro told me that Chibás "had gotten into a terribly difficult situation because he could not prove his charges." [13] Driven to desperation, he chose the drama of public self-immolation as a way of proving the moral superiority of his position and of galvanizing public opinion.

Fidel kept constant vigil at the hospital as Chibás lingered near death. Newspaper photos show him guarding the door to Chibás's room surrounded by men and women awaiting the latest news about their hero. [14]

When Chibás died in the early-morning hours, Orthodox-party leaders, among them Fidel, spent four hours debating where his body should be taken to lie in state so that the public could file past his bier. Some insisted that it be the capitol building, a right to which Chibás was entitled as a senator. Fidel and others violently opposed the idea: the capitol was too much the symbol of the corruption that Chibás had fought. [15] Others favored the Orthodox Liceo, the headquarters of the party. It was argued that the Liceo was too small for the massive turnout that could be expected.

Fidel led the fight for taking Chibás's body to the University of Havana campus. One of the arguments was that Chibás had begun his political life at the university. But

Castro's main reason for advocating the campus was that the national police were prevented by tradition from setting foot there, and therefore, the organizers would have more discretion in keeping out unwanted persons. When the pro-university position finally won, Fidel pugnaciously told the press: "It is best that we hold it there because then certain degenerates will not be able to go to the university and profane the memory of Chibás." [16] Fidel's was one of the few defiant statements made on that day of mourning. Other political figures mouthed the accustomed platitudes on the meaning of Chibás's death.

At the *Aula Magna* of the university, the usual niceties of political protocol were ignored by the militant wing of the Orthodoxy to which Fidel belonged. When wreaths and flowers of corrupt politicians arrived, they were taken out and burned. When Grau or Prio supporters came to shed crocodile tears, they were firmly ushered out. One congressmen, the ex-president of the bus company that Fidel had fought during the fare-increase protests, came and went with lightning speed. One newspaper described the episode whimsically: "He is asked to leave, light resistance and an 'air trip' to the exit." [17]

Fidel was among those in the first guard of honor. One photo shows him directly behind the open coffin of Chibás, pensively looking down at him.[18] Later, in a meeting of the national committee in the home of Chibás's successor, Roberto Agramonte, Fidel made an impassioned speech about the legacy of Eddy Chibás. The populist ideas of Chibás must not be betrayed, he insisted. The party had to become more dynamic than ever in combatting the enemies of the people.[19]

Castro, for one, heeded his own advice. Following Chibás's death, he became the *enfant terrible* of a strife-torn Orthodox party and one of the most fearless muckrakers in Cuba. Following Danton's dictim of audacity and more audacity, he personally took on the police department, the *pistoleros,* and the government of President Prio.

A month after Chibás's death he once again locked horns with the police, but this time as a lawyer bringing suit. He charged that they had unlawfully used violence and caused the death of a young worker during a demonstration against another attempt to raise Havana bus fares. Castro personally took the case to court and singled out two police lieutenants as those responsible for the police violence. One of them, Lieutenant Salas Cañizares, had taken part in the attack on students during the Martí-statue incident two years before. When the government sought to divert responsibility away from the lieutenants by offering up a few sacrificial patrolmen, Castro told the judge:

> I am not interested in just any patrolman being arrested when responsibility for the affair should fall on the shoulders of the officers who gave the orders.[20]

Fidel tenaciously pursued his quarry. When the government moved to mollify public opinion by agreeing to try the two officers, but in a military court, Fidel rejected the compromise. Finally, in a criminal-court trial Castro skillfully presented overwhelming evidence of their guilt and won the case. The two lieutenants were fined five thousand pesos each and put on probation. The verdict must have given Fidel great satisfaction, but the victory was short-lived. Within a year, Lieutenant Salas Cañizares would be the chief of police.

Castro's rostrum was no longer the campus and its Escalinata. Roberto Agramonte had been chosen as the Orthodox party's presidential standard bearer for the 1952 elections, and Fidel threw himself into party politics. He campaigned throughout Havana, attended Orthodox meetings,

and won followers at the grass-roots level. He used his
frequent radio appearances to make slashing attacks on corruption. No one else went so far in touching the sensitive
points of Cuban politics and, by doing so, courting retaliation by the *pistoleros* or police.

In late September 1951, Fidel began to launch frontal
attacks on the corruption that surrounded Prio and his regime. The lessons of Chibás's righteous but evidentially
unsubstantiated attacks on the Minister of Education were
not lost on Fidel. He was fully conscious that if his exposés
were to be effective, he would have to present irrefutable
proofs. Nor was he satisfied with tidbits. His aim was to
create a scandal of major proportions, one that would rock
the government. To this end, he spent the final months of
1951 digging deeply and systematically into Prio's financial
machinations and the history of his enrichment at the expense of the Cuban taxpayers.

Fidel's first leads came from a young member of the
Orthodox party, Pedro Trigo, who lived in the tobacco hub
of Santiago de las Vegas near Havana. It was general knowledge there that serious violations of the labor laws were
taking place on a farm in the vicinity that was rumored to
belong to President Prio.[21]

Accompanied by Trigo and two other Orthodox-party
members,[22] all of whom would later participate under him
in the attack on the Moncada barracks, Fidel began his
investigation. A visit to the local real estate registry office
turned up the fact that the farm had been registered under
the name of a corporation whose ownership was traced back
to Prio. The original 166-acre farm holding had grown to
some 2,000 acres since Prio had become president in 1948.
Further detective work led to the discovery that the corporation had bought other large farms during the same period.

The Prio farm at Santiago de las Vegas employed wage
workers under conditions of virtual slave labor: two pesos

for ten hours' work, from which fifty cents was deducted for lunch and twenty-five cents for transportation. The farm also made ample use of army personnel, in clear violation of the law. From a rooftop near the farm's entrance Fidel's friends took photographs of soldiers arriving by truck to begin their daily chores.

Fidel delved deeper into the origins of Prio's landholdings. He discovered that four years before he became president, Prio had been the lawyer for a wealthy businessman who had been accused of raping a nine-year-old girl. The businessman had been found guilty, sentenced to six years in jail, and ordered to pay ten thousand dollars to the girl's family. On assuming the presidency in 1948, Prio pardoned the businessman and appointed him presidential civil secretary. Property belonging to the businessman had been transferred to a new corporation in which Prio held a controlling interest. One of the civil secretary's tasks was to speculate in new properties for the corporation.[23]

With incontrovertible facts in hand, Castro asked for time on the Sunday radio program of the Orthodox party to air his findings. His request met with opposition from an influential group within the party who viewed Castro as too critical of the party's moderate course and, moreover, as a future political threat. They were not disposed to cooperate in any venture that would increase Fidel's prestige and popularity.

The persevering Fidel was not daunted. He raised funds from those who sympathized with him and bought time on Radio Alvarez. The story was so hot that the newspaper *Alerta* picked it up and splashed it across its front page as an exclusive.[24]

Castro carried his *j'accuse* into the courts. He filed suit against the president for "prostituting the spirit of presidential pardons," violation of labor laws, illegal use of Cuban

soldiers as farm laborers, and contributing to unemployment and *latifundismo,* the Cuban expression for big land
ownership. He signed his brief: "Fidel Castro, January 28,
1952, the day of Martí's birth."

When twenty-four-year-old Fidel Castro decided to run
for congress, he did not receive the enthusiastic blessing of
the Orthodox-party leadership. He already had the reputation as a radical within their ranks, and he did not fit neatly
into their political game. For them, Fidel was too righteous,
intransigent, and undisciplined. Some still recalled his ef-
frontery during the 1948 presidential campaign when he
warned Chibás that he and the university students would
fight any treason to the cause. It was no secret that Fidel
had much less respect for the latter-day leadership of the
party. He condemned the wealthy conservative elements
within it and was critical of the flaccid liberalism of Agramonte and those like him.

The general elections were scheduled for June. In early
February Agramonte announced a list of potential congressional candidates for the party, men who presumably
had his support. Castro's name was not among them.[25] By
then Fidel had decided that he wanted to run for congress.
Accompanied by friends, he visited the home of Manuel
Bisbé, the president of the Orthodox party in Havana province. There, at the front door, he told Bisbé what he
thought of the political opportunists in the party and served
notice that he was a contender for one of the congressional
seats in Havana province.[26] Castro described to me how he
had conducted his campaign:

> I went directly to the people. I had a radio program,
> and there were also the newspapers with my exposés.
> A tremendous political vacuum existed. There were
> no leaders. And since the rank and file of the party

was very honest and spontaneous, the machine couldn't impose its will on them.

I had the addresses of eighty thousand party members in Havana province. I would send out letters to everyone of them. A group of friends helped me stuff envelopes. I used the party's parliamentary franking stamp. I had no right to do it, but there was no other way. . . .

The leaders couldn't hold me back. It was something I had given a lot of thought to. There was no way they could block me. This didn't please them, but I was supported at the grass roots. For that reason it was impossible for them to prevent me from running. Of course, my popularity was still only within the party, although my exposés did have repercussions among the people as a whole.[27]

Fidel would often speak at as many as four meetings a night. At times he would arrive at a town near Havana at one in the morning and Orthodox supporters would come out to hear him blast the Prio government, the *pistoleros,* and the pusillanimity of some of the leaders of their own party. "These details indicate just how I was penetrating the grass roots," Castro told me earnestly.[28]

Although voting for congressional candidates was province-wide, nominations were made by party clubs on a precinct level. Fidel's bastion, the one that nominated him, was the Cayo Hueso district of Havana, a *barrio popular* dotted with warehouses, repair shops, and slum apartments. His candidacy was endorsed by other party clubs in the province. The last club to nominate him, less than a week before the campaign was brought to a halt by a military coup, was that of Santiago de las Vegas, where he had initiated the investigations that led to his exposé of Prio's land operations.[29]

Political pundits of the period gave the Orthodox-party candidate, Agramonte, a good chance of winning the election. The prestige of the Authentic party under the Grau and Prio administrations had fallen to a new low. A national poll showed that in December 1951, 50.54 percent of those asked were against the Authentic government and only 33.79 percent were in favor of it.[30] The Authentic presidential candidate, Carlos Hevia, had neither the popularity nor the skill to reverse the trend.

The third candidate of consequence was Senator Fulgencio Batista, who had been president of Cuba from 1940 to 1944. Before that, however, as head of the army, he had been Cuba's strongman, the power behind several corrupt governments. Batista had led the sergeants' revolt that helped to topple the dictator Machado in 1933. He had then been handpicked by President Franklin D. Roosevelt's special envoy in Cuba, Sumner Welles, as the man to stifle the revolutionary movement that had developed during the anti-Machado struggle. He had done his work well and often brutally. Cubans held him directly responsible for the assassination of the young revolutionary leader Antonio Güiteras and for crushing the March 1935 general strike.

The Communists had no presidential candidate of their own. The Authentics, who had carried out the cold-war attacks on the party, were anathema to them. So was Batista, whom they had supported for president in 1940 as part of their "united front against fascism" strategy. They had long parted ways with Batista. "Once again," a party document declared, "he has the same position he had in March 1935."[31]

The Communists recognized the broad popular appeal of the Orthodox party and believed, as Fidel did, that it could play a progressive role once in power. For that reason, they offered a unity pact with the Orthodox party, a pact that would have committed them to support Agramonte's presidential candidacy while leaving them free to run their own senatorial and congressional candidates.[32]

The leadership of the Orthodox party rejected the Communist proposal. One day at the Canadian ambassador's residence in Havana, I asked Fidel why, and he answered, "It was the period of McCarthyism, and they believed that any pact with the Communist party would block the road to the presidency." He attributed this to "a bourgeois conception, principally the fear of the United States." [33]

Despite the refusal of the Orothdox party leadership to accept the proposal, the Communists decided to push ahead unilaterally with their strategy. Two weeks before the military coup, the Communist party's general secretary, Blas Roca, declared, "Orthodox members on the grassroots, you can be assured that the PSP will not fail you." [34] I asked Fidel what he thought at the time about the Communist position. "There is no doubt," he answered, "that the Communists would have voted for the Orthodox presidential candidate to ensure the defeat of the very corrupt and reactionary party in power. . . . This was, in my opinion, the most correct policy." [35]

Fidel came out with his second major exposé of government corruption, the most audacious lunge of the entire election campaign and, without exaggeration, one of the most sensational exposés in the fifty years of Cuban republican history. He whetted the appetites of Cubans by announcing on a February 19 radio program that he would shortly offer definitive proof of the link between the Prio administration and the *pistolero* groups. *Alerta* picked up the story and published it next to a caricature of Fidel.[36] Other politicians had mentioned collusion between government and gangsters before but had stopped short of offering specific details. Fidel's exposé was awaited by many with the same sense of expectancy as precedes a death-defying circus act.

Castro's exposé came in the form of charges filed against Prio in the fiscal-watchdog court (*tribunal de cuentas*). The mass-circulation *Alerta* published the story, a verbatim reprint of Castro's brief, accompanied by a photograph of the author.

Castro began by delving into the history of the *pistolero* groups. Their origins, he said, were in the so-called revolutionary-action groups that surged forth after Batista had crushed the budding revolutionary movement following the fall of the Machado regime in 1933. They had sprung to life again when Grau became president in 1944, as instruments of terror and vendetta against Bastista and his henchmen. "The Grau regime degenerated," Fidel said, "and all those groups, sooner or later, became lost in the absence of ideological and social content." The *pistolero* groups "are made of the old elements of the action groups and of youth attracted by an erroneous concept of heroism and revolution." He charged that "politicians without scruples gave them their backing and aid in exchange for services." [37]

When Prio came to power in 1948, his Authentic-party regime was "saturated by obligations to these groups." Castro charged that to assuage public opinion, shortly after his victory, Prio had promulgated a decree that was heralded as a blow against gangsterism but in fact only caught some minor offenders in its net. The more powerful groups not only continued to operate with impunity but were actually subsidized by the government through payroll padding and sinecures. The Prio administration had helped to establish an *entente* among the groups that over the years had divided and subdivided.

Until this point, Castro had couched his brief in generalities. What followed was the most explosive portion of his revelations, the most audacious, stating names and the number of sinecures given to each of the *pistolero* groups: Guillermo Comellas, 60 sinecures . . . Tribunal Ejecutor Revolucionario, 110 sinecures . . . Acción Güiteras, 250 . . . El Colorado group, 400 . . . Masferrer, 500 . . . Policarpos gang, "the most fearsome," 600.[38]

Castro totaled up more than two thousand monthly paychecks for services *not* rendered in the Ministries of Health, Labor, Justice, and Public Works. Baiting the lion more daringly, Fidel then named the individual from each group who picked up the checks at the ministries. He also alleged that each month Orlando Puente, the secretary to the President, handed out sixty envelopes, each containing three hundred dollars, to these groups, in addition to the sinecure payments.

The brief accused the president of the republic of having "bought and sold assassinations."

> And while this goes on in the capital and while the Presidential Palace becomes a marketplace of cadavers, there, on the farms of Prío, the soldiers of the nation's army are obliged to work as slaves for a miserable wage. . . .
>
> I accuse him before this court and before Cuban history of being responsible for our tragedy, although it may mean that I have to sign the imperative duty of conscience with my blood.[39]

The exposés undoubtedly enhanced Fidel's chances of winning a congressional seat. He had succeeded brilliantly in breaking into print and casting himself in the role of a political muckraker. His flair and courage reminded many rank and filers of Chibás. With four months to go in the election campaign, with more spectacular disclosures to come, it seems reasonable to assume that Fidel would have been able to capture the imagination of the Cuban voters who had shown themselves to be sick of pallid politics. Whether Castro would have won his congressional seat, however, is pure speculation, inasmuch as the election campaign was brought to an abrupt end by a military coup.

Fidel told me that his intentions were revolutionary when he ran for congress. "I put forth a populist platform and had the support of the indigent districts—the poor people and small farmers." He was part of the radical wing of the Orthodox party, without the support of the party leadership, but "I didn't have any problems, because I had succeeded in mobilizing sufficient backing." [40]

When he spoke to me, he sounded as if he never had doubts about winning the election. Once in congress, he said, he would have "presented a series of revolutionary laws." It was a foregone conclusion that the legislature would have rejected his proposals, but in the debates he would have been able to expose the enemies of the legislation and at the same time win publicity for his program and organize a mass following.

When it became clear to the people that the revolutionary program would not be approved through parliamentary means, he would "begin to work in a revolutionary way for these laws." His resources and immunity as a congressman would allow him "to maneuver and conspire more freely."

> Of course, I always inclined toward action. I didn't believe that the problems of Cuba could be solved through parliament. On that score I had no doubts. [41]

His idea was to break with the "institutional legality," with the aim of taking power "at the opportune moment." Of that moment he said: "It's not something you can do on any day you feel like."

The McCarthyite campaign and the incessant bombardment of the press, radio, television, movies, magazines had had their effect on the people. When one spoke to the people of "socialism," they would be terrified.

The people did not yet see the real causes of the social malaise. What they saw was the violation of the Constitution, the nonfulfilment of its precepts, the flouting of the laws, the taxes, the robberies, unemployment. . . . But they did not see the real causes of the malaise.[42]

Castro's strategy was conditioned by his great confidence in the ability of the people to learn in the process of struggle.

I believed that the masses could be led to revolution, but what was necessary was a process of developing a profound understanding (*concientización*). And what was needed was to have a revolutionary program, which the Orthodox party was lacking.[43]

The program Castro had in mind was progressive and democratic in content, not overtly socialist. He viewed it as a "first phase," a platform that would "include the interests of workers, farmers, teachers, and even soldiers."

The tendency of most Western scholars has been to view Castro's affirmations about his revolutionary strategy before 1953 with skepticism. However, knowing what we know now about his intensive political life during his university years and immediately following them, it can be affirmed that he was already highly influenced by Marxism-Leninism and that he was intent on overturning the *ancien régime* in Cuba. In speaking of his agitational campaign, which he launched in the first months of 1952, he used an expression that gave me a clue to the way he viewed himself at that time. He said that he had embarked on this campaign "a bit individualistically, a bit like a guerrilla fighter, because in politics also I had to be a guerrilla. . . . It was a stage in which we didn't have an apparatus." [44]

This can be interpreted to mean that Castro did not believe then that there was an apparatus—that is, a party, movement, or organization—adequate to the revolutionary task ahead. The Communists, he told me, were "isolated" because of propaganda and the cold-war milieu. He viewed them fraternally from an ideological point of view and had close relations with some of their leaders, but he believed it necessary to develop his own strategy and organize his own apparatus, free of terminology and symbols that could only limit its possibilities for growth.

It is a mistake to minimize Fidel Castro at this stage of his development. Endowed with unusual courage and audacity, he was a natural leader with a sense of history, a knowledge of the labyrinths of politics, and a deep understanding of the idiosyncrasies of the Cuban people. He was steeped in the most intimate problems of Cuban society, and for six intensively lived years he had devoted his main energies to battling the Establishment, organizing struggles, and identifying himself with popular and progressive causes.

Castro's greatest strength, perhaps, was in his sense of *realpolitik*. He was aware of the level political consciousness of his fellow countrymen and of the powerful influence of cold-war propaganda. That is why, throughout the insurrection struggles of the fifties, he avoided revealing, by name, his ultimate aspirations for Cuban society. This is the only way to explain his total avoidance of the word *socialism* during these years of battle and his occasional efforts to put to rest fears that his movement was, in effect, Communist.

5.

Seed of Rebellion

Fulgencio Batista's military coup on March 10, 1952, cut short the Cuban election campaign. The takeover was the final blow to the corrupt and crisis-ridden rule of "representative democracy" that had slithered its way through the slime of Cuban politics since 1902.

The coup was carried out with supreme artifice while Cuba slept.[1] Batista drove to the general-staff headquarters at Camp Colombia, where he received an enthusiastic reception from his cohorts. In Havana, without firing a shot, small contingents of his fellow conspirators took over La Punta and the Cabaña, strategic points on both sides of Havana Bay. Police Lieutenant Rafael Salas Cañizares, Fidel Castro's old nemesis, assumed command of the national police headquarters and as a reward for his services was made a colonel and head of the nation's police. Batista called military chiefs of the other provinces by telephone and won their adherence to his seizure of power.[2]

President Prio was informed of what was happening and rushed to the Presidential Palace at dawn. Politicians followed suit. At 7:30 A.M., a delegation from the Federation of University Students arrived. Alvaro Barba, the FEU president, challenged Prio to resist the coup, and Prio answered, "Of course I'm going to fight." He told the students to go back to the campus and await weapons.[3] They did, but the arms never showed up. Among those waiting for them on campus that day was Fidel Castro.[4]

Political organizations immediately condemned the coup. The FEU called "on all parties and groups that are genuinely democratic to join forces with us."[5] The *genuinely democratic* was probably aimed at excluding the Communists. The Communists, for their part, called "on the masses of all parties to regroup, unite, and form united front committees to fight so that the constitution remains in force." They were the only party that accused "the Yankee imperialists" of fomenting the military coup.[6] The Orthodox party's condemnation stressed the legal and ethical aspects of the coup but did not ask its massive following to take direct action.[7]

When Castro left the university on March 10, he and two friends went to a small farm near Havana that belonged to an Orthodox activist. There, Castro wrote a manifesto denouncing the coup. To Batista's claim that his coup was in reality a revolution, Castro answered that it was nothing more than a lowly *zarpazo*—the thud of a heavy body hitting the ground. The manifesto was Castro's declaration of war against the Batista dictatorship.

> We have suffered misrule for many years awaiting the constitutional opportunity to exorcise the evil. And now you, Batista, you who fled for four years and then played useless politics for another three, appear with your perturbing and poisonous remedy, tearing the constitution into pieces when there are only two months to go before arriving at our goal by adequate means.
>
> It would be satisfying to tumble a government of

emblezzlers and murderers. That is what we were attempting to do by following the civic road, with the
backing of public opinion and the aid of the masses.
What right do you have to substitute with bayonets
those who yesterday robbed and killed people without scruple?

This is not peace. It is the seed of hate that has
thus been sown. This is not felicity. It is mourning
and sadness that the nation feels as it views the tragic
panorama. There is nothing so sad as the spectacle
of a people that goes to sleep free and awakens en-
slaved. Once again the boots. Once again Camp Colombia dictating laws, appointing and dismissing
ministers. Once again tanks roaring menacingly
through our streets. Once again brute force overriding
human reason. . . .

Whatever Prio did in three years, you had been
doing for eleven years. Your coup is thus unjustifiable.
It is not based on any serious moral reason nor on a
social or political doctrine of any kind. Reason is found
only in forces, and justification in lies. Your majority
is in the army but not in the people. Your votes
are in rifles, never in will. With all that, you can win a
military takeover but never clean elections. Your
assault on government lacks principles that give legitimacy.[8]

It was a call by a young lawyer whose future would far
overshadow his past exploits. In retrospect, his words are
those of a romantic, full of passion for a cause but without
an organization to ensure victory. This fact did not dampen
his spirit, however.

Laugh if you will, but principles are, in the long run,
more powerful than cannons. The people develop and
are nourished on principles. For principles they
die. . . .

The truth that lights the destiny of Cuba, that guides the steps of our people in this difficult hour, the truth that you will not permit to be heard, will be known by everyone. It will pass surreptitiously from mouth to mouth, to men and women. Although no one says it in public or writes about it in the press, all will believe it. The seed of rebellion will be planted in every heart. It is the compass that exists in every conscience.

I do not know what insane pleasures the oppressor derives from the lash he flails, like Cain's, upon the human back. But I do know that there is infinite felicity in fighting him, in raising a powerful fist and saying: "I do not want to be a slave." [9]

Castro ended his manifesto by invoking the words of José Martí: "To live in chains is to live in infamy and shame." His last line was from the Cuban national anthem: "To die for your country is to live."

As befitting his character, Castro's statement was the most intrepid made by a political figure on those first days after Batista's coup. It was a firm indicator that Castro had already begun his conversion from "political guerrilla" to a guerrilla fighter in the more traditional sense.

It would be an exaggeration to claim that Castro's manifesto reached anywhere nearly the number of people that the declarations of the institutionalized political groupings did. But it would also be a mistake to surmise that his position was totally unknown or that it did not meet with a sympathetic response from the rank and file.

I found proof of this in the newspaper *Alerta*. The article describes a meeting, six days after the coup, at which the head of the Orthodox party and several other Orthodox politicians, among them Fidel, spoke. The meeting was held beside Chibás's tomb at the Colón cemetery. Speaking of Fidel's speech, the *Alerta* reporter commented: "His words, full of feeling, were acclaimed by the crowd, which once more demonstrated the sympathies that he enjoys among the masses of the party of the Cuban people." [10] This one descriptive phrase published at the time takes on historical proportions in the light of Castro's subsequent claim that he had built a sympathetic following among the rank and file of the Orthodox party. The reporter's observations definitely give credibility to that claim.

One of those who listened to Fidel in the cemetery that day told me he recalled the enthusiastic response to Fidel's words: "In the same way that Bastista entered, so he must be booted out." [11]

By contrast, Agramonte's speech was colorless and hesitant. It elicited an open letter from Abel Santamaría, a young man who would be Fidel Castro's second-in-command during the Moncada attack. Agramonte, Santamaría wrote, had given "a doctrinal speech of the fifteenth category" and "should not have presented himself, pallid, nervous, and vacillating, before the followers of Chibás." [12]

Castro, the *enfant terrible* of the Orthodox party, carried his challenge against the Batista coup into the courts on the same day that the Orthodox leaders filed their own charges.[13] Castro was aware his legal appeal would fall into a void, and it did. He was intent, nevertheless, on exhausting all legal means before embarking on the road of legitimate insurrection.

Castro's accusation before the Urgency Court detailed Batista's violation of the Social-Defense Code relating to sedition and concluded that Batista ". . . has incurred in crimes, punishment for which would make him liable to more than one hundred years in jail."

It would be an oversight to sluff over the content of Castro's brief, as many scholars have done. An analysis of it, especially that part dealing with the problem of revolutionary legitimacy, gives us important insights into his philosophy at that time and thus serves as another key to understanding Castro's ideological development. Castro wrote,

> It is not sufficient that the mutineers claim so facilely that revolution is the source of law, since instead of revolution, there is restoration, instead of progress and order, there is barbarism and brute force. There was no revolutionary program, theory, or declaration that preceded the coup. There were only politicians without the people, converted into assailants of power.
>
> Without a new conception of the state, of society, of the judicial order based on profound historical and philosophical principles, there will be no revolution that generates laws.[14]

Castro was saying here that if there had been a real revolution it would have "generated law" and thus would have been legitimate. Revolution is not the simple overthrow of one government and its substitution by another. A revolution must bring progress, be based on a revolutionary program, theory, or declaration and be accompanied by popular support. It must, moreover, posit a new conception of the state, of society, and of the judicial order based on valid historical and philosophical principles. It must, *ipso facto*, bring about substantial transformations in the *status quo*.

The theory of the legitimacy of revolutionary change was the touchstone of seventeenth- and eighteenth-century philosophers who challenged the divine right of kings and advocated bourgeois revolution. The doctrines of Marxism also legitimized revolutionary change. Fidel's application of the revolutionary-legitimacy theory in the mid-twentieth century obviously harbored final aims far beyond those of the philosophers of two and three centuries before. At this stage of his life, he had no faith in bourgeois representative democracy as practiced in Cuba. His idea of "a new conception of the state, of society, of the judicial order" could *not* have meant a simple return to the pre-Batista regime. What Castro must have had in mind was a socialist revolution or one that opened the way for it. For Castro, *socialist* and *revolution* were forbidden words. His theory of revolutionary legitimacy, however, is a good indication that for him, they were not forbidden thoughts.

In Castro's first manifesto written after the Batista coup, he proclaimed: "There arise new Mellas, Trejos, and Güiterases" to confront the tyrant. These three revolutionary heroes had in common the fact that they were all murdered before their thirtieth birthdays.[15] It is an indication that Castro did not expect much from the traditional politicians. Rather, he was asserting his own responsibility and that of other youth in the crucial battles to come.

Among those who opposed Batista were some notables who mounted fake conspiracies, promised imminent action, and avidly sought publicity for themselves and their movements. The integrity of most of their rank-and-file followers was as real as the guns these movements had stashed away. Most of the weapons, however, were not destined to be used. It was politics as usual as they jockeyed for positions of recognition and prestige in the event that Batista did somehow tumble from power.

Notables among these ambitious conspirators were the last minister of education under Prío, Aureliano Sánchez Arango; Emilio Ochoa, the Orthodox-party leader; and the radio commentator Pardo Llado. They boasted of their plots, impressed followers with their bravado, and even announced periodically the fateful day of armed confrontation. The anti-Batista forces waited expectantly for the "supermen" of Ochoa or the "super supermen of Aureliano" to act, but nothing happened.[16]

Castro recalled later: "We waited months for those people. We thought that a movement would be organized around the university. It was a crazy stage, with a proliferation of organization and great internal dissension."[17]

It was during this period that Fidel Castro began to act conspiratorially. To the casual observer, Fidel had simply submerged himself in his legal practice and in his Orthodox-party political activities. In a business-as-usual atmosphere, he received visitors in his small office in the Orthodox headquarters on the Prado and made periodic trips out of Havana.[18] He was well known as an anti-Batista hard liner, but few suspected that he had begun to build a conspiratorial movement whose final purpose was to overthrow the dictatorial regime.

Castro made contacts among known activists of the Orthodox party, some of whom had been his friends for years and had supported him in his political campaigns. One of his most important contacts was José "Pepe" Suárez, the Orthodox Youth leader of Pinar del Río province, who lived in the city of Artemisa. In a discussion with Suárez at Prado 109, Castro told him, "Pepe, we have to do something. These politicians are simply playing around with us. They are definitely not going to do anything against the dictator."[19] Suárez agreed, throwing his support behind Castro, and Artemisa became a bulwark of the fledgling movement Castro had begun to build.

A fortuitous meeting on May 1, 1952, between Castro and several members of a small anti-Batista group led to one of the most significant additions to the incipient movement. The meeting took place during a commemorative event among the tombstones of Colón cemetery.

The group was out in force: Abel Santamaría, his sister Haydée Santamaría, Jesús Montané, and Elda Pérez. Abel Santamaría was one of those who had acclaimed Castro's defiant speech at the same Colón cemetery six days after the Batista coup. Montané, the personnel manager of the General Motors Inter-American Corporation in Havana, knew Fidel by reputation and had actually spoken to him when Fidel wanted to trade in his old car.[20] Montané and Abel approached Castro at the cemetery and confided in him.

This group, of whose existence Castro learned that day, had been organized only recently. It had bought a used mimeograph machine for seventy-five pesos and run off the first issue, five hundred copies, of a bulletin called *Son los Mismos* (They Are the Same), referring to the fact that Batista and his followers were the same ones who had crushed the revolutionary movement after Machado's fall in 1933.[21]

The *Son los Mismos* group soon became absorbed into Castro's larger and more ambitious scheme. Montané, Abel, Haydée, and others would become part of the inner family of the new movement, and Castro would use Abel's apartment as a meeting place and second home.

A week after their meeting at the cemetery, Castro, Montané, and Santamaría drove to Matanzas and recruited a physician, Dr. Mario Muñoz, into the plans. Muñoz was a radio ham and agreed to build two radio transmitters that could be used for clandestine propaganda activities.[22]

Castro did not like the name of the bulletin, *Son los Mismos*, because it lacked appeal and combativeness. He suggested that a new bulletin be issued with the more aggressive name, *El Acusador* (The Accuser). On June 1, the first issue of *El Acusador* rolled off the mimeograph machine. Castro wrote an article under the name Alejandro, a pseudonym that would later become his *nom de guerre*.[23]

Fidel continued to attend grass-roots meetings of the Orthodox party, which were still legal, although elections were not. He made no secret of his critical line within the party and was not universally supported. At one meeting during the summer, at the Sociedad Artística Gallega, he proclaimed defiantly: "We are going to make the revolution ourselves. You can't make a revolution with a bunch of politicians." Both applause and shouts of derision met his words, and the meeting ended in a shoving match.[24]

On August 16, 1952, the Movement, as members of Fidel's group now began to call it, had its first brush with the law. It was the anniversary of Chibás's death, and Orthodox-party followers had organized a parade up the broad thoroughfare of 23rd Street toward a silent memorial service in Colón cemetery. Castro marched among the stalwarts, and members of the Movement distributed a new issue of *El Acusador*.

The fracas at the Sociedad Artística Gallega had shown that a minority of Orthodox loyalists interpreted Castro's criticisms of the party leadership as divisionism. This was proved once again on August 16, when a faithful party member ripped to pieces her copy of *El Acusador* and berated the man who had given it to her. Castro happened to be close by at the time. He rushed in to persuade the woman that she should read the entire document before forming an opinion and told her that in any case, diversity was salutary to the party.[25]

While copies of *El Acusador* were being distributed on the street, agents of the Military Intelligence Service (SIM) swooped down on the house where the underground bulletin had been run off and arrested Abel; Montané; Melba Hernández, a young lawyer who had also joined the Movement; and several others. Mug shots were taken of them;

then they were released. It seemed that the government had no desire to give ammunition to those who daily attacked it for its violations of legality.[26] Years later, following the victory of the Cuban Revolution, the records of SIM were confiscated. Among them was found Abel Santamaría's dossier with a reference to his arrest: ". . . caught by surprise along with others when he was mimeographing the subversive publication *El Acusador*, which calumnied General Batista and his government." [27]

The most effusive article in that issue of *El Acusador* was written by Fidel and signed "Alejandro." "Fulgencio Batista!" the article declaimed. "The dogs that daily lick your sores will never be able to hide the fetid odors that they emit." Castro used the Spanish familiar *"tú"* as a sign of disrespect in addressing himself to Batista. He castigated the dictator for his "refined cynicism and perfidious hypocrisy." [28]

One formulation in Castro's diatribe against Batista is worth noting. "You speak of progress, and you align yourself with powerful Cuban and foreign interests. . . . You are a faithful dog of imperialism." The term *faithful dog of imperialism* is out of character with Castro's usual public language, which carefully avoided terms that might have limited his broad appeal. It might be explained in part by the fact that Castro was using a pseudonym or, less likely, unable to control his wrath. What is certain is that over the years to follow, he scrupulously avoided similar political clichés.

Another article by Alejandro in the issue reflected Castro's open break with the Orthodox-party *leadership* and his determination to organize a militant movement within the party and especially among its youth. Alejandro declared that Chibás had left behind a movement that "had placed [the party] at the very door of power." However, he alleged,

the leaders of the Orthodox party had misused the legacy
and had engaged in

> sterile battles . . . for motives that were not precisely
> ideological, but rather, of a purely egotistical and per-
> sonal nature.
>
> The immense majority of the party is on its feet,
> more decided than ever. It asks, in these moments of
> sacrifice, "Where are those who aspired to power . . .
> those who wanted to be in the spotlight at meetings;
> those leaders who visited towns and made policy and
> who, at big assemblies, demanded positions of honor
> on the stage and who now don't travel or mobilize
> people or demand positions on the battle line . . . ?
>
> Whoever has a traditional concept of politics will
> feel pessimistic before this picture of reality. For those,
> however, who have blind faith in the masses, for those
> who believe in the irreducible force of great ideas, the
> indecision of the leaders will not be reason for weak-
> ness or loss of heart, because the vacuum will soon be
> filled by the uncorrupted that arise from the ranks.[29]

Two elements in these passages characterize Castro's
political philosophy. They are his "faith in the masses" and
his belief in the "irreducible force of great ideas." In subsequent years, during the multiple stages of the battle,
before and after victory, he was to consistently repeat these
ideas as integral parts of his political outlook. They are
concepts reminiscent of the Marxian dictum that when
ideas take possession of the masses, they become a material
force.

Castro went on to say that "the moment is revolutionary
and not political. . . . A revolutionary party ought to have
a leadership that is revolutionary, young, and of grass-roots
origin."

Engineering student Pedro Miret recalls being visited at the beginning of the fall 1952 term by an emissary from "a person who was not exactly among the favorites on campus despite his correct and defined attitude of opposition to the tyranny . . . but what could one expect when the favorites were the *señores* who . . . had been objects of his virile denunciation?"[30] He was referring to Fidel Castro.

Castro sought Miret's help in organizing target practice and other military training for his followers. Miret knew of Castro by reputation, and the fact that Fidel was being slandered by the *políticos* only made him more credible. Miret accepted the responsibility and was co-opted into the inner circle of the semiclandestine movement.

The men Miret helped to train over the next few months were mostly workers in factories, warehouses, and stores. There were some farm laborers and a few poor *campesinos* among them. For the most part they came from the ranks of the Orthodox party, from Havana and Pinar del Río provinces.

Castro's Movement had few resources. Its strength lay in the loyalty of its members and their dedication to the struggle. Castro had very little money. The income from his law practice was negligible. He spurned cases in which he did not believe or forfeited payment for those in which he did.

On one occasion, Castro and Melba Hernández, also a lawyer, were offered a case by Eugenio Sosa, a wealthy businessman who sought to file a suit against some poor farmers in Matanzas. Predictably, they ended up defending the farmers against Sosa.[31]

Castro had almost no time for his legal practice, however. He was obsessed with building his Movement for the confrontation with Batista, which was still not wholly defined. By January 1953, his followers numbered in the hundreds.

1953 was the centennial of José Martí's birth. Batista's official celebration of the event was viewed with cynicism by millions of Cubans. Ways were sought to vindicate the name of Cuba's independence hero by demonstrating abhorrence for the dictatorship. Anti-Batista actvities, originating in and around the University of Havana, began early in January and reached their high point on the 28th, Martí's birthday.

The month began with a commemoration of the anniversary of the assassination of Julio Antonio Mella on January 10. A special committee handled arrangements for the commemoration. Among the active members of the preparatory committee were engineering students Pedro Miret and Lester Rodríguez, both members of Fidel's Movement and future participants in the Moncada attack. Raúl Castro, also a student at the university, was another organizer of the meeting, as was Alfredo Guevara, Fidel's old Communist friend.

Mella's death was commemorated in a little plaza across the street from the Escalinata. A white plaster bust of the hero was unveiled in an act of open defiance to the government. The authorities acted with restraint, however, to avoid a violent student reaction of the kind so current during the Grau and Prio administrations.

On the morning of January 15, students found the white bust of Mella splashed with tar. A student strike was immediately organized. Glass, nails, and garbage were thrown into the streets around the university, and traffic had to be rerouted. In anticipation of retaliatory attacks on the university, students began to build barricades. An audacious commando group burned an effigy of Batista in a major intersection some blocks from the university.[32]

The FEU called for a protest march from the Escalinata to a patriotic monument near the entrance of Havana Bay, some miles away. Along the route, the police blocked the street and firemen played their high-pressure hoses on the demonstrators. The police then moved in, swinging their clubs, and some fired their guns. Sixteen demonstrators were injured. One of them, a worker-student, was wounded in the stomach. He died several weeks later, the first victim of the Batista dictatorship in the years of the centennial celebration.[33]

The events of the first half of the month created a propitious climate of opinion in Havana for a militant celebration of Martí's centennial birthday. On january 25, an assembly was held on campus to plan for a commemoration that, in fact, would be a demonstration of popular opposition to the Batista regime. During the meeting, Fidel Castro, as a spokesman for the most radical wing of the Orthodox party, made a blistering denunciation of the dictatorship. Flavio Bravo, president of the Young Communists, followed suit. Lester Rodríguez, a member of Fidel's Movement but also president of the organizing committee of the Martí Unity Congress for Youth Rights, a united-front group initiated by the Communist party, also spoke. Flavio Bravo told me many years later that Abel Santamaría, the number-two leader of Fidel's Movement, was also a member of the Martí Unity Congress, as were Raúl Castro and "Ñico" López, both of whom participated in the Moncada attack and later in the *Granma* landing.[34] The fact that these men were close collaborators of Fidel and maintained fraternal ties with the Communists is of historical note.

The assembly decided to celebrate the *centenario* with a torchlight parade beginning before midnight on the twenty-seventh and continuing into the early hours of the twenty-eighth.

The Movement decided to march as a unit. Several hundred of Fidel's followers, many of whom had received elementary military instruction over the previous months, took part. Menacing nails ran through the upper parts of the staffs holding their torches. Fidel, Abel, Raúl, Melba Hernández, Haydée Santamaría, Montané, Ñico, and other founders of the Movement marched in the ranks.

The Movement's bloc was distinguishable from the others by its compact, disciplined, and martial appearance. As it marched by, some of the streetside spectators commented aloud: "Look, there go the Communists!" [35]

Fidel Castro's activities continued after the Martí-centennial celebration. The February 8 *Bohemia* carried his scorching denunciation of a destructive police raid on the studio of the sculptor Hidalgo, an Orthodox-party member. Hidalgo had brought down the authorities' wrath by producing death masks of Eduardo Chibás and statuettes of José Martí on whose base was imprinted, "For Cuba who suffers." [36]

Only days after the article appeared, Castro was charged with disorderly conduct for incidents that occurred while marchers accompanied the body of the worker-student whom police had wounded several weeks before to the cemetery. Castro had been in the front ranks of the procession, along with other known public figures. Some of the marchers had purportedly thrown rocks at the residence of a well-known Batista supporter along the route and at a car that flew the regime's special pennant. The police report on the incident declared that one of the two principal leaders of the demonstration was "Doctor Fidel Castro, ex-member of the FEU and a leader of the Orthodox Youth." [37]

Following his brush with the law, Castro decided to assume a low profile and concentrate on preparing his Movement for action. He did not take part in a frustrated attempt to overthrow the Batista government in April or in a massive anti-Batista May Day rally.[38]

The April uprising was the work of the Movimiento Nacional Revolucionario (MNR), the brainchild of philosophy professor Rafael García Bárcena. García Bárcena had given classes to military men at the Camp Colombia army base and had naïvely counted on them to support his Easter rebellion.

One writer notes disparagingly that Fidel Castro "found it impossible to fit in with García Bárcena, leader of one of the most politically promising groups of the years 1952–1953." [39] This leaves the impression that Castro's ambitions kept him from cooperating with the idealist professor. The reason, however, was much more profound than that. It had to do with Castro's own ideology, his strategic concepts, and the advanced state of his own preparations at the time of García Bárcena's exploit.

García Bárcena, like Fidel Castro, made a special appeal to the youth whom he considered the only force capable of saving the country. In fact, he addressed himself primarily to the Orthodox Youth, the same reservoir from which Fidel drew his forces. [40] But here the similarities ended.

García Bárcena drew his followers in large part from petit-bourgeois families, mostly students at the university. Castro's Movement was made up primarily of wage wokers. Moreover, García Bárcena's social philosophy had an undisguised bourgeois liberal focus and an explicit rejection of Marxian theory. It called for "a completely just social system based on conciliation between capital and labor, the rich and the poor." Its program stated, "The MNR rejects the inevitability of class war and fights for the establishment of full harmony among workers, technicians, and businessmen." [41]

Castro believed in a broad movement with bourgeois aims as its first stage, but never did he reject, even implicitly, the inevitability of class war. Influenced as he was by Marxism, Castro was convinced that class struggle was

·the motive force of history and that the masses played a dominant role in any social revolution.

It was not likely, either, that Castro, schooled in the arena of practical politics, could have been attracted to García Bárcena's ingenuous strategy for overthrowing Batista. The good philosophy professor led forty-six men, some with guns, others with knives, on a march through the streets of Havana to Colombia military base, where he believed he would be joined by enough military men to force the dictator's resignation. The cause was righteous and the men brave, but the scheme was doomed to failure. Before the contingent could get to their destination, they were intercepted and arrested.

By the time of García Bárcena's courageous debacle, Fidel had come to some firm conclusions about the strategic conceptions of other anti-Batista groups:

> The plan to organize a contingent and take over the army barracks within a twenty-four-hour period seemed absurd to us. The army had tanks, discipline, and military training—the masses didn't. . . . We realized that a civilian organization, armed but without training, could easily be defeated . . . in the *putschist* movement that was being projected. That is to say, it was not the kind of insurrection that had indispensable conditions for overthrowing a government—for example, a big and powerful mass movement. Neither did the objective conditions exist for the organization of a general strike. It was nothing more than an adventurist type of action.[42]

Castro's own plan of action did not posit an overnight victory. It, too, would begin by taking a major military barracks, but this would only be the first step in a more prolonged unfolding of events. His essential idea was expressed in the phrase "It is necessary to rev up a small motor that will help start up the big motor." [43]

His concept of extended struggle, the escalation of mass involvement after the initial action, was, by definition, a rejection of *putschism*. Castro's overall strategy, however, was not revealed until well after the events, and the fact that the plan depended on a dramatic blow struck by a small contingent without an organized mass base laid it open to the *putschist* charge.

•

At the time of García Bárcena's Easter action, Castro's Movement was well into the preparatory stage of its own operation. A careful selection had been made from among his original followers. Those selected, fewer than two hundred, knew they were being prepared for battle, but just where and when the battle would occur, they had no idea.

Security now became a more serious matter. The Movement was compartmentalized into cells of about ten men each. Contact from the upper echelons was made directly with the cell chief through intermediaries.[44] The fact that there were no arrests during the months of target practice and training at the university and on isolated farms in Havana and Pinar del Río shows that members took security seriously. The funds needed to support the Movement were raised internally.

In his first session on the stand after the Moncada attack, Castro was asked if ex-President Prio had underwritten the operation. Castro replied, "Just as José Martí refused to accept ill-gotten money from Manuel García, known as 'The King of the Cuban Countryside,' so we did not accept the money of Carlos Prio or any other politicians." [45]

Castro dramatically accounted for the $16,480 contributed to the cause by individual members of the Movement. Pedro

Marrero, a brewery worker, for example, sold his refrigerator and furniture to raise money. Jesús Montané gave his severance pay from his General Motors job to the Movement. Others made the same kind of sacrifice.[46]

They had acquired most of the weapons through legal purchases. They had made one attempt to buy ten Thomson submachine guns at $250 apiece from a Spaniard, but they discovered in time that he was a police agent. They concluded that purchase of military-type weapons would be too risky and too expensive.[47] When others would tell Castro of the impressive arms cache of some other organizations, he would answer, "There are places with thousands of guns —greased and cared for. And one doesn't have to buy them or import them. One just has to take them." [48] When the time for action finally came, Fidel's group had brought together a motley array of weapons: one ancient .45-caliber Browning machine gun, one M-1 rifle, a few Winchester .44-caliber rifles, and a large assortment of shotguns and semiautomatic .22s.[49]

Who were the people Fidel Castro finally took to the final action? Herbert Matthews was still chafing from his error of having called them predominantly students when I spoke to him in 1972.[50] In the early sixties, the Cubans themselves had corrected this original impression by publishing the names and occupations of those who died at Moncada. The list shows that most had earned their living by working for a wage—they were the Cuban equivalent of blue-collar workers, hard hats, and stevedores. Their class origins can be derived from the types of jobs they held and by the fact that most of them had not gone beyond primary school.

The choice of *humildes* for his seemingly suicidal venture was not fortuitous. He had given orders to his followers to search out people of humble origin, "who can understand what we have to do and what will remain to be done." [51] In other words, Castro was already thinking of a revolution that would go far beyond the achievements of his projected first stage.

Of the 147 who participated in the attack on the Moncada fortress, we have been able to identify the occupations of 127. As one studies the biographies of these 145 men and 2 women, it becomes clear that many of the men did not actually have a profession or a skill. For instance, José Testa, a flower vender, had a third-grade education, began working when he was thirteen, and held numerous jobs before being forced by necessity, sometime before the Moncada attack, to sell flowers on the street. Roland San Román, who had a little oyster stand near a bus depot, had quit school at fifteen to support his family and had worked as a construction laborer whenever he could. This same pattern repeats itself time and time again.

Keeping in mind that many of the men were, in fact, *casual* workers, here is the occupation category of 127 of them shortly before the Moncada Attack in July 1953: [52]

Factory and shop workers (including truck drivers, stevedores, construction workers, and one taxi driver	44
Office workers and store clerks (including restaurant workers)	33
Students	13
Agricultural laborers	11
Professionals	4
Small-business men	6
Self-employed workers and traveling salesmen	10
Teachers	1
Housewives	1
Soldiers	1
Employed in father's business	3
Occupations unknown to author	20

6.

The
Moncada

No one can claim that Fidel Castro's Movement was Marxist. It was not. However, there was a Marxist influence among its members. This has been ignored by most students of Cuban affairs. In searching into the background of the members of the Movement, I've discovered numerous links to Marxist tendencies, more than I had foreseen.

Castro, in speaking of the period of preparations for the attack on the Moncada barracks in July 1953, has stated that "we walked around with our books of Marx, Engels, and Lenin. We were studying . . . and when we went to the Moncada, we were reading those books." [1]

Juan Almeida, a black who later became a hero of the guerrilla war against Batista, was a hod carrier earning "hunger wages" when he first met Fidel months before the Moncada attack. Castro, he recalls, "was carrying a book by Lenin." [2] Pedro Miret, another hero of the struggle, characterizes the Movement's number-two man, Abel Santamaría, "with a cigar always in his mouth . . . and his book of Lenin's selected works under his arm." [3]

A selected group within the leadership of the Movement held study sessions in which they analyzed Marx's and

Engels' *Communist Manifesto,* Lenin's *State and Revolution,* and Mehring's biography of Karl Marx. A number of these sessions were held at the beach town of Guanabo, not far from Havana.[4]

The army found one volume of Lenin's selected works at Siboney, the point of departure for the Moncada attack. When Castro was asked about this in court, he answered, "It's possible. I don't deny it, since we read all kinds of books. A person who has not interested himself in socialist literature is an ignoramus." [5]

Castro has said that "the first thing we did with every member of the organization was to indoctrinate him." [6] The indoctrination was not Marxist. It consisted of lectures and discussions on themes related to the plight of Cuba and the need to fight, both analyzed from anti-imperialist and anti-oligarchical positions. The total absence of diatribe against Communism in this indoctrination is highly significant.

The anti-Batista *políticos* were all supporters of the cold war, and for them anti-Communism was the litmus test of patriotism. Castro's and Santamaría's idea of patriotism was obviously very different. Santamaría, concerned with his sister Haydée's ideological development, took her to talk with a veteran woman Communist about various political matters.[7]

The link between certain followers of Castro and Marxism has never been adequately explored. Admittedly, it is often difficult to trace the political antecedents of Castro's followers, and the facts I have uncovered give only a partial picture. They prove that a number of Castro's comrades in arms did have links with Marxism. It is logical to assume that a full picture would give even more dramatic evidence of this. Consider the following people, all participants of the Moncada-barracks attack.

The Movement cell leader, Fernando Chenard, had a

long history of left-wing activity within the Communist party and the trade-union movement. An older member of the Movement, he had been secretary general of the Retail Grocery Clerks Union until 1944 and in charge of the party's work within it.[8]

Miguel Angel Oramos, twenty-one-year-old son of a brewery worker, was employed in Chenard's photo laboratory, and Chenard recruited him into the Movement. Oramos, who died in the Moncada attack, left behind a notebook with the following handwritten quotation: "The slavery to which the worker is subjected by the bourgeoisie shows its true aspect in the factory. —Engels."[9] One can suppose that Chenard also educated other members of his cell along Marxist lines.

José de Jesús Madera, who was only eighteen when he died at the Moncada, was brought up under the influence of his uncle, a Communist. There is a photograph of him as a child holding a Soviet flag.[10] Ñico López was a man "with clear Marxist ideas."[11] Renato Guitart had a great deal of socialist literature in his Santiago de Cuba home.[12] A forty-year-old worker, Luciano González Camejo, was a veteran Communist.[13] Jacinto García, a longshoreman on the Havana docks from 1944 on, was an ardent follower of Arcelio Iglesias, the Communist dock leader.[14] The parents of one of those who died at the Moncada, José Labrador, were poor *campesinos* and open sympathizers of the Communists.[15] Lester Rodríguez, the engineering student, worked closely with the Communist Youth on campus.[16] Raúl Castro, Fidel's brother, became a Communist-party member shortly before the Moncada attack.[17] Elpidio Sosa borrowed Abel Santamaría's *Selected Works of Lenin* and had an active interest in socialism.[18] Andrés Valdéz, a worker, considered himself a Marxist and studied at the Cuban-Soviet Friendship Society,[19] a subversive organization according to the government. The Movement cell headed by Hugo Camejo was composed of Pablo Agüero, Pedro Véliz, Lázaro Hernández, Rolando San Román, and José Testa, all poor men. They organized a Marxist study group in early 1953.[20] According to Valdéz, José Ponce was another Artemisan who had definite socialist ideas before the Moncada.[23] All these men followed Fidel into battle on July 26, 1953, and most of them were killed.

These men exemplify political tendencies that must have been more widespread within the Movement. It cannot be inferred, however, that most of the men who followed Fidel Castro knew what Marxism was. There is little doubt that the vast majority were radical, but in the sense that they had no desire to have their country return to the pre-Batista *status quo*. Their radicalism was based solely on the Cuban reality, their interpretation of the populist ideology of José Martí, and the crusading spirit of Eduardo Chibás. Most of Castro's followers came from poor families, and their predilections tended toward substantial changes that would ensure social and economic justice for the dispossessed of Cuba.

Fidel Castro and Abel Santamaría were convinced Marxists by this time. Why did they not try to impose their complete political position on their followers or express it in their written documents? The answer is that they were extremely sensitive to the anti-Communist atmosphere that surrounded them. They knew that the Communist stigma could effectively limit the breadth of their vulnerable political movement.

Pedro Trigo, one of the Movement's cell leaders, had experienced the effects. of the stigma. He had run for union office at the TEDUCA textile plant where he worked. The day before elections, a leaflet appeared at the plant, allegedly signed by the Popular Socialist party. It congratulated Trigo on having joined the organization. The leaflet was spurious, but the hoax worked, and Trigo, the favorite, lost the election.[24] Castro did all he could to prevent the Communist smear from being used against the Movement. To reveal his full political position would have led only to isolation. This perception of Cuban reality served as Castro's guideline throughout the insurrectional struggle of the fifties and into the first stage of the Revolution. It explains why he avoided open espousal of socialism and why he felt forced at times to be circumspect in order to protect his Movement. His brother Raúl, who joined the Communist party before the Moncada attack, followed the same guidelines in court after the attack by parrying questions about Communism.[25]

Much of what we know about Castro's thinking in those days comes from his retrospective statements. They deserve credence, in view of the knowledge we now have of Castro's growing ideological commitment to Marxism at that time. Castro asked himself how the door could be opened to the fundamental transformation of Cuban society—"How could the masses be led in that direction?" He answered:

> by the revolutionary struggle itself, with defined goals that would imply their most vital interests and that would bring them into confrontation with their exploiters on the field of events and would educate them politically. Only a class struggle unleashed by the Revolution in action would sweep away, like a house of cards, the most vulgar prejudices and atrocious ignorance in which they had been maintained by their oppressors.[26]

Some writers have challenged Castro's claim to being a Marxist on the grounds that an unbridgeable gulf exists between the teachings of his mentor, José Martí, and Marxism. In Castro's case, however, admiration for Martí complemented, rather than conflicted with, his acceptance of the Marxian world view. Both Martí and Lenin "were well represented" on the bookshelves of the house on 25th Street where Castro made his headquarters during the months before the Moncada.[27] Fidel and Abel saw Marxist-Leninist ideas through the prism of Cuba's problems and as an extension of Martí's vision of Cuba. For them, Martí's thought was the national bedrock on which the other ideas flourished. It can be said with certainty that even today Castro is a Martí-influenced Marxist.

While exploring Castro's ideological outlook, I made what some will consider a sensational discovery about his contacts with Communists shortly before the Moncada attack. These contacts do not mean that Castro was a member of the Popular Socialist party, or that he agreed with their tactics and strategy. What it does prove is that even in the cold-war atmosphere of 1953 he respected the Communists and, even though it entailed a danger to his secret undertaking if discovered, was willing to maintain certain relations with them.

One revealing example was his continuing contact with Luis Más Martín. One day not long before the Moncada, Más Martín accompanied Castro to the Communist-party bookshop in Havana. Among the books Castro bought that day were some dealing with the Russian Revolution and the Soviet military campaigns against the Nazis. Castro did not have the money to pay for the purchase, and as was customary, Más Martín, a party functionary, signed as guarantor. Castro had always been a good risk, but this time he never got around to returning the money. He must have had pangs of conscience, however, because from prison two years later he wrote his sister about the money he had borrowed to buy books, ". . . and the day I get together a few pesos, I promise to pay those I still owe."[28]

When Más Martín went into the Sierra shortly before victory in 1958, he joshed with Castro about the money still owing to him.[29]

Only a few days before the Moncada attack, in July 1953, Castro met with Carlos Rafael Rodríguez, now one of the top men in the Cuban government and, at that time, the national propaganda chief of the PSP. Rodríguez told me this story in his spacious office at the Communist party's central committee building in 1972. Castro, it seems, had come to the party bookshop, where he often bought books. "While there, in the same doorway that led to the offices of the national committee of the party, Flavio Bravo appeared. Together with Castro he came up to the propaganda department. . . . We had a long conversation about the national situation."[30]

Rodríguez's version does not indicate that Castro tipped his hand about his imminent attack on the Moncada barracks during the interchange. "The conversation," Rodríguez says, "was that of two leaders, two revolutionaries, speaking about the struggle against Batista." Rodríguez says he does not recall everything they talked about that day. "If I had known what Fidel would do in a few days," he explained, "I would have made it a point to remember what he spoke about that day with much greater precision."[31]

•

The central thrust of the operation worked out by Castro and his military committee was an attack on Santiago de Cuba's Moncada barracks, the second-largest army base in the nation. Once the Moncada had fallen, the next targets in the city were to be the headquarters of the National Police, Maritime Police, and Cuban navy. Simultaneously, a previously prepared program would be transmitted on

Cadena Oriental de Radio. The people would be armed, and Santiago, five hundred miles from Havana, would become a liberated area. It was hoped that these events "would unleash a revolutionary storm over the entire country." [32]

The key element of the radio program was to be the Moncada Manifesto, prepared under the direction of Fidel Castro. The manifesto, largely hortatory in nature, described the immediate political and economic goals of the insurrection. The central portion of the manifesto was an eleven-point revolutionary program presented by those "unconnected to past errors and vile greed who desire a new Cuba." [33] The program declared itself "free from the fetters of foreign nations and from the influences and ambitions of the nation's own politicians and personalities"; affirmed its respect for the Constitution of 1940; and announced its decision to put Cuba on the road to economic prosperity by safeguarding its subsoil, geographical integrity, agriculture, and industry "that have been exploited by illegitimate and spurious governments with excessive greed and culpable interest."

It is not true, as Hugh Thomas says, that "the theoretic ideas of Castro and his friends in 1953 can be gauged most exactly from the proclamation to be read after the capture of the radio station." [34] Like the proverbial iceberg, all that is, is not seen. If one takes into account Castro's idea of presenting a broad "first stage" unifying program, we can see that Thomas's assessment is a serious misconception. More apt might be a comment of Armando Hart, a member of Cuba's CP politburo, who told me, "Only a Marxist could have written the Moncada Manifesto." [35]

One of the main arguments of critics who deny the essentially radical nature of the Moncada Manifesto centers around its advocacy of a return to the Constitution of 1940.

Inasmuch as this is a consistent plank in Castro's program right through to the revolutionary victory, it is worth examining.

The constitution, hammered out with Communist participation on the eve of World War II, was generally considered the most progressive constitution of the Americas, and a broad interpretation of it would have allowed for fundamental social and economic changes. For instance, it declared punishable by law, all discrimination because of race and sex (article 20). It assigned to the state the responsibility of assuring "to all manual and intellectual workers the economic conditions for a decent existence" (article 60). It announced that the "subsoil belongs to the state" (article 88) and proscribed the big landholdings so prevalent in Cuba (article 90). It left another loophole for nationalization by requiring that foreign property must "correspond in every case to the socioeconomic interests of the nation" (article 272). Even the clause that explicitly defended private-property rights allowed for state confiscation of property "by competent judicial authority and for justified reasons of public utility and social interest" (article 24). None of these articles had ever been fully implemented.

The secret of the nature of the Revolution foreseen by Fidel may well be contained, not in the 1940 Constitution, but rather in Point F of the Moncada Manifesto, which declares that the coming revolution "follows the ideas of Martí contained in his speeches and the principles of the Cuban Revolutionary party in the Montecristo Manifesto and takes for its own the revolutionary programs of Young Cuba, ABC Radical, and the Party of the Cuban People (Orthodox)."

The ideas of José Martí, of course, represent a huge storehouse of commentary on many critical themes. Martí has been many things to many people. But there is little doubt that for Fidel Castro what was important were the explicitly progressive aspects of Martí's writings. One of the essential ideas of Martí was contained in his warning of the danger of United States hegemony over Cuba. Another, contained in the Montecristo Manifesto, warned of the dire consequences of racial prejudice. Still another, contained in the principles of the Cuban Revolutionary party, emphasized the need for unity and organization in the struggle. Martí had also espoused the identity of interests of "our America," meaning Latin America, an idea specifically included in Point G of the Moncada Manifesto. One can assume that the "ideas of Martí," so ample in their anticolonial and democratic content, could be interpreted in the context of mid-twentieth-century Cuba as a guide to radical change.[36]

More intriguing are the references to Young Cuba, ABC Radical, and, to a lesser extent, the Party of the Cuban People.

Chibás and his Party of the Cuban People symbolized confrontation with corruption in government. Certainly in the popular mind, his name was not associated with socialism, although for many people he did represent the battle against powerful foreign interests and the *status quo* in general. Fidel Castro, however, had memories of the origins of the party. As a twenty-year-old student, he had heard Chibás call for a new party based on "nationalism, anti-imperialism, socialism, economic independence, political liberty, and social justice." [37]

It might well have been these original ideas that the manifesto referred to when it spoke of the "revolutionary ideas" of the Orthodox party.

The reference to ABC Radical seems strange, since only a handful of Cubans could have been expected to know anything about the tiny grouping that had existed several generations before. The ABC, better known to the older generation, had played a largely destructive and even counterrevolutionary role in the struggle against Machado in the early thirties. After Machado's fall, a small group split off from the ABC under the name *ABC Radical* and put forth a program of socialism for Cuba. This must be the reason the virtually unknown group was included in the manifesto.

The mention of Antonio Güiteras' Young Cuba is perhaps the most significant in terms of defining a specific economic system for the new revolutionary Cuba. The *Program of Young Cuba,* published in October 1934,[38] explicitly attacked foreign control of the Cuban economy and put forth a socialist solution for the nation. In doing so, it planted the idea of necessary stages for achieving this goal. "We will approach the socialist state by successive preparatory stages. . . . We pursue historical certainty, not antihistorical forcing."

When one understands the nature of the examples Castro cited in the Moncada Manifesto, one can see their real implications. Yet despite these very clear but indirect references to socialism, nowhere was the idea or the word specifically mentioned. The wording of the Moncada Manifesto was broad enough to attract all social classes and, at the same time, allowed for a flexible interpretation of the Revolution's socio-economic goals.

Fidel viewed the Moncada Manifesto and the program it defined as "an essential part of the revolutionary strategy."[39] As it happened, very few learned of the Moncada Manifesto. Castro explained a half year after the attack that it was not broadcast "because we adopted the criterion of not taking the radio stations until victory at the barracks was assured, in order to avoid any massacre of the populace."[40]

•

If Castro was essentially a Marxist thinker at the time of the Moncada, then he must have had a special faith in the Cuban proletariat and its historic role. We have already seen that the men he chose to accompany him on his history-making mission were mainly workers. Castro's choice of workers, rather than students, should not be passed over lightly, inasmuch as Castro knew the student community and could have recruited his force from it. That he chose not to is proof of his strategic outlook.

Another significant decision he made has never been disclosed before. It concerns his contingency plan in the event the Moncada attack failed and they were unable to hold Santiago de Cuba. That Castro did have a contingency plan is known. He once said:

> The truth is that we always had in mind to first carry out the insurrection in one region and try to hold it and, if that did not succeed, to go to the mountains with all those weapons and initiate the struggle there.[41]

A clue to at least part of that contingency plan was given me by Más Martín, who joined Castro in the Sierra Maestra during the last stage of the guerrilla war. He recalled that at one of the guerrilla camps, Castro had mentioned in a casual conversation that in the event of being forced to flee Santiago de Cuba after the attack, he had planned to take whatever men he could muster to Charco Redondo, a small mining town in the foothills of the Sierra Maestra, arm the workers there, and retire with them into the mountains to initiate a prolonged guerrilla war.[42]

Más Martín's remark led me to search for information about Charco Redondo and any connection Fidel might have had with it. I found out that the manganese mine at Charco Redondo was operated by the Guamá Company and that it exported its entire production to the United States. It was widely known as a living hell, and periodic exposés were made of the horrible conditions that existed there. One account of a visit to the mine was published in a 1954 issue of Cuba's largest-circulation magazine, *Bohemia:* "We are in the tomb of men . . . without adequate medical attention, without safeguards in their work, without protection of any kind." Charco Redondo, according to the *Bohemia* writer, was "the cruelest kind of exploitation of man by man." [43] He wrote that "a reign of terror" prevailed at Charco Redondo. It was for him a "Dante-esque vision that reminds one of a concentration camp."

There is evidence that Fidel Castro visited Charco Redondo, which is eight miles off the main highway from Bayamo to Palma Soriano, to the north of Santiago de Cuba. That visit, as far as I could determine, took place one day before García Bárcena's futile march on Camp Colombia in April 1953.

Castro spent that Good Friday evening in Palma Soriano, at the home of Oscar Ortega, a member of the Movement. The following day Castro visited Charco Redondo mine with Ortega and Pedro Aguilera, another member of the Movement.[44] Aguilera, a dentist, had a practice at Charco Redondo. Ortega, a worker with a primary-school education, acted as Aguilera's assistant. Years later Aguilera recalled Castro's visit to Charco Redondo:

> Fidel was very struck with the conditions at the mines. He almost organized a meeting there. . . . Miners began to gather around him, and he questioned them . . . about their way of life, the causes of sickness, and a whole series of things.[45]

Following his visit to the mine, Castro ordered the Palma Soriano group to concentrate on building a solid organization in the region. Aguilera writes: "We strengthened our activities at the Charco Redondo mines—[Fidel] instructed us to attract as many as we could from there." [46]

The decision to take the city of Bayamo, at the same time that the Moncada in Santiago de Cuba was being attacked, thus had two purposes. The first was to prevent reinforcements from arriving in Santiago. The second was related to the Charco Redondo contingency plan—to allow Castro and his men to retreat to Charco Redondo if Santiago had to be abandoned.

The fact that Castro planned to retire to Charco Redondo and recruit exploited miners for a subsequent guerrilla war is additional evidence that he was influenced by socialist theory and practice at the time of the Moncada attack. It suggests again that Castro intended the coming revolution to be fought by the dispossessed of Cuba and in their interests.

•

July 26 was the day chosen for the audacious attack on the Moncada barracks. It was the Sunday of Santa María, and the annual carnival would be in full swing, allowing a large group of young strangers to pass unnoticed. Fifty-eight years before, for the same reason, Juan Gualberto Gómez, a black who was Jóse Martí's delegate in Cuba, had chosen a carnival Sunday to initiate the last phase of the war against Spain.[47]

The specific plan of attack was known to only a few within the Movement. Haydée Santamaría claims that five men knew the details: Fidel Castro, Abel Santamaría, José Luis Tasende, Renato Guitart, and Pedro Miret, all members of the Movement's military committee.[48]

Fidel spent July 24 in Havana dispatching his army toward Santiago de Cuba. They traveled in small groups, by car, bus, and train. Housing had already been arranged in both Santiago and Bayamo. An isolated house at Siboney, outside Santiago, had been rented as a "chicken farm"; it was to be the staging area. In Havana, Melba Hernández's house was used as the supply center. From there, on the twenty-fourth, cartons of uniforms were shipped to Oriente province, where Castro was meeting with cell leaders. At two in the morning on July 25, Castro and another member of the Movement left Melba's house with some Batista September 4 pennants that would be used as part of the planned ruse.

Before leaving for Oriente on the twenty-fifth, Castro made an audacious visit to the police department's bureau of investigation, ostensibly to make inquiries about a client.[49] His real reason was to ascertain whether the bureau had any inkling of what he was planning. It seemed that they had no hint of the armed attack the Movement would soon carry out. After midnight on the morning of July 26, Fidel arrived at the Siboney farm, where 130 men and 2 women were gathered. Castro told them of the plans to attack the Moncada barracks. Ten men decided to drop out—four university students, five Havana-cell members, and a radio technician.[50]

The Moncada was a high-walled citadel with a normal garrison of four hundred men.[51] The attack force was divided into three groups. Twenty-four persons were assigned to the city hospital, which could control one access point to the Moncada. Six men were sent to the rooftop of the courthouse, whence the .50-caliber machine gun on the Moncada's roof could be covered. Eight men were to storm Post 3 to open the way for penetration of the citadel by Castro's group of eighty-four men.

Success would depend on a surprise, on a commando attack carried out without firing a shot. The strategic sectors of the base would be overrun before the enemy could rally an effective defense. The attackers' .22-caliber rifles were no match for superior arms of the soldiers in open battle.

The two women, Melba Hernández and Haydée Santamaría, were included in the attack force only after their insistent pleading. They were taken as nurses and sent to the hospital.[52]

Because of a series of unforseen events, the decisive need for surprise was lost, compromising their chances for success. The attack became a defensive battle doomed to failure. After two hours of positional firing, Castro ordered a retreat. The courthouse operation, which was being successfully executed, had to be abandoned. The group invading the city hospital knew nothing of the retreat, and by the time they became aware of the situation, their escape was impossible. The military operation in Bayamo was equally disastrous. There, a ten-minute attack ended with the retreat of Fidel's group of attackers.[53]

The plan, prepared for many months to begin the armed revolutionary war, became a rout in a few hours. The people of Santiago who heard the firing did not know its meaning. Many thought it was a battle among Batista's soldiers, since Castro's men were dressed in army uniforms.

The aftermath of the attack was bloodier than the fighting. At the Moncada, eight of Fidel's group and sixteen soldiers were killed. At Bayamo, only one soldier died in battle. Yet the final toll of the Movement's dead reached sixty-one,[54] a measure of the criminal retaliation practiced by the Batista armed forces against prisoners they captured during the next three days.

Only later, after wide public protest in Santiago, was Colonel Río Chavino forced to announce that the lives of the prisoners would be spared. Archbishop Pérez Serantes asked for permission to enter the areas in which fugitives were hiding, to guarantee their safety.[55] Thirty-two revolutionaries finally surrendered through his mediation.

Castro's capture came on August 1. For five days he had wandered around the mountains near Santiago with a small group of followers. Exhausted by their arduous retreat, they were caught by a rural-guard patrol while they were sleeping.

●

Castro had given orders to his men to return to Siboney in the event of failure of the Santiago attack, so that they could make their way to the Sierra Maestra to continue the struggle.[56] However, one participant declares that on leaving the Moncada, Castro decided to lead several carloads of men to Caney to attack a police station.[57] This version states that the driver missed the northeast cutoff on Garzón Avenue in Santiago and thus took the road to Siboney. Once on the Siboney road, there was no turning back, since by this time police and army vehicles had been alerted.

Caney is on the road from Santiago to Palma Soriano, which lies on the main highway to Charco Redondo. A victory for his Bayamo group would have permitted Castro to reach Charco Redondo without interference from Batista's forces. He could then have picked reinforcements among the workers and headed for the nearby Sierra.

The return to Siboney put Castro's men in a much more critical situation. Only one road passed through Siboney. In one direction lay Santiago and in the other, La Gran Piedra, the highest peak of the zone. To reach the Sierra Maestra on foot would have taken days, perhaps weeks.

Of the forty men who gathered at Siboney, seventeen decided to follow Castro on foot toward Gran Piedra.[58] During the following days they wandered through unknown terrain. They were especially helped by a black woman who treated one of the wounded and sent her grandson to guide the rest.[59] A farmer gave them a veritable feast—pork and *malanga* (arum). Castro left him his chrome-plated [60] pistol and, half in jest, told him to use it when the landowner came to collect taxes or dispossess him. At another shack, that of Feliciano Heredia, they were given food and Castro was able to listen to a speech by Batista on a portable radio. Batista blamed the Moncada attack on "millionaires, resting on a cushion of money, proclaiming revolution . . . buying arms overseas . . . and making run of blood, but not their own." The targets of this denunciation were obvious: Prio and Aureliano. Batista had other targets, however. He claimed that his soldiers had found "Communist documents, Soviet propaganda, and books of Lenin" at Siboney.[61]

Castro was captured on August 1 by a rural-guard squad led by Lieutenant Pedro Sarría, a black man. Among Castro's followers captured with him were Armando Mestre and Juan Almeida, also black. According to an account by Sarría, several of his black soldiers felt consternation on seeing other blacks in such a perilous situation and shouted: "'And you? What are you doing here with these whites? You're blacks. What are you going to gain? Now you're chained together with them.'" [62]

Sarría had ordered, "Silence. I don't want any of that. Not one word that criticizes the opinion of anyone.'" [63]

Sarría was later arrested, tried for insubordination, and convicted. Three months before Batista fled, Sarría was allowed to leave jail but remained under house arrest. After the Revolution he became adjutant to the President of Cuba. When he died in 1972, Fidel Castro attended his funeral.

III.

Genesis

of

Revolution

With what joy I would revolutionize this
country from top to bottom.

Fidel Castro, letter from prison, April 14, 1954.

I knew what the final goal was. My program
was like the antechamber to a socialist revolution. To get to the third floor, one must start
from the first.

Fidel Castro to author on the Moncada program,

June 20, 1975.

7.

"History will
Absolve Me"

On September 21, almost two months after the attack on the Moncado barracks, Case Number 37 of the Urgency Court of Santiago de Cuba was brought to trial. The defendants numbered more than one hundred.[1]

The high point of the first day's session was Fidel Castro's testimony. During his two hours on the stand he proudly admitted his role in the Moncada events and explained his motives for organizing the attack. He denied having received support from any party or politician and scoffed at the idea that former President Prio was the "intellectual author" of the attack. In a phrase that has since become famous in Cuba, he declared, "The only intellectual author of the attack on the Moncada is José Martí, the apostle of our independence."[2]

Near the end of the first session, Castro asked for and received permission from the court to act as his own defense attorney. On the following day, he used his newly won powers with devastating effect. He showed extraordinary skill in eliciting proof, from the prosecution witnesses, of tortures and assassinations committed by the army after the attack. He was, it seems, too effective. When the list was called at the beginning of the third session on September 26, Castro was not in the courtroom.

The judges were told that Castro was sick and could not attend the session. Raúl Castro, one of the defendants, shouted, "Fidel is not sick!" Not long afterward, Melba Hernández, a prisoner herself, handed the court a letter she had spirited out of Boniato prison. In it, Castro denied that he was ill and alleged that his assassination was being planned. He asked the court to appoint physicians to examine him.

That evening, the three judges of the Urgency Court visited Castro at Boniato and later signed an affidavit that he was in a "good state of health and showed absolute serenity." [3] Despite this, the director of the prison refused to allow Castro to attend the subsequent sessions of the trial at the courthouse "because he is under treatment by doctors in this prison." [4]

The trial proceeded without Fidel and two of his wounded comrades. By the tenth session, on October 5, all those who had denied their guilt had been exonerated.[5] On the following day, twenty-seven men and two women, all of whom had confessed their participation in the Moncada assault, were found guilty. Three, including Raúl Castro, were sentenced to thirteen years in prison; twenty received ten-year sentences; three received three-year sentences; and the two women, Haydée Santamaría and Melba Hernández, were each sentenced to seven months at the Guanajay women's reformatory.

Castro's trial, along with that of a wounded co-defendant, was resumed on October 16 in the nurses' salon of the local hospital. In his cross-examination of Major Andrés Pérez, Castro asked how, in three supposed battles with insurgents after the Moncada, the army had killed eighteen and lost none. "Is it," he commented with sarcasm, "that you were using atomic weapons?" [6]

That same day Castro was handed a fifteen-year prison sentence. But the day is historically memorable for his long defense speech, which has become part of the classical literature of revolution. "Condemn me, it doesn't matter," he concluded. "History will absolve me."

Critics have accused Fidel Castro of having subsequently betrayed liberal goals projected in his "History Will Absolve Me" defense plea. Castro's future radicalism, his communist outlook, they claim, was in no way anticipated in the impassioned speech he made in the makeshift courtroom in Santiago. Theodore Draper, for instance, dismisses the speech as "little more than an anthology of familiar ills and cures, long the staples of Cuban politics." [7] Castro has never contended that the ideological thrust of "History Will Absolve Me" was socialist or communist. It was, he has averred, an "advanced program." [8]

To buttress the argument that the ideals Castro projected were essentially moderate, critics point to his advocacy of a return to the Constitution of 1940. I have already shown that this constitution was extremely progressive and that a loose interpretation of it would have left the way open for fundamental transformation of Cuban society. More important, however, the constitutional-restoration theme is simply the visible part of a much more radical philosophical outlook expressed in "History Will Absolve Me."

It would be hard to imagine Fidel Castro as an idolator of the 1940 Constitution. He had grown to political manhood under it and knew how the constitution could be used in the interests of the rich and the corrupt. He was obviously not interested in returning to the Grau and Prio way of life. The Batista regime was the apex of antipopular government, but the previous regimes that had operated *under* the constitution had exhibited many of the same evils. "If the previous regime was full of political quackery, thievery, pillage, lack of all respect for human life, the present regime has multiplied political quackery by five, pillage by ten, and the lack of respect for human life by one hundred." [9]

In his quest for legitimizing radical change, Castro put aside the question of constitutionality and sought his answers in political philosophy. He recalled the defense of the right of rebellion against tyrannical government by generations of antifeudal and bourgeois theorists: John Salisbury, Francis Hotman, John Knox, John Locke, Jean Jacques Rosseau, and Thomas Paine by such documents as the American Declaration of Independence, and the French Declaration of the Rights of Man.

"I admit, because I so believe that revolutions constitute a source of law." [10] He had espoused the same doctrine in his suit against Batista shortly after the military takeover. At that time he had defined the essence of revolution in negative terms: "Without a new conception of the state, of society, and of the judicial order based on historical and philosophical principles, there can be no revolution that generates law." What he was saying quite clearly is that only a profound social upheaval generates a real revolution, generates its own legitimacy.

For Castro the constitution was not something sacrosanct. When he speaks of restoring it as the supreme law of the land, he significantly adds "until such time as the people would decide to modify or change it." [11] But after victory, "the revolutionary movement, as the momentary incarnation of that sovereignty which is the only source of legitimate power, would assume all the faculties inherent in sovereignty, such as the power to legislate, to enforce laws, and to judge." [12] He then states candidly that "a government acclaimed by the mass of combatants would receive and be vested with the necessary power to proceed to establish effectively the will of the people and true justice." [13] This was exactly the line followed when the revolutionary victory did come in 1959.

If Castro had been primarily interested in a return to pre-Batista conditions, he would not have needed to project a popular revolutionary dictatorship in "History Will Absolve Me." Certainly his legal defense would have been more acceptable to powerful anti-Batista forces if he had simply advocated the immediate return to the *status quo ante,* the restoration of deposed President Prio, and the traditional political-party system. It is precisely on the question of state power and its assumption by the revolutionaries that one discerns the influence of Marxist thought on Castro. He obviously felt the need to guarantee, by a revolutionary dictatorship, the processes of necessary change.

•

In "History Will Absolve Me," Castro advanced a limited program that would have had the effect of a head-on collision with the Cuban power elite and U.S. investors. By extending to the *campesinos* full ownership of farms of less than 165 acres, it would have eliminated sharecropping, the most common form of land tenure in Cuba and the basis of semifeudal relationships in the countryside. By assuring workers a 30-percent share of the profits of all large enterprises and sugar-cane farmers 55 percent of the profits made from the sale of cane, it would have meant a clash with foreign and domestic business interests. A confiscation law for all property embezzled from the state under previous administrations was open to broad interpretation and could have included vast areas of land obtained fradulently by Cuban and U.S. businessmen. Never had Grau, Prio, or Agramonte proposed such radical changes.[14]

This *immediate* program is only the tip of the iceberg, however. It represents nothing more than the first stage of revolutionary reform. Castro makes it plain in "History Will Absolve Me" that once these immediate goals were made law, others would be studied and implemented, including agrarian and educational reform and the nationalization of the U.S.–owned electric and telephone monopolies.[15]

The details of agrarian reform were not spelled out, but Castro did note that "more than half the best crop lands are in foreign hands," and he singled out the United Fruit Company as an example.[16] It is logical to assume that his agrarian reform would have eliminated the huge landholdings of both United States and Cuban *latifundistas*.

Nationalization of the electric and telephone companies might have been contemplated as the beginning of a broad nationalization program. Castro explicitly declares in "History Will Absolve Me" that it is the responsibility of the state "to employ all the means within its reach to provide work to all those who might need it and to assure dignified living to every manual and intellectual worker."[17] Under conditions of a revolutionary dictatorship the key words, *all the means within its reach,* could mean a broad nationalization policy as a solution to Cuba's chronic unemployment.

That Castro hints at a socialist solution in "History Will Absolve Me" can be derived from his scornful attitude toward those "mouthing nonsense about absolute freedom of enterprise, guarantees for investment capital, and the law of supply and demand."[18]

"The future of the nation and the solution to its problems," Castro declared, "can no longer depend on the selfish interests of a dozen financiers nor on the cold calculation of profits by ten or twelve magnates in their air-conditioned offices."[19] Castro's defense plea was a sharp condemnation of the entire Cuban socioeconomic system. He speaks of the burden of unemployment, the tragedy of the housing situation, the absence of public health care, the parasitic nature of the cities, the plight of the farmers, and the omnipotence of the big landholders.

A correction of these ills would have required drastic changes in the power structure through class struggle. This struggle would pit *the people* against the political and economic elite. Who does Castro mean by *the people?*

"When we mention the people in connection with struggle, we mean the unredeemed masses . . . *six hundred thousand* Cubans who are out of work . . . *five hundred thousand* farm workers who live in miserable huts . . . *four hundred thousand* industrial workers and laborers . . . *one hundred thousand* small farmers who live and die working land that is not theirs." [20]

Castro's intention was to put an irreversible revolutionary process in motion. Revolution was to be the source of law. The legislation decreed by the revolutionary government could not be decreed unconstitutional, Castro argued, "because when people achieve what they have eagerly sought for various generations, there is no force in the world strong enough to take it away from them." [21] In this formulation perhaps, we find the key to Castro's strategy for deepseated change, his ultimate reliance on the people moved to revolutionary action.

"History Will Absolve Me" posited a political philosophy and program that struck at the roots of class privileges in Cuban society. It is in this sense, as Castro commented many years later, that it contained "the germ of all the subsequent development of the Revolution." [22]

Why wasn't Castro more explicit in defining his goals? Because, he once answered, such an approach "would have scarcely been able to win over anyone." [23] The program was designed to unite the Cuban people against the immediate enemy, Batista.

"It was written with sufficient care so as to put forward a series of fundamental points without, at the same time, making formulations that might limit our field of action within the Revolution; that might prevent the movement, which we believed could bring about the defeat of Batista, from being very small and limited. That is to say, we had to try to make the movement as broad as possible." [24]

Castro has observed that the program presented "the maximum aspiration at that stage, given the objective and subjective conditions." However, he adds, "we were socialists; we had the opportunity to study the fundamental works of Marx, Engels, and Lenin." [25]

Skeptics refuse to believe that Castro could have been sufficiently astute to have hidden his deepest aspirations for the Cuban Revolution. But an analytical study of "History Will Absolve Me" shows, beyond doubt, that Castro *did* have in mind a revolution that went far beyond "the familiar . . . cures, the old staples of Cuban politics."

Castro's credentials as a revolutionary have been impugned by some critics who claim that he was blind to the "black question." One writer affirms erroneously that before 1953 Fidel Castro "never had anything to say on the problem of the Negro in Cuba." [26] I have already proved the baselessness of this claim by showing that Castro had been an active member of the Committee to Fight Racial Discrimination at the university and had spoken out against racism.

The same writer asserts that "it would have been possible to have read 'History Will Absolve Me' without knowing there were Negroes at all in Cuba" [27] and that "Castro never mentioned the matter in any of his speeches or programs before the Revolution." [28]

In "History Will Absolve Me," Castro did not specifically mention racial discrimination in Cuba. But he did make poignant reference to the matter after the Moncada, only three weeks before he delivered this speech. It occurs in his reference, during his first appearance in court, to Antonio Maceo, the black general who was a hero of Cuba's independence struggles.[29]

PROSECUTOR: Tell me, young man. On what political prestige did you bank that led you to believe that an entire people would join you, a people as astute as the Cuban people and one that has been deceived so many times?

FIDEL CASTRO: . . . On the same prestige . . . that the black muleteer Antonio Maceo counted on when he rebelled. . . . He was not yet then the Maceo of the Baraguá protest, nor of the Invasion, who was capable of predicting that it was dangerous to contract debts of gratitude with such a powerful neighbor, referring to the United States of North America.

In those first years of battle, Maceo was not known and did not have the prestige to which you refer. . . . History has many times tried to depreciate him because he was black. They have portrayed him as a simple warrior, when, in addition to being a warrior, he was a statesman, a man who had developed himself extraordinarily and whose civic qualities awakened respect and admiration from his enemies.

But Maceo was a muleteer and black, and because he was a black mule driver, they belittle the legitimate place in the history of his country he deserves for his irrefutable merits.[30]

The prosecutor's question had not been concerned with the problem of racial prejudice in Cuba. It was, "On what political prestige did you bank?" Yet Fidel chose to answer by using Maceo as his example. Even so, Maceo's name could have been invoked without coming to grips with the problem of racial prejudice. Castro could have simply answered that Maceo had begun as a simple man without prestige and that he had gained it in the course of the struggle for Cuban independence. Out of choice, Castro brought out the problem of racial prejudice, a clear indication of his own thinking on the matter.

It is also significant that the part of Maceo's ideological heritage Castro emphasized was the warning against the threat of the "powerful neighbor . . . the United States of North America"—a sign of Castro's own ideas on the matter.[31]

Like Maceo, one of Castro's followers, Juan Almeida, was unschooled and black. The same writer who wrongly criticizes Castro for his blind spot on the black question calls Almeida a person "of limited intellect but loyal to Castro as a leader and willing to follow him anywhere under any circumstances."[32] This same Almeida fought with Castro at the Moncada and later, during the prolonged guerrilla war, became a *comandante,* the highest rank in the rebel army. Since the Revolution he has held a succession of vital posts in the army and government.[33] Almeida's "limited intellect" was demonstrated when he was cross-examined during the Moncada trial:

PROSECUTOR: (*in disbelief*): Someone had to convince you to take part in the attack on the Moncada!

ALMEIDA: No, sir, no one had to convince me. I came on my own, inspired by my own idea. . . . No one induced me to it except my own ideas, which coincided with those of *compañero* Fidel Castro and which, in my case, come from reading the works of Martí and the history of our independence fighters. And I believe it was the same in the case of Fidel, although he had the opportunity to go to the university and has great knowledge of all those things.

PROSECUTOR: Did you give or receive orders?

ALMEIDA: I received them. I did not have the honor to give them.

PROSECUTOR: But surely you would have liked that revolution to triumph so that you could give orders?

ALMEIDA: That was not my intention. I want the revolution to triumph so that the people give orders. Others have given them until now and things have not gone well. Thus, the moment has come for the people to give the orders, for the people to manage things.[34]

How can we explain the absence of an explicit reference to racism in "History Will Absolve Me"? It is possible that Castro felt an emphasis on race under Cuban conditions was not necessary. Maceo and Martí, symbols of black-white unity and intellectual mentors of Fidel Castro, had both believed that the struggle was Cuban before it was black or white. Maceo had proclaimed that "the flag of Cuba . . . is that of all Cubans; join together, then, beneath it." [35] Martí had declared that to be "Cuban is more than white, more than mulatto, more than black." [36]

Castro had *the people* in mind "more than white . . . mulatto . . . black." Certainly blacks counted heavily among the "unredeemed masses" for whom he appealed in "History

Will Absolve Me." However, like Maceo and Martí before him, he surely viewed Cuba as a nation whose majority, without distinction of race, shared a common fate of poverty, corrupt government, oppression, and foreign domination, requiring a spirit of common purpose.[37]

•

In his inventory of the items found by the army at Siboney, Captain M. E. Aguila listed "The first volume of the selected works of Communist dictator Lenin." [38] The discovery of the volume with the signature of Abel Santamaría on the flyleaf was given wide publicity and used by the government to shore up the thesis that Communists were involved in the Moncada attack.

The Batista government had immediately taken advantage of the Moncada attack to shut down the Communist news paper, *Hoy,* "for complicity . . . in the bloody criminal assault in Santiago de Cuba." [39]

The situation of the Communists was prejudiced by the coincidence that a large contingent of its national and local leaders happened to be in Santiago de Cuba during or shortly before July 26. The Communists had gone to the city for a national-assembly meeting. Ostensibly, however, the gathering had assembled to celebrate the birthday of the Communist party general secretary, Blas Roca. Many of the delegates, including Blas Roca, left the city when the assembly ended, and other delegates stayed on until the next day, which happened to be July 26.[40]

Shortly after the attack the military-intelligence service began picking up PSPers who had been or were in Santiago. More than a dozen, including Juan Marinello, the president of the PSP, and Blas Roca, were arrested and immediately sent to the Vivac in Santiago. A few were picked up in Havana and later sent back to Santiago. Nine Communists were included in Case Number 37 and later acquitted.[41]

During their imprisonment in the Vivac, Raúl Castro suggested that the Communist leaders there organize a study circle for the thirty-eight men in the cellblock. One of the discussions was based on a Martí dictum: "Unity is the order of the day." [42]

The Communist witnesses truthfully denied any involvement in the Moncada attack. Lázaro Peña, the veteran trade-union leader, declared, "I am not in any way responsible for the events, nor have I had any dealings with its protagonists." When the prosecutor asked Peña if "the declarations of the PSP are directed toward the broad masses?" Peña answered with a simple "Exactly." [43]

After the attack the PSP had issued a statement repudiating the "*putschist* method peculiar to bourgeois political factions." It characterized the attempt to take the Moncada barracks by storm as "adventurism." At the same time it recognized the heroism of the men, although it considered it to be "false and sterile." [44]

Two decades later I asked Carlos Rafael Rodríguez, a leading Communist then as now, about his Party's attitude. The vice-president of the Cuban state council told me:

> We did characterize it as a *putsch*. Fidel later showed that this was not his criterion. . . . He demonstrated this, and he was right because he had an overall plan. The plan did not consist of a simple attack on the barracks but an attack on the barracks in order to arm the people and unleash a general insurrection. And he had a political program.
>
> That is to say, he did not intend to seize power through a single blow. He conceived of an integral process, but we did not know that. We knew all that only later, because Fidel had not made his entire plan explicit. We understood this only when Fidel explained all the steps in his proposed plan of action—the barracks attack, the requisition of arms, the appeal

to the people calling on them to organize a mass movement, and, in later stages, a large-scale armed struggle. He had even prepared a radio appeal calling on the people to fight for a political program.

But at that time we judged things by their external character, and we called it a *putsch*. It should be noted that at the same time, we lauded the bravery and courage of the Moncada attackers.[45]

Although the PSP divorced itself from the Moncada attackers on theoretical and practical grounds, its leaders were impressed with Castro's audacity and integrity. They knew that the leader of such an attack, facing a long prison sentence, could very well have played on the anti-Communist sentiments so much in vogue at the time, making his own defense more palatable and thus reducing his sentence. Castro had not done this. He had instead adopted a principled stance by attacking the Batista government, exposing the ills of the Cuban body politic, and presenting a program that the PSP itself could easily support. It was logical, therefore, that the Communists respected Castro despite their differences with him over tactics and strategy.

Immediately following his release, Lázaro Peña told a local party leader in Havana, "You know, that Fidel Castro will be around for a long time." [46]

In mid-October, the twenty-eight male prisoners were sent to the *"Presidio Modelo"* on the Isle of Pines, south of the Cuban mainland.[47] Their cell was a long, high-ceilinged ward of the prison hospital.

Almost immediately, Fidel organized a "school"—the Abel Santamaría—for the men's general and political education. Classes in mathematics, grammar, and history were given during the day, and in the evenings there were often dis-

cussions on varied themes. The prison authorities allowed
the men to receive books, and before long they had accumulated a substantial collection.

About a hundred of Fidel Castro's books arrived. Among
them were novels by Balzac, Anatole France, Gorky, and
A. J. Cronin (*The Stars Look Down*). There was a two-
volume history of political ideas and a four-volume edition
of José Martí's works. One could find in the Library such
works as *Economy and Society,* by Max Weber, and *Liberty, Power, and Democratic Planning*, by Karl Mannheim
There were a book of essays by the Peruvian Marxist José
Carlos Mariátegui, works of Lenin and Marx, and a half-
dozen books by José Ingenieros, the Argentine socialist
thinker.[48]

Jesús Montané, one of the prisoners, told me that "it was
Fidel who personally indoctrinated us." [49] For Castro himself, confinement proved to be the proverbial school for
revolutionaries. In an enthusiastic letter from prison he
wrote:

> What a fantastic school this prison is! Here, I have
> forged my vision of the world and have found the
> meaning of my life. Will it be long or short? I do
> not know. Fruitful or sterile? But there is something
> I feel reaffirming itself within me; my passionate de-
> sire to sacrifice and struggle.[50]

Fidel remained with the other Moncada prisoners until
mid-April. His separation came after the men loudly sang
the "July 26 Hymn" during a visit to the prison of Fulgencio
Batista. As punishment Castro was put into solitary confinement.[51]

Castro suffered deeply from the enforced solitude in his
tiny cell across from the prison mortuary. After four months
he wrote:

> I spend the days reading and mastering my feelings.
> . . . If someone's patience has been put to the test, it
> has been mine. . . . there are times when I spend hours
> fighting against the desire to explode, to declare a
> hunger strike and refuse to swallow anything until
> they take me out of this cell or kill me.[52]

Later he wrote:

> I am alive because I have duties to fulfill. Many times
> during these terrible moments which I have had to
> suffer over the past year, I have thought how much
> more agreeable it would be to be dead. I consider
> July 26 to be above my own person, and if I believed
> that I was no longer useful to the cause for which
> I have suffered so, I would kill myself without hesita-
> tion.[53]

By the time Castro wrote this, ten thousand copies of "History Will Absolve Me" had been printed and distributed in
Cuba. From the beginning of his confinement he had begun
to reconstruct the speech, using as a guide his fabulous
memory and the notes made by one of the reporters at the
trial. The manuscript pages were sent out, first between the
double bottoms of matchboxes and later written in lemon
juice between the lines of innocuous letters.[54]

"History Will Absolve Me" brought the entire story of the
Moncada assault and Fidel Castro's revolutionary ideas to
the people of Cuba. Its publication coincided with Batista's
attempt to change his public image by legitimizing his
presidency through elections set for November 1.

Grau San Martín, the old Authentic-party warhorse, announced himself as a presidential candidate. Through no
desire of his own, his campaign meetings would often be
converted into militant demonstrations for change. He

would be interrupted with chants of "Revolution . . . revolution . . . revolution!" or with slogans directed against political repression and corruption.

On October 24, as Grau began a speech in Santiago de Cuba, voices in the crowd began to chant: "Fidel Castro . . . Fidel . . . Fidel Castro!" Grau was literally drowned out. He waited until the shouts died down and then announced: "Friends, the first act of my government will be to free all political prisoners, including the boys of the Moncada." [55]

Fidel Castro, in his solitary cell on the Isle of Pines, had his radio tuned in to the political rally that night. He was elated by what he heard, and later, long after midnight, wrote:

> I carefully studied the multitude from a psychological point of view and the reaction that was manifested there was a phenomenon that doesn't have a precedent. What a formidable lesson for the hierarchy! How loyal the people of our province are! [56]

•

During his more than one and a half years of confinement, Castro worked out the tactics and strategy of the revolution he hoped to lead. He carefully studied the historical and political literature at hand, and his active mind grappled with the practical and theoretical problems of organizing the kind of struggle that would unite the Cuban people on its side. There is no doubt that in his analysis of these problems, his overview was that of Marxian historical materialism. This is clear from a letter he wrote from prison, in which he mentions his reading a work by Karl Marx. It is, as far as I am able to discover, the only time before the revolutionary victory that Castro wrote about reading a Marxist work and gave his opinion of it.

In the letter Castro speaks of having read two works on the Revolution of 1848 and its aftermath, Victor Hugo's study of it, *Napoleon le Petit*, and Marx's work entitled *The Eighteenth Brumaire of Louis Bonaparte*.[57] His comment on the two clearly reveals his ideological outlook. "In comparing these two works," he wrote, "in placing them side by side, one can appreciate the enormous difference between a scientific and realistic conception of history and a purely romantic interpretation." [58]

Castro wholeheartedly identifies himself with Marx's "scientific and realistic conception of history." What conceptions does Marx express in *The Eighteenth Brumaire . . .* ? The pamphlet, basically a study of revolution and counter-revolution in France, challenges all the traditional teachings about bourgeois democracy. Marx speaks of the state apparatus, the laws, constitutions, and "cretin parliamentarianism" and concludes that "the bourgeois republic means the unlimited despotism of one class over other classes."

"Hugo," Castro comments, "does not see the inevitable outcome of social contradictions and the struggle of dominant interests at a precise moment." Castro states that for Hugo, "history is chance"; for Marx, "a process governed by laws." [59]

It would be a mistake not to give full import to Castro's statement. In it Castro is revealed as a convinced Marxist by that time, one who understood the role of class struggle as the moving force of history, and history as "a process governed by laws."

His own study of Cuban reality must have taught him that the road of struggle would be long and complex. Yet he reveled in the vision of a renovated Cuba. In another letter from prison, he wrote:

> With what joy I would revolutionize this country from top to bottom. I am convinced that one could

make its people happy. I would be prepared to incur
the hatred and ill-will of one or two thousand people,
among them relatives, half my friends, two-thirds of
my colleagues and four-fifths of my old college
mates.[60]

There is little doubt that Fidel had in mind a socialist revolution. The absence of explicitness has fostered misintrepre-
tations of his ideology and historical projections. One day
in 1975 I asked him about his Moncada program, and he
answered:

I knew what the final goal was. My program was like
an antechamber to a socialist revolution. To get to the
third floor, one must start from the ground floor.[61]

He then quoted from memory the words of José Martí:

"There are things that, in order to be achieved, must
be hidden. . . . By proclaiming what they are would
only raise difficulties that would make it harder to
attain the desired ends." [62]

When Fidel finished quoting Martí, he pointed his long,
thin cigar at me and declared, "That was Martí's letter to
Manuel Mercado, written on the field of battle one day before his death. When I wrote the Moncada program, I had
Martí's advice very much in mind."

In April 1954, a few days after he wrote of the joy with
which he would revolutionize Cuba "from top to bottom,"
Castro set down his own theory of discretion in a letter to
one of his confidantes, Melba Hernández.[63]

All agreement must be based on firm and clear
foundations, those which will probably succeed and
bring about positive benefit to Cuba. If not, it is
preferable to march alone while you maintain our

standard high until the formidable young men in prison, who prepare themselves with great care for the struggle, are freed. "To know how to wait," said Martí, "is the great secret of success."

Deal with the people artfully and with a smile.[64] Follow the same tactic used in the trial. Defend our viewpoints without making unnecessary enemies. There will be enough time later to crush all the cockroaches together.[65]

8.

Amnesty and Exile

Castro's letters from prison are infused with a goal that went far beyond the simple overthrow of the Batista dictatorship. That goal was a social revolution, and Castro spent his solitary days and nights in fervent thought defining the kind of movement necessary to achieve his purpose. He viewed those who had survived the Moncada assault— the *Moncadistas*—as a vanguard core around which he would build a broader organization. "I ought to organize the men of the 26th of July," he wrote, "and unite them into an indestructible group. . . . A perfectly disciplined nucleus constitutes an incalculable advantage . . . for a legal or insurrectional organization." [1]

His organization would impose iron discipline. Nothing could be expected, he said, "of a movement composed of anarchic men who at the first signs of discord strike out on the path they consider most convenient, thus destroying the machine." Castro projected an apparatus "so powerful that it can implacably destroy anyone who tries to create tendencies, cliques, problems, or who rebels against the Movement." [2]

The disciplined nucleus would be surrounded by "a great civic-political movement." It would therefore be an organization that would have "the necessary force to conquer power by either peaceful or revolutionary means."[3] After victory, the disciplined nucleus and the mass movement would be the principal guarantee for maintaining power. The concept must have been influenced by Lenin's concept of the party as a powerful, disciplined apparatus based on popular support and capable of winning and defending state power and of destroying the counterrevolution.

Castro cautioned against sacrificing principles, but he insisted that "political realities should be taken into consideration; that is, both feet should be kept firmly on the ground."[4] He believed it was necessary "to bring the masses a new and promising message," one like the Moncada program, which took into account the political realities of Cuba. He understood that the revolution would be a prolonged process with different stages. "I know that not even God himself could create all the marvels of the world in a single day," he wrote, "but from the first, we should lay the groundwork that leads to those results."[5]

Perhaps what most sustained Castro's revolutionary fervor during his imprisonment was his impassioned optimism. He believed, as Marx did, and he had so stated in his letter on the *Eighteenth Brumaire* . . . , that historical processes were "the inevitable outcome of social contradictions . . . a process governed by laws."[6] As a man deeply influenced by Marxism, he considered that the dominant contradiction, the class struggle, was the great motive force of the historical process and that it was the masses that made history. This conviction burst forth in his writings: "I am full of faith in the future; I believe blindly in the virtues of the Cuban people."[7]

•

Fidel Castro and his followers were released under a general amnesty decree on May 8, 1955. The decree came as a result of strong public pressure and Batista's desire to improve his public image. After Grau San Martín had made his promise to free all political prisoners if elected, Batista was obliged to follow suit. When Grau withdrew from the presidential campaign because of the dictator's illegal control of the election boards, Batista had even more reasons to worry about his image. By honoring his election pledge on amnesty after he was sworn in as president in February 1955, Batista sought to prove that "democracy" had returned.[8]

Before the general amnesty decree, Castro had been offered his freedom in return for a pledge to change his ways. He responded, "We do not want amnesty at the price of dishonor. . . . Better a thousand years in prison before the sacrifice of integrity."[9] Castro did accept the possibility that "a change of circumstances or a climate of definite constitutional rights" might dictate "a change of tactics in the struggle." But he insisted that he would never change his tactics "by virtue of a shameful and cowardly accord with the government."[10]

Castro and his men were finally released unconditionally. At the prison gate, surrounded by friends, relatives, and reporters,[11] he embraced the chief of the prison guard, Lieutenant Pérez Díaz, and told reporters, "This is a spontaneous and sincere expression without histrionics, because this officer is a gentleman in the full sense of the word." It was a gesture similar to the tribute he had paid to Lieutenant Sarría and Captain Tamayo in "History Will Absolve Me."[12]

Castro held his first news conference before leaving the Isle of Pines and several more after returning to Havana. He announced that he would stay in Cuba "fighting with bared chest" and added:

> Our case will demonstrate whether there are constitutional rights or not. . . . We will gladly serve as guinea pigs. If these rights don't exist, I will be the

first victim of a cowardly attack. I've been informed that there are some people who are preparing to assault my comrades and me.[13]

When asked about his political affiliation, Castro defined his position euphemistically as "revolutionary Chibasism," a way of saying that he would continue to work with the Orthodox party but would not necessarily follow its leaders. He also told an interviewer that there were no ideological differences among the militant anti-Batista groups "that will justify, at this difficult hour, the weakening of these forces. The present moment . . . calls for unity." [14]

In answer to a question about the rash of indiscriminate bombings that were taking place in Havana, he declared that he repudiated "terrorist acts because they are inhuman, antirevolutionary, and indirectly beneficial to the government." [15] Castro suggested that the bombings might be the work of "military or gangster elements, who want to maintain a state of tension that permits their own excesses. No one with any sense," he said, "can think that setting off a bomb in any old doorway can cause the fall of a government." [16] His view is suggestive of Lenin's statement that "without the working class, just plain bombs are totally useless." [17]

Castro announced publicly that "our freedom does not mean enjoyment and rest, but rather struggle and duty, fighting without letup from the first day—arduous work for a nation free from despotism and misery." [18] It was a warning to Batista that the "guinea pigs" would test his promise of constitutional liberties to their limits.

On the ferry from the Isle of Pines, Castro met on deck with a small group of his loyal followers. He told them that in his opinion, the government would not tolerate militant opposition for long. When it cracked down on the legal

A very youthful Fidel Castro as a University student leader rallying his schoolmates on the spot where hero José Martí was once forced to break stones. This was the spring of 1947.

Young Castro in 1947 confronting a high police officer, with some of his followers looking on.

On November 3, 1947, Fidel Castro brought Cuba's "Liberty Bell" to Havana. His idea was to ring the borrowed bell at a mass assembly and ask for a renunciation of President Grau San Martín, whom he accused of corruption.

Fidel in the streets of Bogota, Colombia, after having taken part
in the civil disturbances there in April of 1948. He is in leather jacket.

Temporarily restrained from revolutionary activities by his arrest for
leading the Moncada attack.

Melba Hernandez and Haydee Santamaria meet Fidel as he leaves prison in May 1955. Both women had participated in the Moncada Barracks attack and served jail sentences, being released from prison months before Fidel.

Fidel moments before his release from jail in May, 1955.

Fidel holds a press conference at a local hotel the day he was released
from the Isle of Pines prison. At left, with tie, is Jesus Montane,
one of his closest co-workers. Montane also served a jail sentence and later
joined Fidel on the Granma expedition. Photo date, May 1955.

Fidel reading at the Havana home of his sister, Lidia, the day after his release from prison in May of 1955.

Fidel relaxes at the Miami home of Felix Elmuza (center). Man with cigar is Juan Manuel Marquez who came as second in command on the Granma expedition and was killed in the first battle. Elmuza also joined Fidel and was killed during the guerrilla war.

A pensive Fidel on the eve of victory (circa January 1, 1959). On the
outskirts of Santiago de Cuba, Fidel demands the unconditional
surrender of the city from a Batista officer. Celia Sanchez (center)
observes the history being made.

Fidel holds a news conference in May 1975 during the visit to Cuba of Senator George McGovern. Left to right: Barbara Walters, Fidel, Lionel Martin (with beard), Frank Reynolds of ABC (with glasses and striped tie), and Ed Rabel of CBS.

road, as he predicted it would, only one alternative would be left open, that of armed struggle.[19] Foreseeing this, the July 26 Movement, the name chosen on the ferry for the organization, would operate clandestinely from the beginning.[20]

Castro did not disguise his intention to lead a movement of national proportions. He used the press to make his program public and announced without false modesty that if the people put their faith in his movement, "we will not disappoint the nation." [21] He was clearly announcing that his group would contend for leadership in the political struggles ahead.

Castro's prediction that Batista had little tolerance for an active opposition soon proved correct. After Castro had spoken on a Havana radio station on May 19, the station manager was picked up by police in an effort to intimidate him.[22] When Castro was scheduled to speak at a mass rally on the University of Havana campus on May 20, the government first banned the scheduled broadcast of the event and then, with a huge display of force, banned the event itself.[23] On the same day, the home of Pedro Miret, one of the amnestied *Moncadistas,* was raided by police in a futile search for arms.[24] Another raid on the house four day later discovered three men who, according to a clairvoyant precinct chief, "were having a conversation of a subversive character about insurrectional plans." [25] The police officer described Raúl Castro, who was not in the raided house, as the leader of the "subversive group."

Fidel Castro was in the courtroom when the charges against Miret and Raúl Castro were made. He told reporters that "amnesty is becoming a bloody hoax played on the people and the press. . . ." He said, "Our lives and personal security are exposed to attack," but added that the *Moncadistas* would remain in Cuba despite harassment, "because our departure from Cuba would definitely end any possibility of a peaceful solution." [26]

The gadfly role assumed by Fidel taxed the patience of Cuba's overlords. When Colonel Charviano accused Castro of maligning the army by his assertion that there had been a wanton massacre following the Moncada attack, Castro replied in an audacious *Bohemia* article entitled "You Lie, Chaviano!" [27]

Santiago Rey, the minister of justice, was furious. "This kind of thing will not be permitted!" he raved to reporters. He threatened action against Castro for his "criminal, irresponsible, and intolerable attitude." [28]

Batista commented on Castro's article with a menacing: "I just hope that none of the political parties repeat provocations such as that." [29] A few days later, Batista again broached the subject of the Castro article and declared that "the governing parties have brains, ears, *and also hands*," an undisguised threat of physical violence.

Castro shot back that Batista was "conceited, vain, dishonest, and wrong." [30]

Castro had written in jail that propaganda was "the soul of all struggle." [31] and he showed himself once again to be the master of the art. His effectiveness goaded the government to action, making it difficult for him to speak on radio and television. He continued to make his voice heard, however, from the pages of *Bohemia* and regularly from the newspaper *La Calle,* which was edited by a sympathizer.

One of Castro's articles during this period sheds additional light on his profound sympathy for the workers. When railroad workers went on strike to protest a wage cut, Castro wrote poignantly:

> An 8-percent cut in salaries; 8 percent more hunger, 8 percent more misery, 8 percent more economic crisis, 8 percent more ruin, sickness, and unemploy-

ment. 8 percent less in the hands of the worker to buy at the grocery, the bar, the pharmacy and other stores; 8 percent less food, clothing, shoes, and medicines for the women and children. . . .[32]

He called on the public to support the striker's cause. To a government threat to send in strikebreakers, Castro replied, "No worker who considers himself a Cuban and has a sense of honor will fall into this trap!" He spelled out his sympathies in an impassioned paragraph:

> When servile pens of vested interests write editorials in favor of a foreign company, our heartfelt word has to be for the workers. There is hunger for bread and liberty. To them, as revolutionary combatants, we give our sympathy. We are, and we will always be, with all just causes, with the poor of the world.[33]

The last sentence is reminiscent of José Martí's declaration in his *Versos sencillos,* "I want to stake my future with the poor of the world." But the theme is specifically working class, and it is here that the Marxian influence converges with that of Martí in Fidel Castro.

•

The murder of Jorge Agostini in June was a sign that the government's war against the opposition was escalating into terror. Agostini, a former chief of the presidential guard, had gone into exile after the military coup. When Batista announced the restoration of constitutional rights, Agostini returned from exile. Days later he was gunned down in a Havana courtyard. Castro, in an article published in *La Calle,* was the only political figure in the nation who publicly accused the government of having engineered the murder.[34]

On the night of the murder, seven bombs were set off in

different parts of Havana. Castro was convinced that it was the work of *agents provocateurs* or, at least, of misguided opponents of the regime. "I am so convinced of the immense harm that they are doing to the struggle against the dictatorship," he wrote, "that I would not hesitate to publicly denounce the bunch of savages who render such a valuable service to Batista while pretending to be revolutionaries." [35]

As Castro had foreseen, the rash of bombings gave the Batista government an excuse to clamp down on the opposition. Less than a week after Fidel's exposé of the provocative nature of the bombings, the government charged Raúl Castro with having put a bomb in the Tosca, a Havana movie house.

Raúl was included in a catch-all indictment brought against twenty-seven persons accused of trying "to provoke a revolution in Cuba." The plot, according to the indictment, had been "masterminded overseas by well-known figures of the deposed regime of Dr. Carlos Prío." [36]

The following day, a day on which Batista and Fidel's old enemy Rolando Masferrer held an amicable meeting,[37] police raided the office of *La Calle*. The editor was arrested,[38] and his name was included in the conspiracy case announced the previous day. His newspaper was charged with having "falsely ascribed to certain authorities the commission of persecutions, abuses, and crimes against adversaries of the government." [39] Prima-facie evidence included some of the articles written for *La Calle* by Fidel Castro.

The outlawed Communist party was also dragged into the conspiracy case. The Ministry of Justice declared that *La Calle* was "directed and oriented by Communist elements and subsidized by subversive elements." It was pointed out that *La Calle* used the same print shop as "the Communist magazine *Cuba Deportiva* (Cuban Sports) and that its street venders were "controlled and oriented by elements of the dissolved PSP." [40]

Fidel Castro, who had not as yet been included in the indictment, although his articles had been, showed up in Urgency Court to file a deposition. In it, he accused the government of planning the murder of Raúl and himself and the police of having set off the bomb in the Tosca movie house.[41]

It had already become clear that Batista would not book a really militant opposition aimed at organizing a mass movement against his regime. The "guinea pigs" had proved that the "civic road" to change was blocked. It was time for the young revolutionary leader to initiate phase two of his master plan, that of organizing an armed invasion of the island from overseas. In view of this plan, Raúl Castro sought asylum in the Mexican embassy in Havana and then left Cuba.[42] The day after the *La Calle* raid, Fidel Castro excused himself from a risky television appearance,[43] and from then until his departure he maintained a low profile.

His main efforts were devoted to developing the clandestine organizational apparatus of the July 26 Movement, a decisive element in his insurrectional plans. Most of his old followers remained faithful, and new adherents were sought, among them many who had been followers of García Bárcena's defunct organization.[44]

During the months following amnesty, Castro's popularity among the grass roots of the Orthodox party had grown. He had been the guest of honor at numerous Orthodox meetings and had been selected honorary chairman of an important rank-and-file Orthodox-party conference in Las Villas province.[45] Nevertheless, he spurned several offers tendered by the official leadership of the party—one to become a member of the party's executive council and another to become the Orthodox-party candidate for president of the Havana city council.[46]

By refusing to become part of the official machine, Castro

remained free to build his own freewheeling movement within the Orthodox party and to clash openly with its tactics and policy. He became one of the sponsors of a grass-roots party congress scheduled for mid-August.[47]

Castro built a solid framework for the new July 26 Movement. Men and women were assigned to organize the Movement in the trade unions and among women and youth. Castro considered the work in the trade unions to be "essential" but did not have time, before he left, to oversee the organization of the labor committee.[48] Finance, propaganda, and distribution sections were established, and combat groups began to function.

Great emphasis was placed on building the organization in Oriente province. Castro knew by this time that his home province would be the main scene of his future military operations, and he had sent some of his most trusted followers to initiate the July 26 Movement there. They came into contact with Frank País, the organizer of a small insurrectional group. Castro invited País and his group to join the July 26 Movement, and País accepted.[49] One of País's closest collaborators explained to me that "we saw in the *compañeros* of the Moncada serious revolutionaries, patriots who weren't politicians. . . . We had confidence in Fidel." [50] País met with Castro in Havana and, from then until his death two years later, played a vital role in the Movement.

When Castro felt satisfied that the Movement could survive and grow without his presence, he decided to leave Cuba. The Communist party knew of his plan and sent Raúl Valdés Vivó, secretary general of the Young Communists at the University of Havana, to speak to him. The Communists' respect for Castro had grown over the years, and they suggested that he not leave the country but stay in Cuba to help to organize a united-front political movement against Batista. Castro listened respectfully as Valdés

Vivó presented the Communists' position. He answered with great equanimity that although he favored building a mass movement, he also believed that it must be accompanied by direct confrontation with the enemy. He told the emissary that he was going abroad to prepare the way for a revolution in Cuba.[51]

Vivó's visit with Castro is one more element in the hidden history of the Cuban Revolution. The fact that the interchange took place in a fraternal atmosphere is further proof of Castro's conviction that the Communists were honest allies and of the Communists' confidence in Castro's integrity. There was no doubt that Castro and the Communists differed over tactics and strategy. That they could intimately discuss these differences explains in great part the development of their future relations.

On July 7, Castro left Cuba for Mexico. He gave newsmen his final declaration at the airport. It was a statement for history:

> I am leaving Cuba because all doors of peaceful struggle have been closed to me.
>
> Six weeks after being released from prison I am convinced more than ever of the dictatorship's intention, masked in different ways, to remain in power for twenty years, ruling as now by the use of terror and crime and ignoring the patience of the Cuban people, which has its limits.
>
> As a follower of Martí, I believe the hour has come to take our rights and not to beg for them, to fight instead of pleading for them.
>
> I will reside somewhere in the Caribbean.
>
> From trips such as this, one does not return, or else one returns with the tyranny beheaded at one's feet.[52]

●

Fidel's first days of exile in Mexico were somber. Two weeks passed, and no word came from his followers in Cuba. Desolate, he wrote to Melba Hernández that he felt "more isolated than when they had me in solitary confinement." [53]

On July 26, the anniversary of the Moncada attack, Fidel laid a wreath at the Monument of the Child Heroes of Chapultepec and later met with Latin American exiles at the Ateneo Español in Mexico City. [54] He spent most of his time, however, away from the glare of publicity, working on two position papers: *Manifesto Number One of the July 26 Movement* and *A Message to the Congress of Orthodox Militants*. [55] He planned to pawn his overcoat to pay for the printing. [56]

Finally, on August 1, he received his first report from Havana. The following day, he sent off his own letter, analyzing the situation in Cuba and sketching the tactics to be followed. The greatest danger, Castro wrote to his followers, was the tendency to accept Batista's proposal for legislative elections while Batista remained president. This tendency had to be fought "with blood and fire," he wrote, and the two position papers he was preparing would help to combat it. [57]

The grass-roots Congress of Orthodox Militants, whose call Fidel had sponsored before leaving Cuba, was scheduled for mid-August. In his letter, Castro told the Movement in Havana that they should take full advantage of the congress by sending effective delegates there and carrying out "an ample labor of proselytism." With his characteristic optimism, Castro told his followers, "You will see how we break the curtain of silence and open the road to a new strategy. . . . In the long run, all real revolutionaries will join the Movement when they see how the masses and public opinion support us." [58]

Castro's *Message to the Congress of Orthodox Militants*

represented a bold bid to win over the rank and file of the Orthodox party to the M-26-7 cause. Having learned of its contents, the principal leaders of the party boycotted the session in which it was read aloud.[59]

The message leveled its attack on the Orthodox leadership's willingness to accept Batista's plan for general elections that excluded the presidency. The delegates listened intently as Castro proclaimed that another road was open; "The road is called revolution . . . the one we have already adopted irrevocably. . . . It is one of sacrifice." The message appealed to "the best Orthodox members" for their support and defined the new movement as "the revolutionary apparatus of Chibasism, which is rooted in its cadres and from which it emerged to struggle against the dictatorship when the Orthodox party lay impotent and divided in a thousand pieces." [60]

At the close of the reading, most of the five hundred delegates rose and began a cadenced chant: "Revolución . . . revolución . . . revolución." It was a sign of the July 26 Movement's capacity to capture the allegiance and imagination of the people. Suddenly it was on its way to becoming a mass movement.

•

Manifesto Number One of the July 26 Movement was also distributed in Cuba in mid-August. In many ways it is a more radical document than "History Will Absolve Me," an even more lucid expression of Castro's desire "to revolutionize this country from top to bottom." It is difficult to understand why most writers on the Cuban Revolution have underestimated its revolutionary character and its essentially socialist outlook. If they had studied it with more care, Castro's "conversion" into a Communist in 1961 would not have surprised them.

The manifesto gives us an insight into Castro's disdain

for the system of parties and political representation as practiced in Cuba. "What has petty politics given this country over the past fifty years?" he asked, and answered, "Speeches, *chambelonas*,[61] congas, lies, compromises, deceit, betrayals, the improper enrichment of a clique of rogues, empty talk, corruption, infamy."

Castro appealed in the name of the dispossessed. "The voices are those who suffer hunger in the countryside and the cities, the desperate voices of those who have no work or hope of finding any." [62]

The profoundity of the social upheaval Castro envisioned, its class character, is clearly discernible in a passage that defends the revolution-to-be from those who claimed it would bring anarchy:

> To those who accuse the Revolution of upsetting the economy of the country, we answer: "There is no economy for the rural workers who have no land; there is no economy for the millions of Cubans who are unemployed; there is no economy for the railroad, port, sugar, hemp, textile, and bus workers and those sectors whose wages Batista has mercilessly reduced. And there will be an economy for them only through a just revolution that will redistribute the land, mobilize the vast resources of the country, and equalize social conditions, putting an end to privilege and exploitation.[63]

What kind of revolution was Castro thinking of that would put an end to privilege and exploitation? Marxism had taught him that the "exploitation of man by man" could be eliminated only by the overthrow of capitalism and the victory of socialism. What Castro says in the above passage, I discovered, has a strong similarity to a passage from Marx's and Engels's *Communist Manifesto*. They write:

You are horrified at our intending to do away with private property. But in your existing society, private property is already done away with for nine-tenths of the population; its existence for the few is solely due to its non-existence in the hands of those nine-tenths.[64]

My supposition that this passage influenced Castro was made even more credible by a speech he delivered in Chile many years later. In it he recalled how the *Communist Manifesto* had first come into his hands and how much he had been influenced by "those sentences which I will never be able to forget, like . . ." Then Castro went on to recite *from memory* the very passage cited above.[65]

Castro's manifesto declared that those who accuse the Revolution of "upsetting the economy" must be talking about "the economy of the senators who earn 5,000 pesos a month, of the millionaire generals, of the foreign trusts that exploit the public services, of the great landowners, of the tribe of parasites who thrive and get rich at the expense of the state and the people. . . . Then we welcome the Revolution that upsets the economy of those who so greedily profit from it." [66] In the same way, Marx and Engels had written, "You reproach us with intending to do away with your property. Precisely so: that is just what we intend." [67]

The immediate program of *Manifesto Number One of the July 26 Movement*, like that in "History Will Absolve Me," stopped short of explicit socialist solution. Even so, its implementation would have meant a radical socio-economic transformation. Its first-stage measures included the abolition of big land holdings, distribution of land to farm families; ample participation by workers in the profits of all big businesses; an industrialization drive "made and promoted by the state"; a sharp decrease in rent; state construction of low-cost housing; the conversion of every tenant into owner; nationalization of public services; and the construction of ten children's cities to house and educate two hundred thousand children of workers and farmers.[68]

Castro's understanding of Cuban reality dictated his projection of an audacious but still limited program. It is of interest to note that the *Communist Manifesto*'s first-stage revolutionary program does not posit socialist measures any more than Castro's program does. Marx and Engels admit that these are measures "which appear economically insufficient . . . but which, in the course of the movement, outstrip themselves, necessitate further inroads upon the old social order, and are unavoidable as a means of entirely revolutionarizing the mode of production." [69]

9.

". . . Or We will Be Martyrs"

Raúl Castro introduced Fidel to a young Argentinian physician, Ernesto "Che" Guevara. Che had come to Mexico from Guatemala following the CIA–directed overthrow of the progressive Arbenz government.[1] In Guatemala, while absorbing the experience of what he hoped would be a profound social revolution, he had met Ñico López, the exiled *Moncadista*. From Ñico he first heard of Fidel Castro's integrity and courage as a revolutionary leader.

Che was searching for a Latin American war of liberation in which he could participate. He and Fidel, a doctor and a lawyer, intellectually sophisticated and sharing a broad culture, had much to talk about. Despite his reluctance to include non-Cubans, Fidel accepted Che as part of the future expeditionary force.[2]

Andrés Suárez, in his book *Cuba—Castroism and Communism*, writes, "I have not been able to find a single document showing that Guevara was familiar with the classics of Marxism."[3] When I mentioned Suárez's passage to Dr. Alberto Granados, the fellow physician with whom Che had toured Latin America in 1951, he replied resoundingly, "Nonsense!"[4] When Fidel and Che met in Mexico City, they were both well versed in Marxist classics.

Che had been a member of the Young Communist League of Argentina for a short time.[5] It is highly improbable that a serious student and thinker such as Che would have joined the movement without familiarizing himself with their doctrine. Hilda Gadea, Che's first wife, attests to the fact that Che had read *The Communist Manifesto*, Engels's *Anti-Duhring* and *Origins of the Family, Private Property, and the State*, and Lenin's *Imperialism* and *What Is to Be Done*, all "classics" of Marxism.[6]

After he had arrived in Guatemala in December 1953, Che took part in the activities of the Alianza de la Juventud Democrática, the youth movement of the Guatemalan Communists.[7] Dr. Edelberto Torres, a Central American scholar and mentor to revolutionaries, recalls that Che wanted to go to a peace conference in Peking in 1954, stay in China for a while, and learn more about the revolution.[8] Later, in Mexico, he wanted to go to the World Youth Festival with the Guatemalan delegation and then go on to the Soviet Union and China.[9]

The testimony of Harold White, a maverick American friend of Che's, throws additional light on his ideological outlook. White, a serious student of Marxism, was already past middle age when he met Che in Guatemala.[10] The two men would spend hours in conversation. White quickly discovered that Che had a deep knowledge of Marxism.

White had brought to Guatemala a four-hundred-page manuscript of selected Marxist writings, arranged according to theme, that he had compiled. Che was enthusiastic about the usefulness of the book and offered to translate it into Spanish by seeking out the equivalent passages in Spanish editions of Marx, Engels, Lenin, and Stalin. When Che fled to Mexico, he continued working on the project until he joined Castro's group.[11]

Many years later, Castro characterized the Guevara he

had met in Mexico City: "He had read, naturally, the works of Karl Marx, Engels, and Lenin, and although he did not belong to any party, he was already a Marxist thinker at that stage." [12]

•

The core of Castro's tiny army was made up of *Moncadistas,* among them his brother Raúl, Jesús Montané, Ñico López, Juan Almeida, Armando Mestre, and Calixto García. The last three were blacks. An important addition to Fidel's organization was Juan Manuel Márquez, a forty-year-old former city councilman from the Marianao district of Havana. In late October 1955, Castro and Márquez spent seven weeks visiting Cuban communities in the United States, organizing the July 26 Movement, and raising funds.[13] Most of those who turned out for the meetings were Cuban workers who had left their homeland for economic reasons. The audience cheered when Castro said in New York's Palm Gardens:

> The Cuban people want something more than a simple change of command. Cuba longs for a radical change in every aspect of its political and social life. The people must be given something more than liberty and democracy in abstract—decent living must be given to every Cuban. The state cannot ignore the fate of any of its citizens who were born and grew up in this country. There is no greater tragedy than that of a man capable of and willing to work, who suffers hunger with his family because he lacks a job.[14]

Castro left behind a July 26 organization in the United States to complement the clandestine apparatus within Cuba. Before returning to Mexico, he issued *Manifesto Num-*

ber Two of the July 26 Movement,[15] in which he declared
that "a revolution, unlike a *putsch,* is the work of the people." He was now able to do what he had not been able to
do before the Moncada attack. He wrote,

> publicly appeal to the people to help us, to prepare
> the country for revolution on a major scale without
> possibility of failure. We shall set forth the actions the
> masses must carry out everywhere when national re-
> bellion breaks out like a storm so that the fighting
> detachments, well armed and led by the active youth
> cadres, will be supported by the workers throughout
> the country, organized from below in revolutionary
> cells capable of unleashing a general strike.[16]

In only four months, the July 26 Movement had moved
toward the center of the anti-Batista stage, and ambitious
opposition politicians began to see Castro and his Movement as a threat. The column "Cabalgata Política" (Political Calvacade) in *Bohemia* commented,

> Fidel Castro is too dangerous a competitor for certain
> leaders of the opposition who, during three years and a
> half, have failed to take a correct stand toward the
> Cuban situation. Those leaders know it too well. They
> now feel displaced by the size the 26th of July Move-
> ment is acquiring in the battle against Batista. The
> logical reaction of the politicians in the light of this
> evident fact should be to face the revolutionary action
> of *Fidelismo* with a resolute political stand.[17]

Instead of resolute political action against Batista, there
came a succession of articles attacking Fidel Castro in order to undermine his prestige, his appeal to the Cuban
people, and ultimately his Movement. One article in *Bohemia* was petulantly entitled "The Country Is Not Fidel's." [18]

Castro lashed back in a defiant article called "Against Everyone." [19] The art of polemics was Castro's forte, and he used this opportunity to review his consistent record of opposition to corruption under the Authentic administrations and to the Batista regime. In answering the charge that he was using July 26 Movement funds for his personal benefit, he described his near penury despite the tens of thousands of dollars that passed through his hands. As always, Castro appealed over the heads of the politicians to Cuba's poor, to the farmers, "tired of speeches and promises of agrarian reform," to the unemployed, to the sick without medical care, to the "hundreds of thousands of families living in huts." He denounced the bleeding of the nation's riches by foreign trusts, grafters, and gamblers. "But for them," he affirmed, "Cuba would be one of the most prosperous and rich countries of the Americas."[20]

•

For the July 26 Movement 1956 was the time of testing. It was the year the Movement survived the exposure of its clandestine presence in Cuba, a plot to kill Fidel Castro in Mexico, the arrest of Castro and his expeditionary force, a nearly disastrous landing in Cuba, the failure of the urban uprising and the general strike, and the near destruction of its expeditionary force. Yet the Movement and its leaders survived this fateful year.

At the beginning of 1956 Cuba's Military Intelligence Service (SIM) announced that it had unearthed "a subversive plot to overthrow the government, masterminded by Fidel Castro overseas." [21] SIM agents raided homes in each of Cuba's six provinces and made many arrests.

In Mexico, Castro was engaged in a surge of activities directed toward four interlocking objectives: to strengthen the underground network in Cuba; to build a support base in the

United States and other centers of Cuban emigration; to continue his ideological campaign to prepare the Cuban people for insurrection; and finally, to train his small expeditionary force for its landing in Cuba before the end of the year. Castro recognized this as the year of decision. He announced publicly: "In 1956 we will be free or we will be martyrs." [22]

In early spring, Castro announced his formal break with the leadership of the Orthodox party. "Who has said that leaders are eternal, that situations do not change, and even more in a process of convulsion where everything is altered with dazzling speed?" [23] Castro wrote. He now called his movement "the vanguard of the struggle against the regime." [24] "It is not different from the Orthodox Party. . . . It is the Orthodox party without a leadership of landlords like 'Fico' Fernández, without sugar-plantation owners like Girardo Vázquez, without stockmarket speculators, without commercial and industrial magnates. . . ." He appealed to "all revolutionaries of Cuba, without miserable sectarian differences and regardless of any previous differences," to close ranks around the July 26 Movement.[25] He did not exclude the Communists from his call for unity.

Not long afterward, Castro was forced to answer allegations that he and his movement were Communist tinged. These charges followed the arrest of the M-26-7 leader and about twenty of his men by the Mexican Federal Security Agency (DFS).[26]

Prior to his arrest, Castro wrote that he had learned of plans by Batista's henchmen to have him murdered. When it became clear that Castro would not be an easy target, "they threw the Federal Security Agency on us." [27] The Mexican agents arrested Castro and some of his followers in Mexico City and later swooped down on the training camp at Santa Rosa, about twenty miles from the capital, where they caught a dozen of his men.

The prisoners were charged with violation of the immigration law that stipulated, "An immigrant or nonimmigrant who devotes himself to illicit or dishonest activities will have his immigration status canceled and will be deported." [28] They were sent to an immigration detention center in Mexico City.

After a week of investigation the Federal Security Police sent a report to the president of Mexico in which they affirmed that "the 26th of July group has no Communist ties nor aid from the Communists." [29] Nevertheless, the Mexican press singled out Che Guevara as a sinister figure. The Mexico City newspaper *Excelsior,* allegedly quoting police sources, wrote that "Dr. Guevara, who also figures in other political movements of an international character in Guatemala, the Dominican Republic, and Panama, was identified as an active member of the Mexican-Soviet Institute of Cultural Exchange." [30]

Alberto Bayo, the elderly ex-colonel of the Spanish Republican Army, who had been training Castro's group, escaped arrest. Bayo, an expert on guerrilla warfare,[31] sent a letter to the police and the press in which he "confessed" to being leader of the group.[32]

In Mexico, the DFS recognized that Fidel was *not* a Communist. Nonetheless, an article in the Cuban magazine *Bohemia* informed the Cuban public that "the Mexican Federal Security Police affirms that it has proof of Fidel's membership in the Communist party." [33]

Castro answered the charge against him in an article written from jail. He used expressions that have been cited by a number of writers to prove that Fidel Castro had declared open war on the Communists.[34] The polemical paragraph reads:

> The intrigue is ridiculous . . . and without the least foundation because I have been a militant in only one

Cuban political party, and that is the one founded
by Eduardo Chibás. What moral authority . . . does
Mr. Batista have to speak on Communism when he
was the Communist party presidential candidate in
the elections of 1940, if his electoral posters took
shelter under the hammer and sickle, if his pictures
beside Blas Roca and Lázaro Peña are still around,
if a half dozen of his ministers and trusted collaborators were well-known members of the Communist
party? [35]

Blas Roca and Lázaro Peña later became highly respected
members of the central committee of the Cuban Communist party headed by Fidel Castro.[36]

I had occasion to ask Blas Roca about Castro's mention
of him and Peña in the 1956 article. "It was a tactic," he
commented simply.[37] Castro had written in this manner to
parry a blow that might have crippled his budding movement just as it was beginning to pose a real threat to the
regime. If Batista could not succeed in murdering Castro,
as he attempted to do, the next best thing was to attempt to
pin the Communist label on him, thus narrowing the appeal of his Movement.

Any serious analysis of Castro's reply shows that he
strictly circumscribed ideological content in his reply
to charges that he was a Communist. One can compare his reply with that of former President Prio, when he
had been charged with collaborating with the Communists
the previous year. Prio had defended himself by pointing
with pride to his anti-Communist record. "I threw the
Communist leaders out of the trade unions," he boasted.[38]
But Castro simply limited himself to denying that he was a
Communist-party member and stating a historical fact well
known to every Cuban adult, that the Communists had supported Fulgencio Batista's candidacy for the presidency in
1940 and collaborated with him.[39] He used Batista's accept-

ance of this support to undermine his credibility. In this way, Castro parried the blow without doing damage to his own principles.

In Mexico City, Castro sought recourse in the courts and won freedom for himself and members of his Movement.[40] Once free, he hastened his plans for the invasion of Cuba.

•

If Castro's article had actually been an authentic attack on the Communists, he would have avoided further relations with the Popular Socialist party. The opposite was the case. After his release, he met twice with Communists from Cuba, resulting in the PSP's decision to support Castro's plan, contingent on developments in Cuba following the invasion.[41]

At the first meeting, the Communist emissary, Oswaldo Sánchez, told Castro that the party believed he should postpone the invasion until the sugar harvest in January so that a strike movement, similar to that of December 1955, could be organized among the sugar workers. Castro's invasion could then be a signal to convert the economic strike into a general political strike, thus unleashing a revolutionary situation similar to that which had toppled the Machado dictatorship in August 1933.[42] Castro told Sánchez that he had already made a public commitment to the people of Cuba and that the invasion plans could not be postponed. He informed Sánchez of his plan to time an urban uprising, principally in Santiago de Cuba, with the landing of the invasion party.[43] His revealing his general plan to the Communists attests to his faith in their integrity.

Sánchez returned to Havana, where the Communist leadership discussed Castro's plan and decided to send out orders to regional organizations of the party. The party was to make preparations to support the insurrection when it began by organizing strikes among the workers.[44]

In Oriente province, the landing place of the coming invasion, contacts between the July 26 Movement under Frank País and the Communists were already established. Lester Rodríguez, a *Moncadista* and the coordinator of the M-26-7 Movement in Oriente during Castro's absence in Mexico, later recalled, "There is one thing that has never been mentioned by anyone—the contacts that were established with the Popular Socialist party." [45]

Shortly before Castro's expedition was to depart from Mexico, Flavio Bravo, Castro's old Communist friend, was sent to talk to him. Despite Castro's great prestige, his Movement would have small chance of successfully mounting coordinated uprisings throughout Cuba. However, if, once begun, they found sufficient support to transform themselves into a struggle of major proportions, the party would join the struggle and work to bring about a general strike. [46]

Bravo's meeting with Castro took place in November 1956. He told me that he was with Fidel "almost to the very moment he left Mexico." [47] The contacts between Castro and the PSP were understandably cloaked in secrecy. To have made them public would have fatally disrupted the unity that had been painfully achieved by the heterogeneous July 26 Movement.

The PSP was not exclusive in its reservations. Frank País, the July 26 action chief in Oriente, had visited Castro in Mexico and told him that preparations for a general strike were still incomplete. The action cadres in Santiago were still "defenseless, unprepared, and without coordination."[48] País recommended that the invasion be postponed, but Castro convinced him that postponement would be a serious psychological setback in view of the Movement's promise to act in 1956. Fulfillment of that promise would add new impetus to the anti-Batista struggle. Convinced, País went back to work with renewed vigor to prepare support for the coming invasion.

The invasion was so important to Castro that he presumably accepted money from ex-President Prio to buy the invasion yacht, *Granma*. Castro justified this later to Herbert Matthews: "We made no concessions to Prio afterward. ... I have no regrets about it. We were willing to do anything for the Revolution." [49]

Frank País covered the province of Oriente, organizing cells, working out military plans, desperately seeking out more weapons and working out contingency plans in case of failure or partial success. País has been described in a number of books published outside of Cuba as a "Baptist schoolmaster" [50] who came from a well-to-do family. In fact, País came from a family of modest means, and although he had taught civics in a Baptist school, he had become a radical as a result of the anti-Batista struggle.[51] One day, in a conversation about religion, he told one of his intimate co-workers of the Movement, "I stopped believing in all that when I killed my first man." [52]

País had been a student leader at the teachers' college in Santiago before the Batista coup. His conversion to armed struggle followed Fidel's attack on the Moncada barracks. During the night of the attack and for days afterward, he and some of his friends scoured the hills around Santiago in search of survivors and arms. "They kill all of them, even those who surrender," he wrote to a friend three days after the attack. "They are assassins. It enraged and pained me to see how those boys were dying." He added, "I'm not mixed up in anything, but I wish I were." [53] Three weeks later he was picked up · by the police and charged with having put out a subversive leaflet entitled *"Assassins."* [54] He later organized his own urban-guerrilla group and in mid-1955 incorporated it into Fidel Castro's newly organized M-26-7.

País's populist sentiments can be easily recognized in an essay he wrote in 1954 called "Five Students and the Mountain." He and several university friends made a pilgrimage to Realengo 18, a backwoods area that had a long history of struggle, much of it under the guidance of the Communist party.[55] In the essay, he quotes a local farmer to the effect that the prolonged struggle for land in the region "gave us all a spirit of class." País, not yet twenty when he wrote the essay, reproduced the purported words of another Realengo *guajiro:*

> "Cuba is in a bad way, brother, in a bad way. God! Listen to your unprotected children and don't let them die of hunger and misery." But we will all die of those things, supporting palaces and skyscrapers, riches and duck feathers. And two tears welled up in our eyes on seeing the misery of the poor farmer, his noble spirit, and the dog's life he lives. How sad is Cuba's future when so many men live dying from daily worries, suffering pain, deception, treachery, and abandonment! . . .
>
> The farmer continued, "But I have faith in you, the youth of Cuba, the youth that left behind the joys of a day off in order to come and listen to this poor farmer."
>
> We have no other hope than to die waiting for someone with a heart of the people, the soul of a poet, and sentiments of a man—not a hyena—to come to the countryside, not to ask for votes, but to give brotherly love; not to figure ways of cheating the poor farmer, but instead, believing that the future is in the mountain.
>
> Don't forget. Don't forget.[56]

•

In keeping with Castro's general instructions, Lester Rodríguez and Frank País made contact with diverse civic and
political groupings, including the Communists. País, like
Fidel, believed in the integrity of the Communists and recognized that they were an important force among the organized workers. Fidel Domenech, Young Communist leader
in Oriente province, took part in the first official contacts
with the July 26 Movement in Santiago. Later, Francisco
"Paquito" Rosales, who had been Communist mayor of the
Oriente of Manzanillo, was assigned to maintain contact
with the Movement.[57] Rosales and Domenech on one occasion attended an important meeting in the home of Ramón
Alvarez, head of the July 26th labor front, to discuss coordination between the two organizations within the trade-
union movement.[58]

After Oswaldo Sánchez's discussions with Fidel Castro in
Mexico City, the PSP national committee sent out orders to
its provincial leaders to be ready to organize a general strike
when Castro's forces landed in Oriente and the urban uprising began. Several days before the impending landing,
País met with Communist representatives and told them that
the uprising would take place on November 30, the expected
date of the invasion. The PSP agreed to issue a public call
for a general strike in Santiago de Cuba for that day.[59]

The real motive for the general strike was to be disguised
as a call alerting the workers to the threat of a Trujillo-
directed *putsch* in Cuba. The Communists drafted a strike
call with this as its basic theme.

When this information was given to me, I must admit
that I was skeptical. But both Juan Taquechel and Laslao
Carvajal, two old-time Communist leaders who were active
in Santiago at that time, told me the same story inde-
pendently, and both remembered vaguely that the strike
call had been published in a Santiago de Cuba newspaper
one or two days before November 30.[60]

The National Library in Havana did not have a complete set of Santiago newspapers, but I finally found what they were talking about in the Santiago de Cuba library in the November 29, 1956, edition of the daily newspaper *Oriente*. The item was headlined, "Workers Launch Slogans against Trujillo-inspired *Putsch*." The article began: "A workers' delegation visited our offices and asked us to publish the following call."

The declaration accused known Trujillo followers of planning a *putsch* in Cuba. The Batista government, it claimed, was using the legitimate threat of a *putsch* to present all opposition activities as Trujillo-inspired, in order to confuse the Cuban people. The article ended with a call to action:

> We propose the largest possible mobilization of our class, together with the people in general, against the Trujillo plot—to denounce it, to unleash protests, to call meetings, demonstrations, strikes. . . .
>
> If the *putsch* takes place, to oppose it with a general strike of all workers and action of the masses in the streets. . . .
>
> We should begin to protest against the danger of the *putsch* immediately, by carrying out on *November 30* a half-hour stoppage in all work centers—factories, the docks, banks, commercial establishments, the buses. . . . Hour of the stoppage: 10 to 10:30 A.M.[61]

The call was signed "Committee for the Defense of Workers' Demands and for the Democratization of the Trade-union Movement." The names affixed to the call were all of labor activists and members of the PSP.[62] In this way, the Communists alerted Santiago workers for the insurrectional activities of the following day.

A last-minute order by the PSP national committee to

hold back on the general strike, contingent on the success of the July 26 Movement's armed uprising, was received in Santiago de Cuba when preparations for the strike had already been made. The Guantánamo Communists, however, never received the order, which accounts for their full participation in the abortive general strike in the city.[63]

On November 27, a July 26 leader in Santiago received a cable: "Work requested out of stock." [64] It meant that the yacht *Granma* was on its way to the southern Oriente coast. It was estimated that the crossing would take three days; the uprisings were thus set for November 30. What no one could foretell was that the *Granma* would arrive far behind schedule. On the thirtieth, the eighty-two men aboard the yacht listened helplessly as the radio told of the Santiago uprising.

The strategy of the Santiago uprising was to blockade the Moncada barracks and, if all went according to plan, take control of the city. Simultaneous insurrectional activity in and around Guantánamo city, to the east of Santiago and to the north of the big U.S. naval base, was aimed at tying up Batista's army in that area and cutting highway and railroad traffic off from the rest of Oriente province. In the north of the province, there were to be armed operations around the sugar port of Puerto Padre and in the isolated town of Baracoa. The July 26 action groups in Bayamo and Manzanillo had instructions to join Fidel Castro's landing party as soon as they made contact with it and to help the party get into the Sierra Maestra.

The strategy in Santiago was to seal off the Moncada barracks and carry out several commando actions designed to win control of the center of the city and to secure weapons. The captured weapons would then be used to attack the Moncada and bring about its surrender. The seizure of the weapons was fundamental to the plan's success. The July

26 arms deposit in Santiago contained only about fifty semi-automatic and automatic weapons, as well as a few museum pieces, a Mexican musket, and an ancient Spanish harquebus. For every person who actually took part in the November 30 action, five or six could not do so for lack of firearms.[65]

The two main targets for the commando attacks were the National and Maritime Police headquarters. Operations began at dawn. The attack on the National Police headquarters ran into heavy resistance from the first. When it proved impossible to take the building, it was set afire. The Maritime Police headquarters operation was more successful. After a brief firefight, the station was occupied and the arms seized.

The weakest link in the plan of action proved to be the blockade of the Moncada barracks. By midafternoon it was clear that the insurrection could not be sustained. Frank País sent scouts to the highways leading out of the city to see if escape into the Sierras was possible. They found the roads blocked by the army.

By nightfall, the sporadic resistance had ended. Hundreds of Santiago youth were behind bars, and the *Granma* was still far from the Oriente coast.

IV.

Guerrilla
of War
and
Politics

Lenin has already said it—a policy of principles is the best policy.

Che Guevara to Fidel Castro, personal note, Sierra Maestra, January 6, 1958—one year before victory

In the history of revolutions there is a substantial subterranean part that does not become public.

Che Guevara, October 28, 1964.

10.

Battling on
Native Soil

The *Granma,* with eighty-two men aboard, made an inauspicious start, an augury of the tribulations to come in the days ahead. A gale was blowing out of the north. Che remembered "men with anguish reflected on their faces, grabbing their bellies, some with their heads inside pails, others arched in strange positions without moving, their clothes full of vomit." [1]

The Caribbean was calm on the last two days of the journey. But the *Granma* was overdue, and the uprising in Santiago had already been crushed.

The plan had been to land north of Niquero, on the southwest coast of Oriente province. Celia Sánchez, the daughter of a local doctor, had supplies and vehicles waiting for the men. The landing party would be taken to the Sierra Maestra, whose foothills began only thirty miles from the coast. She waited in vain. The *Granma* pulled into shallow water *to the south* of Niquero. It was more of a shipwreck than a landing, Che observed. The men slipped over the side of the yacht and then began a two-hour trek through a mangrove swamp, an immense quagmire of mud and tangled foliage. [2]

The first Cuban brought before Fidel Castro on shore was Angel Pérez, a poor charcoal maker. "I am Fidel Castro, and we have come to fight for Cuban freedom," Castro told him. Pérez knew Castro by reputation and invited him to his shack.[3] While they were there, a Cuban navy ship began to fire into the surrounding bush, and planes flew over, strafing the area. The advantage of secrecy had been lost.

The men started inland, guided by a local farmer. At dawn the following day, Castro's troops, "ghosts that walked as if following the impulse of some obscure psychic mechanism,"[4] halted in a cane field not far from hilly country. During the morning hours the exhausted men slept, and in the afternoon they wandered out into the cane field to cut stalks of succulent cane.

Disaster struck at four in the afternoon. Alegría del Pio almost became the graveyard of the undertaking that had taken so long to prepare. The men suddenly came under attack from a group of Batista's soldiers. It was a day of capture and death, escape and dispersion. Twenty-one of Castro's force were killed, a few at Alegría del Pio and the rest during the next few weeks.

Castro escaped with two men. It took them two weeks to get to the ragged Sierra Maestra range. They were later joined by tiny groups that included Raúl Castro and Che Guevara. At one point there were only seven armed men.[5]

It has often been stated that Fidel Castro is a master at converting adversity into victory, demoralization into optimism. He would have been only too human had he called off the entire plan to bring guerrilla war to the Sierra Maestra. Yet Castro was as sanguine as ever. He told his small band of surviviors. "And now we're going to win."[6]

The fact that his handful of men were able to survive and reach the Sierra Maestra was due in large part to the aid they received from *campesinos*[7] of the region. The two most prominent of these local heroes were Crescencio Pérez, an old farmer patriarch, and Guillermo García, a cattleman. These men organized an underground peasant network to aid the survivors of the Alegría del Pio disaster.[8] García soon joined Castro's rebel band and went on to win its highest rank, *comandante*.[9] In 1965 he became one of the eight members of the political bureau of Cuba's Communist party.

At the end of December, Celia Sánchez made contact with Castro's tiny force in the Sierra. She returned to the *llano* [10] to report to Frank País and the other leaders of the July 26th urban underground. Within a few months Celia Sánchez would return to spend the rest of the war as Castro's aide.[11]

Not all the *campesinos* helped. Some betrayed the small group of strange men who had come into their lives so abruptly. It is likely that a *campesino* guide betrayed the presence of Castro's men to the army, resulting in the surprise attack at Alegría del Pio. Che suspected the guide and observed in retrospect, "We shouldn't have let our guide go." [12] Once in the Sierra Maestra, Castro ordered the execution of "Chicho" Osorio, the foreman of a big local farm who had cooperated with the army in its search for the guerrillas.[13]

Osorio's execution coincided with Castro's first offensive action, the attack on a small army post at La Plata, manned by about a dozen soldiers. The guerrilla force began the attack with twenty weapons. They captured eight Springfield rifles, a Thompson submachine gun, and thousands of rounds of ammunition. The attack was successful. This was the only time during the guerrilla war when the Movement had more weapons than men.[14] Still, Che Guevara, the rebel army's first historian, wrote, "The *campesino* was not prepared to join the struggle, and communications with the urban bases virtually didn't exist." [15]

La Plata was a morale booster for the tiny guerrilla band. Five days later, the "battle veterans" ambushed the vanguard of an army column sent in their pursuit and killed five soldiers.

•

In the summer of 1972 Herbert Matthews, already in semiretirement from his long career with the *New York Times,* arrived in Cuba. We were both at the Hotel Nacional, where I had long discussions with him about Cuba. He is a man of great integrity with a Jeffersonian-populist outlook. I remember his preoccupation over the professional ethics of having his broken tooth fixed by Cuba's free dental service.[16] Though critical, he had great sympathy for the Cuban Revolution. It was clear that he did not at all regret the role he had played in bringing Fidel Castro to the world's attention.[17]

When Matthews interviewed Castro on the morning of February 17, 1957, in the Sierra Maestra, the rebel army had only eighteen men. It was a roving guerrilla band with no permanent base or fixed destination—"the nomadic phase," as Che Guevara characterized it.[18] In the month since the attack on La Plata, they had made contact with many poor farmers but had not yet penetrated the farmers' pervading fear, sown by the army's terror tactics.

Several days before Matthews arrived, Castro's forces had been bombed from the air and almost ambushed on the ground. Their location had been betrayed by a *campesino* guide, Eutimio Guerra, who had helped them through some of their roughest periods. Guerra was executed a few days after Matthews left the Sierra.[19]

Matthews was contacted by the July 26 Movement in Havana and agreed to go into the Sierra to meet Fidel. Guevara wrote, "At that time the presence of a foreign journalist, preferably an American, was more important to us than a military victory." [20]

The interview was published in the *New York Times* on February 24. The Cuban censors cut out the article in the *Times* before it was put on the newstands in Havana. Batista's Minister of Defense denied that Matthews had personally interviewed Castro. "A chapter from a novel of fantasy," he called it,[21] whereupon the *New York Times* printed the now famous photograph of Matthews and Fidel in the bush, both with big cigars in their mouths.

Fearing censure by the forthcoming meeting of the Inter-American Press Association, Batista's government finally allowed the interview to be published in Cuba. *Bohemia* emphasized the importance of Matthew's story:

> Thanks to him we know that: 1) the insurrection in the Oriente mountains is alive and on Cuban soil, 2) its leader is alive and on Cuban soil, leading the combatants of the July 26 Movement, 3) his position is so secure that he can afford to invite a distinguished American correspondent to interview him.[22]

Matthews's story condemned the Batista dictatorship and predicted that Castro and his movement were a force to be reckoned with. Matthews saw Castro's program as "radical, democratic and therefore anti-communist." [23]

Matthews was mistaken.

There is a curious element in Matthews's report that should be questioned. Matthews wrote that Castro's organization "is a revolutionary movement that calls itself socialistic." [24] It is curious, because Castro never used the word *socialistic* to describe his Movement in any public statements, and it is not likely that he made an exception in Matthews's case. Moreover, Castro told Che Cuevara that Matthews had asked him if the movement was *anti-imperialist*, and he had answered in the affirmative.[25]

Matthews's overestimation of the size of the rebel outfit

created a sense of expectancy in Cuba.[26] The army was ordered to wipe out the guerrilla band, and its frenetic activity around the Sierra only reinforced the rumors that the guerrillas were already a formidable force.

Unable to capture the guerrillas, Batista's army began driving the farmers from their homes in the Sierra foothills to the beaches of the southern coast. Then the depopulated zones were indiscriminately bombed. *Campesinos* suspected of aiding the guerrillas were treated with criminal brutality.

The Communists, in one of their underground publications, *El Campesino*, condemned the government's savage policies and said that they were designed "to stop the *campesinos* from joining the rebels."[27] The PSP, still following a policy of conditional support for the guerrillas, continued to differ with Castro on the overall strategy and tactics of the anti-Batista struggle. The Communists believed that only broad united-front tactics and mass action could create the conditions for the overthrow of the Batista regime.[28] Juan Marinello, the president of the Communist party, reiterated these differences in a letter to Herbert Matthews written in the middle of March. He stressed, however, that the rebels were "inspired by noble intentions."[29] Marinello's letter was written only four days after the failure of students to kill Batista and spark a national uprising.[30]

About the same time, Castro's band received much-needed reinforcements from the *llano,* sent by Frank País. By April, Fidel's army had about eighty men in its ranks, including some *campesinos.* "Little by little," Che wrote, "a change in the farmers' attitude toward us was taking place, impelled by the repressive measures unleashed by Batista, the assassinations, and the destruction of homes."[31] The rebel army was becoming a fish in the proverbial sea of peasants. During its first year of operation, it became in large part a *campesino* army.

What has never' been given due importance is the *kind* of peasant who inhabited the Sierra. Without understanding this, it is difficult to explain the militant support given by so many Sierra *campesinos* to later socioeconomic transformations that went far beyond the agrarian reform.

The *campesinos* of the sierras of Oriente were not typical peasants. "At least half of the economically active population of the Sierras belonged to the agricultural proletariat." [32] They were wage workers who earned their living by working for the landowners and therefore could be considered part of Cuba's working class. Another 10 to 15 percent were "semiproletariat" who farmed a tiny parcel of land and spent part of the year working for wages as agricultural laborers. [33] This explains why peasant-worker solidarity was achieved from the very beginning of Cuba's revolutionary process.

Moreover, the *campesinos* of the Sierra Maestra were experienced in the struggle. Most of them had close connections with Cuba's factories in the field, the sugar mills. Entire zones had a tradition of organization and militancy. There were thirty-nine sugar mills spotted around Oriente province, nineteen of them concentrated around the Sierra Maestra. The experience of workers' struggle in the mills and sugar plantations spread working-class consciousness over these zones. [34]

In many areas, farmers confronted powerful economic interests in a long and hard struggle in defense of their land, for higher prices for their crops, and against eviction. I've heard many farmers from Oriente speak about these experiences. [35]

The Communists were active in these struggles, which dated back to the thirties. They controlled the Sugar Workers Union, the most powerful labor organization in the country. Within it they organized agricultural laborers, most of whom were landless or tenant farmers. The Communists had also founded and led the Farmers' Federation, which directed many battles wages by the *campesinos* of the province.[36]

Over the years, the Manzanillo–Mabay sugar mill–Bayamo east-west axis formed a line from which working class ideas radiated into the areas around the sugar mills and up into the Sierra Maestra. The Mabay sugar mill had been the center of one of the short-lived "soviets" set up by workers after the fall of the Machado dictatorship in 1933.[37] Manzanillo had had a Communist mayor and congressman [38] in the forties and fifties.

I asked Carlos Rafael Rodríguez whether the Communist party had penetrated up into the Sierra Maestra. He answered with a drawn-out "Ooooo, we had a great many members among the farmers of the Sierra." [39]

In my conversation with him, Rodríguez revealed, for the first time, that the Communist had made official contact with Fidel's group only weeks after the *Granma* landing. They had sent an emissary, Gottwald Fleitas, leader of the Bayamo PSP, into the Sierra to speak with him. "He went into the Sierra when there were only twelve men . . . at the beginning of 1957," Rodríguez said. Fleitas was commissioned to tell Castro that the PSP had sent out directives to its *campesino* members in the sierra to offer their cooperation to the guerrillas.[40]

In accordance with party directives, some Communist *campesinos* helped Castro's guerrillas in subsequent months. For instance, one member of the PSP in San Lorenzo de las Mercedes, in the heart of the Sierras,[41] and another, Conrado,[42] who lived on a hilltop named after him (the Heights of Conrado), aided the small band almost from the beginning of their operations in the Sierra. Conrado, who had joined the party in the thirties, is mentioned by Che Guevara, who wrote that "this comrade was a member of the PSP and from the very beginning had established contact with our troops." [43]

It should be reiterated that the Communist position was that an armed struggle had little chance of success at this particular moment. However, their *conditional support* of Castro's guerrilla force is historically significant, inasmuch as it provides us with one more link in the long chain of fraternal contacts between Castro and the PSP.

The world knows that Castro has never spoken publicly about these contacts. Nonetheless, the historical facts lead to the inevitable conclusion that he welcomed them and considered the Communists as his political allies in the long run. This is established by his political tactics during the guerrilla war and his leadership after victory.

•

If Matthews proved Castro's physical presence in the sierra, the Battle of Uvero might be said to have proved his fighting presence. The battle took place on May 29, 1957, ten days after CBS Television broadcast a film on Castro's rebel army, the work of Bob Tabor and Wendell Hoffman. [44]

The attack on the Uvero army post, near a sawmill close to the Caribbean seacoast, ended in victory for the guerrilla band. Enemy casualties were nineteen dead, fourteen wounded.

The rebels also suffered high casualties—six dead and nine wounded. [45] But the psychological and propaganda impact of the Uvero battle possibly justified this high price, since news of the battle reverberated throughout Cuba and the Cuban exile communities.

Uvero made it difficult to obscure the fact that while Cuba's exiled politicians talked and jockeyed for position in anticipation of Batista's fall, Castro and his Movement acted. The armed struggle in the Sierra gave Castro an authority he could not have gained by political public relations.

By the middle of 1957, former President Prio, exiled in the United States, began to plan to co-opt Castro for his own ends. He saw the advantage—even more, the political imperative—of identifying himself with Fidel Castro and thus sharing in the prestige that had already accrued to the July 26 Movement. He was well aware that Castro's freedom to maneuver politically was severely restricted by his isolation in the mountains of Oriente—"a prisoner of the Sierra," as Che put it.[46]

Accordingly, in July,[47] two important figures of the Miami-based exile community made their way to the Sierra Maestra. One was Raúl Chibás, leader of the Orthodox party in exile and brother of Eduardo Chibás. The other was a Prio representative, Felipe Pazos, former president of the Banco Nacional. Che's assessment of these two men was harsh. He wrote of Pazos' "small Machiavellian brain" and of Chibás, who "lived only from the prestige of his brother . . . but had none of his virtues." [48]

The two men came to convince Fidel of the need to issue a joint manifesto. Castro agreed to do so and tried to make the declaration as radical as possible, a difficult task, Che noted, when dealing with men "insensitive to the call of the popular struggle." [49]

As soon as the Sierra Maestra Manifesto was signed and appropriate photographs taken of Pazos and Chibás with Fidel for publicity purposes, the two men left the Sierra.

If the Moncada program was not all that Castro dreamed of, the Sierra Manifesto was even less so. It did, however, spell out some progressive measures to be put into effect after the overthrow of Batista. Castro recognized that it was not yet possible to impose the program of those who were fighting in the mountains. It was "a necessary compromise and progressive at that moment." [50]

The manifesto contained a number of formulations that were clear victories for Castro's point of view. Castro had insisted on the formation of a revolutionary front that would include "all opposition political parties, social organizations, and revolutionary sectors." [51] A strict interpretation of this clause meant the inclusion of the Communists, a position anathema to the majority of exiled politicians.

The Sierra Manifesto rejected a military coup as a means for overthrowing Batista and explicitly excluded "mediation or intervention of any kind from another nation in the internal affairs of Cuba," [52] obviously referring to the United States. It called for a provisional government and the appointment of a provisional president.

An important concession on the part of the exiled politicians was the recognition that the "Sierra Maestra is already an indestructible bulwark of freedom." [53]

Castro wanted to include a more radical agrarian-reform program, but Pazos and Chibás would not go beyond a formula for distributing unused land, with indemnification of the owners.

Pazos and Chibás left the Sierra intending to play the manifesto as a trump card in Miami. When Batista's army launched an offensive in the fall and stepped up its terror against the *campesinos* in the Sierra, the politicians proved that they were really more interested in politics than in helping Castro and the armed struggle. Lester Rodríguez, Castro's emmisary in Miami, asked the exile groups for weapons but was turned down. He wrote to Castro, "There is no commitment to these people and I do not believe that in the future it is desirable to have any." [54]

In October 1957, Ursinio Rojas, veteran leader of the

PSP and the sugar workers, made his way to the Sierra Maestra to meet secretly with Fidel Castro. I have been told that they had a frank exchange of opinions about the rabid anti-Communism that existed among certain leaders of the July 26 Movement in the *llano* and especially within the Movement's National Labor Front (FON). Castro believed in unity with the Communists, but he was not yet in a position to impose this policy on the Movement leaders. He and Rojas explored the problem and discussed the organizational form that a unified movement could take.[55]

About that time, the PSP was reviewing its policy toward Castro's guerrilla movement. It was decided to give permission to some Communists to join the rebel army, although not as open representatives of the PSP.[56] It is probable that Rojas informed Castro of the party's decision.

The PSP's outlook was slowly changing. In January 1958, the Communists declared that "the struggle *has still not reached the point* where the majority of the people are in favor of armed struggle, of war." [57] The formulation is revealing because it implicitly recognizes that at some future time the struggle *would* reach that point. The PSP accepted as established the efficacy of Castro's guerrilla war in the Sierra but did not believe that conditions were the same elsewhere: "There is a great difference between the level of the struggle in the Sierra Maestra, where for more than a year a group of Cubans has been battling the tyranny with weapons in hand, and the level of struggle in the rest of Cuba; that is, in almost all the rest of Cuba." [58]

The unity policy Castro and Rojas discussed bore some fruit, although more with the grass-roots membership than with the city leaders of the Movement. For instance, in the industrial Luyano section of Havana, the Communists and July 26 organizers worked in close harmony. Más Martín, Fidel's old friend who had become head of the Luyano Communists, told me how he and the July 26 coordinator,

Caamaño, worked together to build the July 26 Movement in the shops. When Luis Cabrera, a national leader of the July 26 Labor Front, found out about the joint work of the two organizations, he warned Caamaño that he would have him expelled from the organization if he continued to cooperate with the Communists. Más Martín says that cooperation did continue but more discreetly.[59]

It is interesting that the July 26 Movement had within its ranks men who considered themselves Marxists and who had been influenced by the PSP. This explains the red flag that was raised by July 26 militants above the Príncipe prison yard in November 1957 in celebration of the Russian Revolution.[60] The three who raised the flag were all workers and all subsequently died in the struggle. Another July 26 hero, Arístides Viera, left a last will and testament in which he wrote: "The fundamental ends to which I aspire, with full consciousness of the key revolutionary factors, do not differ one molecule from those of Marx and Lenin." [61] But there were leaders of the July 26 Movement in the *llano* who refused to cooperate with the Communists under any circumstances.

•

In January 1958, a year before victory, Che Guevara penned a note to Fidel Castro, who was at another base in the Sierra Maestra. Che's note was an enthusiastic endorsement of a political declaration made by Castro in an open letter to exile groups in Miami. "Lenin has already said it," Guevara wrote; "a policy of principles is the best policy." [62]

As far as I can discover, Che's little note has never been quoted in any book about Fidel Castro. Yet the casual "Lenin has already said it," in a note meant only for the eyes of Castro, informs us of a certain ideological identity between the two men.

In this note, Che was congratulating Castro for his public

rejection of the Miami Pact, which had been drawn up in Miami without his participation and signed there on November 1, 1957. Among the signatories were ex-President Prio; Manuel Antonio de Varona, the ex-president of the Cuban senate; Roberto Agramonte, of the Orthodox party; and three members of the July 26 Movement whom Castro had not authorized to sign the document.

It had taken twenty days for the full text of the Miami Pact to reach Castro in the Sierra. By that time it had already been made public. On the day the text arrived Castro's Column 1, "José Martí," fought three battles with the Batista forces. Castro wrote in his open letter to the so-called Cuban Junta in Miami: "The arrival of those papers, as another irony of fate at a time when what we needed were arms, coincided with the most intense offensive launched by the tyranny against us." [63]

On receiving the text, Castro had called the July 26 Movement leadership to a meeting in the Sierra to discuss the Miami Pact, "in which not only the prestige but also the historical rationale of the 26th of July Movement is at stake." [64] Then Castro formulated his powerful denunciation of the Miami Pact.

Castro said that the pact was not binding because the July 26 delegates subscribed to it "without even the consideration—not to mention the elementary obligation—of having consulted its leaders and fighters." [65] Castro wrote that although this procedure was "bitter and humiliating . . . we would have accepted [the pact] . . . if we were not simply in disagreement with essential points." [66]

One of the first lines of the Miami Pact must have irritated Castro. It stated that the pact was being written "in the free land that belongs to this great democracy, the United States of America." Castro didn't mention this phrase. He did, however, characterize as "cowardly the absence of a clause rejecting foreign intervention in the domestic affairs of Cuba,[67] a formulation that had been included at his insistence in the earlier Sierra Manifesto. The July 26 leader also criticized the absence of a clause explicitly rejecting substitution of the dictatorship by a military junta, another point that had been included in the Sierra Manifesto.[68]

Castro was especially incensed over a clause stating that after victory "the revolutionary forces will be incorporated into the regular armed forces with their weapons." Castro asked, "What is meant by revolutionary forces? Are uniforms and authority to be granted to persons who today have their weapons hidden, only to bring them out on the day of victory, and who remain with their arms crossed while a small group of compatriots fight all the forces of the tyranny? . . ."[69]

"What is most important for the Revolution," Castro declared in his open letter, "is not unity itself but the bases of such unity."[70] He said years later that he was not interested in unity with exile organizations on the basis of the Miami Pact because it would have given a majority to the conservative elements. He noted that Prio and others in Miami "were contrary to total unity; they were always in favor of excluding the PSP from this unity."[71]

Castro knew that accepting the Miami Pact at that moment would mean forfeiting his dream "to revolutionarize this country from top to bottom."[72] He was well aware of Lenin's cautionary remarks on state power and understood that the dissolution of the rebel army at the end of the war,[73] which the Miami Pact called for, would destroy the only force in Cuba capable of ensuring the further development of the Revolution. For these reasons, the full meaning of Che's intimate little note—"Lenin has already said it; a policy of principles is the best policy"—was not lost on him.

The Communists agreed with Castro's and Guevara's assessment of the Miami Pact. A few weeks after the letter to the Cuban Liberation Junta was made public, they printed their own declaration, which stated that "the masses of the July 26 Movement and popular democratic opinion have welcomed with sympathy the decision of the July 26 high command." [74]

11.

My True
Destiny

By the end of 1957, the rebel army consolidated its claim to the Sierra Maestra by successful ambushes of enemy detachments and attacks on army posts. In November, a rebel platoon ambushed a truck convoy carrying three hundred soldiers, inflicting seventy enemy casualties. Batista's high command was forced to alter its tactics. In December, the army pulled back from the Sierra and attempted to seal it off with a ring of army posts. They had been unable to destroy the guerrillas. They now sought to quarantine them, but in vain.

Castro proved himself adept at guerrilla war in the mountains. He demonstrated his mastery in the equally decisive war of politics. Castro knew that as the war against Batista grew in scope, the U.S. government would be confronted with a crucial question. Should it continue its support of the dictatorship or begin to seek a substitute pawn? It was common knowledge that Batista was only as strong as his American backers wished to make him.

If the State Department considered Castro's goals "Communist," adequate U.S. military support would be mounted to ensure his destruction.[1] With Castro defeated, the way would be open for a safe, "democratic," obedient alternative to the Batista dictatorship.

In these circumstances, Castro knew it was essential to allay U.S. fears about his movement and to convince the Americans that their economic and political interests would be safeguarded by his victory.

It is against this background that one must interpret his words appearing in the mass-circulation U.S. magazine *Coronet* for February 1958. It provided, he wrote "the opportunity to state our aims and to correct the many errors and distortions circulating about our revolutionary struggle." In the article he told Middle America and the State Department what they wanted to hear: "We will aid in setting up a provisional government to be made up of delegates of our various civic organizations: Lions, Rotarians, professional bodies such as physicians' or engineers' guilds, religious associations, and so forth." Absent were his comments of two and a half years before that petty politics had given Cuba only "lies, compromise, deceit, betrayals." [2]

Castro's statement on free enterprise was a parody that could have served as a public-relations blurb for the U.S. Chamber of Commerce. "I personally have come to feel," he wrote, "that nationalization is, at best, a cumbersome instrument. It does not seem to make the state any stronger; yet it enfeebles private enterprise. . . . Foreign investments will always be welcome and secure here." He spoke in terms Americans were accustomed to: "The single word most expressive of our aim and spirit is simply—*freedom*."

Castro's words, winging like bullets out of the Sierra, were intended to disarm Cuba's historical enemy, and subsequent events bear witness to their deadly accuracy. The threat of American intervention in the event of a rebel victory had its historical antecedents. [3] In 1895, José Martí had warned against the dangers of American domination in bitter words:

Here I am, in danger of losing my life daily, in the course of my duty to my country—because I know it and have the spirit to fulfill it—to prevent, in time, through the liberation of Cuba, the danger of the United States' extending itself through the Antilles and falling with all its weight on our lands of America. All that I have done and will do is for that end. I've had to do it silently and indirectly because there are things that, to be achieved, must be hidden. . . . by proclaiming what they are would only raise difficulties that would make it more difficult to attain the desire ends.

This testimonial to his heirs, which Martí wrote on the day before he was killed in battle, ended: "I have lived in the monster and known its entrails. My sling is the sling of David." [4]

These last words of Martí are echoed in the equally bitter words of Fidel Castro, written in a scribbled note to Celia Sánchez four months after his "Pablum Declaration" in *Coronet*. The oath contained in this intimate note was provoked by a rocket attack by U.S.–built fighters on the house of Mario Sariol, a mountain villager who had helped Castro's army since its arrival in the Sierra. Castro wrote:

I've sworn that the Americans are going to pay dearly for what they are doing. When this war is over, a much wider and bigger war will begin for me, the war that I am going to wage against them. I realize that that is going to be my true destiny. [5]

•

By the beginning of January 1958, the July 26 leadership in the *llano* was insisting that the time was ripe to organize a general revolutionary strike. [6] Faustino Pérez, the leader of the M-26-7 Havana forces, [7] went to the Sierra from Ha-

Campamento de Dos Ríos. 18 de Mayo de 1895.

Sr. Manuel Mercado

Mi hermano queridísimo: Ya puedo escribir, ya puedo decirle con qué ternura y agradecimiento y respeto lo quiero, y á esa casa que es mía, y mi orgullo y obligación; ya estoy todos los días en peligro de dar mi vida por mi país, y por mi deber —puesto que lo entiendo y tengo ánimos con que realizarlo— de impedir á tiempo con la independencia de Cuba que se extienda por las Antillas los Estados Unidos y caigan, con esa fuerza más, sobre nuestras tierras de América. Cuanto hice hasta hoy, y haré, es para eso. En silencio ha tenido que ser, y como indirectamente, porque hay cosas que para lograrlas han de andar ocultas, y de proclamarse en lo que son, levantarían dificultades demasiado recias para alcanzar sobre ellas el fin.

José Martí

Jose Marti's letter to Manuel Mercado, written the day before he died (see page 209).

Sierra Maestra
junio 5

Celia:

Al ver los cohetes que tiraron en casa de Mario, me he jurado que los americanos van a pagar bien caro lo que están haciendo. Cuando esta guerra se acabe, empezará para mí una guerra mucho más larga y grande: la guerra que voy a echar contra ellos. Me doy cuenta que ese va a ser mi destino verdadero.

Fidel

Castro's letter to Celia Sanchez written during the guerilla war (see page 209).

vana to convince Castro of the necessity to call for a general
strike. He painted a rosy picture of its possibilities for success and told Castro that the *llano* action groups were ready
for the long-awaited action.

It is very possible that Castro was not sanguine about
the chances for success of a general insurrectional strike at
that time. He felt obliged, however, by the very insistence
of the *llano* leadership, to give his backing as leader of the
July 26 Movement to the general-strike call.[8]

On March 12, he and Pérez signed a joint call for the
strike. It pointed to the dictatorship's suspension of constitutional rights as a sign of "tremendous weakness" and
asserted that there was "a general-strike atmosphere" in
Cuba.[9]

The Communists, who had strong bases in the ports, factories, and sugar mills, immediately sent out their own call
to back the general strike.[10] Consistent with its tactical outlook since Batista's takeover, the PSP conceived of the process as a series of struggles for immediate economic and
political demands that would reach a peak and end in a
national strike accompanied by a general insurrectional
situation.[11] *Carta Semanal,* the underground PSP newspaper, launched the slogan "Factory workers, unite! Organize
united-front committees." [12]

For the most part, however, the July 26 leadership in
Havana, and especially that of its labor front, Frente Obrero
Nacional (FON), had no intention of developing conditions
for unity with the Communists. Their conception of the
strike consisted solely of a strike call to the people and
simultaneous armed attacks against planned targets in
Havana. Preparatory organization of the strike in factories
and shops was not essential to the plan. The PSP, which was
ready to take part in the strike, was not allowed to share in
the preparations.

By the beginning of April, the Communists were convinced that the strike would miscarry if the situation was not rapidly corrected. They sent a veteran militant, Oswaldo Sánchez, to the Sierra to advise Castro of their views. Castro was undoubtedly impressed by the arguments of Sánchez, who claimed that the *llano* leaders, especially in Havana, had overestimated their strength and had failed to organize the strike on a shop level. They had refused cooperation with the Communists and depended too much on spontaneity for the success of the strike.[13]

Castro was disconcerted about the turn of events, especially the FON leaders' refusal to create the necessary conditions of unity for a successful general strike. On March 26 he issued a directive that, by implication, was critical of many of the strike organizers in the *llano*. The main thrust of this directive was its call for unity, evidently with the Communists. Castro wrote:

> In calling the people to this final struggle against the tyranny, our Movement does not make exceptions of any kind. All Cuban workers, no matter what their political or revolutionary affiliations, have a right to participate in the strike committees in the work centers. The Natonal Labor Front is not a sectarian body. It was formed as an instrument to unite and lead the workers in the struggle against the tyranny.
>
> The leadership of the National Labor Front will coordinate its efforts with the labor sections of the political and revolutionary organizations that combat the regime and with all organized groups that fight for economic and political demands of the working class, so that no worker remains separated from his patriotic task.[14]

Castro's March 26 Directive was sent to Havana with a *campesina* messenger, Clodomira.[15] However, it did not have the desired result. July 26 leaders in Havana, and especially those of FON, gave Castro's directive a minimum of publicity and continued to make plans unilaterally. In effect, Fidel Castro's leadership from the Sierra was being sabotaged by a small but powerful group of July 26 Movement *llano* leaders.[16]

Ironically, it was the Communists who tried to give publicity to Castro's March 26 directive. Even before they had received a copy of it in Havana, their *Carta Semanal* reported that "a radio program from the Sierra Maestra tells us that Fidel Castro has called for unity of all opposition forces and for the organization of joint strike committees in the work centers." [17] The following day they raised the slogan "Forward! Toward the general strike." *Carta Semanal* wrote, "We feel the spirit of unity is growing. But we know that the forces of disunity are present." [18]

The July 26 *llano* leaders suddenly launched the strike on April 9, 1958. An armed group took over a radio station in Havana and announced that the strike would begin immediately. It was a bolt out of the blue and not the culmination of a process, of careful grass-roots preparation.[19]

The response of the people of Havana was sporadic. In most places, confusion reigned. Many shop workers did not hear the strike call. Those who did went out into the streets but found no leadership. The armed action groups of the July 26 Movement behaved heroically but were largely ineffective, and there were too few of them. Workers in some shops finally responded by work stoppages, but this had little effect in hampering the government's ability to control the situation.

Greater success was achieved in Cuba's central province, Las Villas, where there had been coordination among groups as diverse as the PSP and Catholic Action.[20] The Communists played a key role in their traditional strongholds, the sugar mills, where they worked side by side with the FON.

The strike's defeat was a critical blow to the *llano* movement. Batista's forces began a general campaign of repression. July 26 activists, as well as many PSP members, were forced to make their way to Oriente to join the guerrilla movement.

The Communists were bitter about what they considered adventurism on the part of the July 26 *llano* leadership in Havana. "We have suffered the effects of disunity, of the unilateral call for the strike without taking into account the rest of the opposition or the workers themselves. . . . Strikes cannot be made lightly by simply calling for them by radio." [21]

Less than a month after the April 9 strike, a meeting was held in the Sierra Maestra to evaluate it, fix responsibility for its failure, and reorganize the July 26 Movement in the *llano*, which had been severely damaged by the subsequent repression. Fidel presided at the meeting. Che Guevara has given the most complete account of it, in his article "A Decisive Meeting." [22] Tension filled the air, but Fidel's moral authority and prestige guided the meeting's conclusions.

Describing these conclusions, Che wrote that the *llano* leaders had "underestimated the strength of the enemy and subjectively exaggerated its own." [23] He observed that the most violent criticism was directed against the leaders of the FON "who had opposed any participation of the Popular Socialist party in the organization of the struggle.[24] . . . The adventurist policy of the labor front leadership had crashed head-on against inexorable reality," Che noted. The strike had been "saturated with subjectivism and *putschist* concepts." [25]

Enzo Infante, who attended the crucial meeting in the Sierra after the failure of the strike, told me that "in some ways, events had represented a struggle for power between the *llano* and the Sierra, which in turn represented two ideologies on revolution." [26] He was referring to the serious political differences that had developed between the two.

Important leaders of the July 26 Movement in the *llano* had come to believe that their field of battle was more decisive than the guerrilla struggle in the mountains. More important than this military assessment, however, were their political differences with the men of the mountain. Castro's policy was aimed at establishing a government to represent *primarily* the dispossessed workers and farmers. He intended to lead Cuba on a road to socialism if the possibilities presented themselves. An important group of *llano* leaders, on the other hand, had in mind a bourgeois-democratic state and economy, purged of the old vices.

Che observed that the April 9 experience "initiated an ideological struggle within the July 26 Movement." [27] Fidel's prestige and authority were consolidated. From then on until victory there was only one center of leadership of the July 26 Movement: the Sierra Maestra. A new lesson was learned, said Che, "that the Revolution did not belong to any one group." [28] Significantly, after the meeting in the Sierra, the July 26 National Labor Front (FON) changed its name to *United* National Labor Front (FONU).

The April 9 strike also marked the turning point in the Communists' attitude toward the guerrillas. Following the strike, increased numbers of PSP members, in danger of being caught in the stepped-up police repression, made their way to the Oriente mountains to join the rebel army.

Following the failure of the April 9 strike, the Batista regime carried out a general offensive against Castro's guerrilla army in the Sierra Maestra. The offensive, launched by ten thousand soldiers, was a total failure. Castro's three hundred guerrillas outwitted the Batista forces on almost every occasion. Two months later, when Batista called off his attack, the rebel army went on the offensive. Che writes, "We captured more than six hundred new weapons, more than double the number we had started with, and we inflicted more than a thousand casualties on the enemy." [29]

Castro's leadership position in the anti-Batista movement was growing from strength to strength. There was now general recognition among the opposition forces that the Sierra would inevitably play a vital role in Batista's defeat.

The old Establishment forces began to realize that their future lay in hitching themselves to the victorious movement. Castro continued to assure the opposition politicians, the Cuban capitalists, and the United States government that he was not a wild radical. "Never has the July 26 Movement talked of socialism." [30] he told Jules Dubois of the *Chicago Tribune* in May 1958. Castro now felt the time had come to negotiate a unity pact with other opposition elements, including those with unsavory reputations for politicking. He was not yet ready to reveal his final aims. His strategy, as always, was to unite as broad an anti-Batista movement as possible without sacrificing his freedom to maneuver toward higher goals.

On July 20, in Caracas, a unity manifesto to which Fidel Castro had previously subscribed was officially ratified. Besides Castro, the signatories included former President Carlos Prio for the Authentic party; the well-known lawyer Dr. José Miro Cardona; Manuel de Varona of the Partido Revolucionario Cubano Insurreccional; and representatives of other anti-Batista organizations.

The Caracas Pact was much different from the Miami Pact, which Castro had rejected seven months before. His forces had been much weaker then, and he had felt that that pact would have put him in a political straitjacket by giving influence and maneuverabilty to more conservative anti-Batista forces. There was always the danger that after victory, they would be in a stronger position to influence basic political decisions.

In his rejection of the Miami Pact, he had asserted that the leadership in the struggle "will continue to be in Cuba in the hands of revolutionary fighters." The Caracas Pact recognized the ascendancy of the guerrilla movement, especially in Oriente province. It called for the "adoption of a common strategy to defeat the dictatorship by means of armed insurrection." [31] After victory, the pact projected "a brief provisional government . . . to establish full constitutional democratic rights." [32]

The Caracas Pact also closed the door to recognition of military men who might displace Batista through a *putsch*. The Miami Pact had made no reference to U.S. intervention. The Caracas Pact asked "the government of the United States of America to cease all military and other types of aid to the dictator." [33]

The signatories set up a "Frente Cívica Revolucionaria Democrátia." Fidel was named commander-in-chief of the armed forces, and Manuel Urrutia was designated as president of "Cuba in arms." In his rejection of the Miami Pact, Castro had proposed Urrutia as provisional president. Castro had pointed out that Urrutia was "impartial to partisan politics . . . for he does not belong to any political group." [34] For the moment, at least, Urrutia's independent position was advantageous to Castro, inasmuch as it was an obstacle to the *políticos'* ambitions for power.

The Communist party was not invited to sign the Caracas Pact, but it is significant that there was no attempt in the text to define precisely who would take part in forming the government after Batista's downfall. Castro commented years later that the other anti-Batista forces made the ex-

clusion of the PSP one of their main points—"We understood that it would be better not to talk about the problem
but to end the war." [35]

Castro's adherence to the unity pact was an important
tactical move. He was very aware, however, that the struggle would have to go far beyond the limits acceptable to
most of the other signatories.

At the same time as the Caracas Pact was announced,
Castro welcomed an official representative of the PSP, Dr.
Carlos Rafael Rodríguez, to his camp.[36] There was some
irony in the fact that Castro, recognized as commander-in-
chief of the armed forces by the Caracas signatories who
had refused to invite the Communists, now had a Communist
delegate with him in the Sierra.

•

In March 1958, Raúl Castro, newly promoted to *comandante*, left the Sierra Maestra with a group of men to open
up the Second Front, "Frank País," in the eastern third of
Oriente province. There is evidence to indicate that before
he left the Sierra Maestra, the Rebel Army command made
contact with the PSP, which had a long history of militant
activity in the area of the proposed Second Front. The
evidence comes from José "Pepe" Ramírez, the head of the
National Small Farmers Association of Cuba (ANAP) since
its foundation in 1959.

Ramírez was attending an underground PSP school in
Havana, when, *at the beginning of March,* he was ordered
to go to Holguín, in the north of Oriente province, to await
further orders. Raúl Castro left the Sierra Maestra with his
tiny band to open up the Second Front *on March 10.* A few
days after Raúl Castro arrived in the new fighting zone,
the regional secretary of the Communist party in north
Oriente province ordered Ramírez to "go up to the Second

Front and report to Raúl." [37] Inasmuch as the contacts between the Rebel Army command and the PSP must have been established while Raúl Castro was still in the Sierra Maestra, one can fairly assume Fidel Castro, commander-in-chief of the rebel army, had taken the initiative in the matter.

When Ramírez arrived at the temporary headquarters of the Second Front, Raúl told him, "I know you by reputation. The *campesinos* say good things about you, and the big landowners say bad things about you." [38] Raúl gave Ramírez the job of organizing the *campesinos* of the Second Front, a large area extending to the easternmost tip of Cuba. It was familar work to Ramírez. He had been raised in that area by his uncle Pablo Cruz, an illiterate farmer who had joined the Communist party in the early thirties. Cruz had a reputation as a fighter among the peasants, and Pepi Ramírez followed in his footsteps. From 1943 to 1956, before going underground, he had been first an activist and then a leader of the Communist-led *campesino* federation.

Raúl Castro ordered Ramírez to begin planning for a congress of *campesinos* for later in the year. Over the summer months preparatory meetings were held all over the Second Front. Campesino veterans of the PSP worked hard to make the congress a success. [39] The event was held in September 1958. Farmers came on horseback from faraway places and set up around the guerrilla camp. Raúl Castro chaired the meeting. The main report was radical in tone. "The reactionaries, backed by foreign capital," it said, "support the bloody and tyrannical government of Batista so that they can enrich themselves at the expense of the people, even though this foreign backing means the strangulation of our national economy." [40]

Raúl Castro had also chosen Communists for another critical job, that of heading the school at Tumbasiete in the

Second Front, where elementary academic and ideological courses were given to rebel-army troops.[41] The unity between the Rebel Army and the Communists in the Second Front was a hint of things to come after victory.

On October 10, 1958, the anniversary of the independence war against Spain, Fidel Castro signed an agrarian-reform law that gave sharecroppers and squatters title to the land they lived on, without indemnification in cash to the owners as required by the 1940 Constitution.[42] It was an early sign that Castro would not allow the written constitution to stand in the way of fundamental revolutionary changes.

The agrarian reform, promulgated in the Sierra Maestra before the victory, did not include the division of the big landholdings in Cuba, a reform Castro had promised. The absence of such a clause was probably misunderstood by the more conservative elements. Che commented later that the politicians, "incapable of understanding the principles that guided Fidel Castro, believed that the promise to divide up the big landholdings was as demagogic as their typical election promises. They would be sorely disappointed." [43]

In fact, Fidel Castro was determined to go beyond anything most Cubans imagined. He was as aware as ever, however, that the unity he had so carefully nurtured within his heterogeneous movement could wither away if he publicly announced goals that went beyond the political horizons of most of his followers. In a letter from prison four years earlier he had compared Marx to Victor Hugo, to the detriment of Hugo for not seeing "the struggle of dominant interests at a precise moment." [44] Now he told Carlos Rafael Rodríguez in the Sierra that it would be a grave tactical error at that moment to alert the enemy by defining the revolutionary goals and the eventual class enemies too clearly.[45]

A story that Luis Más Martín told me is revealing in this

context.[46] Martín had arrived at rebel-army headquarters at La Plata on September 6. It was his first meeting with Castro after many years. A decade earlier, as the head of the Havana Young Communists, he had worked with Castro in the protest movement against bus-fare increases in Havana. In this connection, the Communist-party newspaper, *Hoy*, had published Castro's photo and mentioned him as one of those who had "adopted the decision to take even more drastic measures if police dare to violate university autonomy." [47]

Castro was having a tooth filled by a dentist using a foot-operated drill when Más Martín first saw him. That evening, Castro and Más Martín went for a walk around the camp. Later, they talked about the past, Más Martín recalls, and about the labor movement in Havana, prisons and prisoners,[48] the general political climate in the country . . .

At one point in their rambling conversation, Castro asked his old Communist friend, "How much do I owe the party bookstore?"

Más Martín recalls answering, "How much do you owe? The amount you bought the last time." The "last time" was the day Más Martín had taken him to the bookstore shortly before July 26, 1953.

"How much was that?" asked Fidel.

Más Martín replied, "I don't know. I think it was about forty-five pesos."

Fidel shot back, "Don't worry. When the revolution triumphs, we will have Marxist books coming out of our ears!"

12.

"Yes, It Is
a Revolution!"

In late August two military columns of about one hundred men each marched down from the Sierra Maestra and began to move toward the west. They were led by two of Fidel's most competent and audacious commanders, Che Guevara and Camilo Cienfuegos.[1] Guevara's task was to set up a fighting front in the Escambray Mountains of Cuba's central Las Villas province. Cienfuegos had orders to carry the war beyond Havana.[2]

Che and Camilo, two soldiers utterly loyal to Fidel Castro, were to carry his military and political policies into the heartland of Cuba. The messages that flowed between them and central command headquarters in the Sierra provide a striking record of their exploits.[3] They show that Castro was informed of the main problems of his lieutenants and that he, in turn, made the major strategic decisions.

Before the two columns were sent off on their crucial mission, Castro sent word to the July 26 Movement in the *llano* to prepare to help the columns along the route. He also forewarned the Communist groups through Carlos Rafael Rodríguez, the official representative of the PSP in the Sierra.[4]

Che thought he would be able to cross Camagüey province in less than a week by using trucks, as Raúl Castro had done when opening the Second Front. This proved impossible, and both the columns of Guevara and Cienfuegos, traveling separate routes, took one month to cross the province on foot.[5]

Che's message to Castro about his crossing of Camagüey province was revealing. He wrote, "We were not able to establish contact with the July 26 organizations, since a couple of supposed members refused aid when I requested it. I received money, plastic sheets, some shoes, medicine, food, and guides only from members of the PSP."[6]

His reception at the hands of another guerrilla group at the Camagüey–Las Villas border was an even greater disappointment. Che received a message from the Escambray Second Front, a largely ineffective and highly conservative guerrilla group led by a businessman, Eloy Gutiérrez Menoyo, and an American adventurer, William Morgan.[7] The group told Che that the Rebel Army could not enter the Escambray Mountains without clearing its plans with them. To stop at that juncture would have meant encirclement and annihilation. "We continued on," Che wrote, "estranged and hurt because we expected more from those who call themselves comrades-in-arms. But we decided to solve each and every problem and to carry out the express orders of the commander-in-chief, Fidel Castro, to achieve unity."[8]

The Escambray Second Front was not the only guerrila outfit operating in the zone. The Revolutionary Directorate, composed primarily of university students, had also set up a guerrila group in the Escambray Mountains. However, its attitude differed from that of the Escambray Second Front. Che and the leaders of the Revolutionary Directorate met to discuss combined operations. Che spoke at length on the need to promulgate an agrarian-reform law in the Escambray. The revolutionary directorate agreed in general with these ideas but argued that the Escambray Second Front was a group of bandits and should be excluded from any unity pact.[9]

On October 26, combined forces under Che attacked the town of Guinea de Miranda, defeating a forty-man military detachment. A highly symbolic photograph, [10] taken on the main street of the newly won city, shows Majors Faure Chamón and Castello of the Revolutionary Directorate standing beside PSP member Captain Juan Miranda, a member of Che's rebel forces.

Two weeks later, Che wrote to Faure Chaumón agreeing that cooperation with the Escambray Second Front had proved impossible but that in his "official conversations with members of the Popular Socialist party, they have demonstrated a frank attitude in favor of unity and have placed their organization in the *llano* and their guerrilla unit of the Yaguajay Front at the service of that unity." [11]

·

The guerrilla unit of the Yaguajay Front had been organized some months earlier by Félix Torres, a Communist. It was his aim to join it to the July 26 Movement detachments operating in that area. Camilo knew of the existence of the Torres group [12] and, toward the end of his arduous and dangerous trek through Camagüey province, had sent out scouts to contact it. Torres, in turn, knowing of Cienfuego's difficult position, had sent out men to find him.

Camilo wrote in his campaign diary, "We have arrived at a camp commanded by Félix Torres, of Communist ideas. It is very well organized. From the first he put all his efforts into cooperating with and aiding us. We are convinced that we have a common cause." [13]

Torres described his first discussion with Cienfuegos:

TORRES: I am a Communist, but some of my men represent different views. Politically I follow the line of the Communist party, but militarily I follow the line of the Sierra Maestra. We have sixty-five men in my guerrilla group. From this moment on, all my men with their weapons are under your command.

CIENFUEGOS: I knew about this guerrilla group before getting here, but I didn't imagine it this way. This is a guerrilla unit with real organization, characteristic of the people of your party. I accept you as part of our force. You will be a *comandante* and as such continue to lead your guerrillas.[14]

•

Camilo found that the July 26 detachments operating in the area were openly anti-Communist and were refusing to cooperate with Torres's group. He sent back a report to central command. Castro's reply arrived as Camilo's troops were preparing an ambush of enemy forces. "It is a crime against the Revolution to foment grudges and divisions," he wrote.[15] Cienfuegos called together representatives of the July 26 Movement and the PSP of Las Villas province. They agreed to maintain separate July 26 and PSP detachments under his general command and to divide captured arms between them.[16]

Camilo chose Gerardo Nogueras, a Communist leader of the sugar workers, to organize a National Conference of Sugar Workers, to take place in the liberated territory of Las Villas.[17] One of the meetings in the mountains brought out eight hundred workers from the sugar mills of the liberated region to form a new trade union.[18] Camilo reported to Fidel,

I spoke to sugar workers. I was more elated than at any time in these years of fighting. . . .

Those men used a rock as a platform. They spoke as they hadn't done in many years. These men, with the weariness of years reflected in their faces, shouted out their suffering and their needs. We will spend our greatest efforts to find solutions today and tomorrow.[19]

The National Conference of Sugar Workers was held at year's end, only days before final victory.[20] Representatives of the sugar-mill workers and sugar-cane cutters came from all over Cuba. On the opening day several thousand men, women, and children marched in celebration through the streets of the liberated mountain town where the conference was to take place.

The sugar worker's conference in liberated territory, like the earlier *campesino* congress, was part of Castro's master plan to rally Cuba's poor farmers and workers behind him and organize them for the struggle ahead. He knew that they were the people who would prevent power from being torn from the revolutionary movement and who would ensure the ongoing radicalization of the Revolution once victory was achieved. When victory came, plans were already underway for convening a National Workers' Congress in the Sierra Maestra.[21]

Castro's preoccupation with organizing of workers and poor farmers was the key to the kind of revolution he would make and to the nature of its leading forces. Fidel, through his loyal lieutenants Raúl Castro, Che Guevara, and Camilo Cienfuegos, sought the support of the Communists as he would continue to do later. At the same time, the PSP was beginning to accept Fidel Castro's leadership. In all this, one can discern the pattern of Fidel Castro's "hidden design."

After September 1958, the Batista government began to disintegrate at an accelerated pace. Its crisis was common knowledge, although complacency still reigned in government circles.

Censorship was clamped down on the nation, but Radio Rebelde broadcasts from the Sierra brought news of the war into every Cuban home. Hundreds of thousands of Cubans bought the illegal "Freedom Bonds" of the July 26 Movement and, in doing so, became active conspirators in the insurrectional war.

The July 26 Movement, which had strong backing among professionals, penetrated some of Cuba's publicity agencies.[22] Cubans still laugh about the advertisements for Tornillo Soap that followed the official government newscasts. After the Batista government handouts were read, the announcer would burst in with, "Don't believe in tales, women —Tornillo Soap washes best of all." Also memorable were the Bola Roja bean advertisements that followed the news. The word *bola* as used in Cuba can be variously translated *ball* (like a round bean) or *rumor*.

Just a week before Batista fled, a two-page advertisement for Eden Cigarettes showed a man with a pack of Edens in one hand and a book in the other entitled *High Fidelity*. Newspapers were ordered to stop running another advertisement showing a man with a watch on his wrist, above the caption "This is the watch that went to the Antarctic." The man's face closely resembled Fidel Castro's, complete with beard and military cap.

The symbols *0-3-C* began to appear on the walls of Havana. The zero-three-C campaign called for a moratorium on frivolity during the holiday season: zero *cine* (movies); zero *compras* (purchases); zero *cabaret* (nightclubs). It also had a more political meaning: zero *corrupción* (corruption); zero *cohecho* (bribery); zero *caudillismo* (dictatorship).

Citizens expressed their sentiments in many ways. When Batista's picture was flashed on the screen, it usually provoked catcalls. When a song known to be one of Batista's favorites was played at dances, couples stood still.

•

The contact and cooperation between Castro and the PSP did not occupy the center of the stage in this period before victory. Therefore, it is mainly in retrospect that one can recognize the trend toward the political convergence that was taking shape—Castro's grand design of historical dimensions. Prominent observers, unaware of this background, have therefore been unable to present a coherent history of the origins of the Cuban socialist revolution.

Some anecdotes of the Sierra throw light on the Fidel Castro who was to lead this first socialist revolution of the American hemisphere.

One night Fidel Castro, Carlos Rafael Rodríguez, and Más Martín were talking at the Las Vegas de Jibacoa rebel-army camp in the Sierra. At one point Rodríguez was explaining his ideas on the political struggle that would develop after victory. He drew a diagram showing the right, center, and left forces. He predicted that the right and left would try to win over the center. Castro asked with amusement, "And where do I fit in?" Rodríguez shot back, "You will be the leader of the left." [23]

The political struggle, though much sharper in the cities, was also in evidence in the Sierra—in fact, right in Castro's command headquarters at La Plata. This led to verbal pyrotechnics on occasions, revealing something of Castro's political ideas.

One day in November, Castro announced that he was leaving La Plata that evening. Later, while talking to a July 26 leader, he happened to hear the daily transmission of Radio Rebelde coming from a radio in the next room.

A voice began to read a document called "A Letter to Militants." It included an attack on socialism and compared Nazism to Communism.

Later, when a second reading of the document began, Castro began listening more carefully. "Turn it off," he ordered. Going outside, he spotted some of those responsible for the radio broadcast on a nearby hillside where the transmitter was. Indignantly, he shouted at them, "Did you think I had already left? Did you think I wouldn't hear it? Why don't you take on Batista and the *yanquis* and leave Communism alone?" [24]

About a month before Batista fled, Manuel Urrutia, the provisional president chosen by the Caracas Pact signatories, came into the Sierra. Shortly before Christmas, only days before Batista fled, Urrutia met with some of the noncombatants of the *llano* and drew up recommendations for a new government. Castro was not present, but he obtained a copy of the document. It suggested that he appoint some members of the July 26 political committee in the *llano* as his advisors. The document failed to include Rebel Army participation in the provisional government after victory.

Castro was deeply annoyed, believing as he did that only the Rebel Army could ensure the type of profound revolution he had in mind. Five years earlier, in "History Will Absolve Me," he had declared that after victory "a government acclaimed by the mass of combatants would receive and be vested with the necessary power to establish effectively the will of the people and true justice." His view had not essentially changed since then. When the group who drew up the document approached Castro to present him with a copy, he shouted at them: "Politicians! Playing politics and dividing up the jobs while men are fighting and dying!" Taken aback, the group left without handing him the document. [25]

In the last months of 1958, Castro's troops launched a general offensive against enemy positions in Oriente and Las Villas provinces. His columns were sent down from the Sierra to take control of new territories. A new Third Front was opened at the very gates of Santiago de Cuba. It had ceased to be a guerrilla war and had become a war of positions.

The rebel victories were impressive. Castro himself led the attack on the town of Güisa. After ten days of fighting, the rebel army captured a large supply of American-made military supplies.[26]

During December it became clear that the collapse of the Batista army was imminent. Its forces were demoralized and incapable of putting up effective resistance. In the cities, urban guerrilla actions were stepped up, bringing the physical presence of the war to millions of people. At the same time, Radio Rebelde from the Sierra continued to blast through the curtain of censorship into Cuban homes.

In the final days of 1958, when victory was within grasp, the idea of ensuring the destruction of the old political apparatus of Cuba, including the army and police, became "practically an obsession" with Fidel.[27] He was wary of any maneuver that might put the government in the hands of a military junta or a civilian government that would simply maintain the socioeconomic *status quo* in Cuba. In August he had felt the same when Colonel Neugart, an emissary of General Cantillo, the chief of Batista's Oriente forces, had tried to win his support for a military coup. Castro had turned down the proposition, insisting that after Batista's fall, power must be handed over to the Revolution.[28]

By the end of the year the Rebel Army had tightened its ring about Santiago de Cuba. Much of Las Villas province had fallen to the troops of Che Guevara and Camilo Cienfuegos, and its capital city, Santa Clara, was already under seige. On December 28 Castro met with General Cantillo. Once again he made it clear that he would not accept a military junta to replace Batista. Cantillo knew that Oriente province was lost and that Santiago de Cuba could not resist the impetuous advance of the rebels. He agreed to lead a military insurrection in Santiago on December 31, have the armed forces *unconditionally* aid Castro's forces, and give tanks to the Rebel Army.[29]

When the interview was over, Castro's forces moved closer to Santiago de Cuba, prepared to enter the city. Cantillo, however, reneged on his agreement. He sent a message to Castro stating that "circumstances have altered greatly in favor of a national solution." [30] He meant that the military men had decided to oust Batista and appoint a new civilian president. Later they chose an aging judge, Orlando Piedra. Castro's answer was to announce that his troops would begin the attack on Santiago at three o'clock on the afternoon of December 31.

The transmitters of Radio Rebelde had been moved down to Palma Soriano, near Santiago de Cuba. There Castro broadcast to an expectant nation:

ANNOUNCER: Here is Radio Rebelde, on the outskirts of Santiago de Cuba, speaking in the name of the July 26 Movement and the Rebel Army.

People of Cuba! The tyrant has fled, as have the other assassins, before the irresistible advance of the rebel army.

Those who supported him yesterday conspire to replace him. They have organized a military junta. Now more than ever, the people have to be on the alert. . . . Now, with the people of Cuba, Fidel Castro:

FIDEL: Whatever the news from the capital may be, our troops should not cease hostilities at any time.

Our forces should continue their operations against the enemy on all battle fronts. . . .

Military operations will continue until a specific order is sent from this command. That order will be issued only after military forces in the capital have arisen and placed themselves under the orders of the revolutionary command.

Revolution, *yes!* Military coup, *no!*

Military coup in agreement with Batista, *no!* This would only serve to prolong the war.

Snatching victory from the people, *no!* This would serve to prolong the war until the people obtain total victory!

After seven years of struggle, the democratic victory of the people has to be complete, so that never again will there be in our homeland another March 10.

No one should be confused or deceived!

The people, and especially the workers of the entire republic, should listen attentively to Radio Rebelde and rapidly prepare all work centers for the general strike. If it should be necessary to stop any attempt at a counter-revolutionary coup, they should begin as soon as the order is given.

The people and the Rebel Army must be more united and more firm than ever to prevent the victory that has cost so much from being snatched from them! [31]

On the same day, in a message to the head of the Santiago army garrison, Castro wrote, "It is not power in itself that interests us but that the revolution fulfill its destiny." [32] The following day, Castro issued a proclamation ordering "a general revolutionary strike in all the territories that have not been liberated." [33] It was a call to the working class to stay the hand of the military men who were conspiring to put Piedra in power.

The people of Havana responded. Transport and power were paralyzed, and the city's economic life came to a standstill while revolutionaries acted to take over the capital. Troops in cars and trucks led by Camilo and Che rushed down the central highway toward the city.

Castro entered Santiago de Cuba triumphantly. He spoke to an ecstatic crowd in the city's Céspedes Square. For the first time an assembly of citizens became electors representing the general will of the Cuban people. He asked:

> Who wants Piedra as president? [Silence.] And if
> no one wants Piedra as president, how are we going
> to accept Mr. Piedra at this moment? [34]

Castro raised the name of Urrutia, whom Caracas Pact signers supported as provisional president:

> Does he have the support of the people? [Affirmative
> shouts.] Well, I want to say that the president of the
> republic, the legal president, is he who has the sup-
> port of the people of Cuba.[35]

Over the years many decisive issues would be presented to mass assemblies of Cubans in this way. This procedure became institutionalized over the first years of the Revolution as a viable form of communications between the leaders and the people, as an expression of popular will.

In his Santiago de Cuba speech, Castro said:

> This time, luckily for Cuba, the Revolution will truly
> arrive at its goal. It will not be like '98, when the
> Americans came in and made themselves the owners
> here. It will not be like '33, when the people began to
> believe a revolution was in the making and Batista
> came and betrayed it, took power, and installed a
> ferocious dictatorship. It will not be like '44, when the
> multitudes ardently believed that at last the people
> had taken power, but those who had taken power
> were the crooks.
>
> Neither crooks, nor traitors, no interventionists.
> This time, yes, it is a Revolution! [36]

Thirty-three-year-old Fidel Castro stood on the threshold
of realizing his dream—"to revolutionarize this country from
top to bottom." He told the people that day of national re-
joicing, "The Revolution will not be made in a day, but rest
assured, we *will* make it." [37]

Notes

Introduction

1. The pre-Revolution Hotel Rosita de Hornedo, now the Hotel Sierra Maestra. ICAP—Instituto Cubano de Amistad con los Pueblos.
2. Eduardo García Delgado.
3. Huberman and Paul Sweezy had recently published *Cuba, Anatomy of a Revolution* (New York, 1960). Morray was writing *The Second Revolution in Cuba* (New York, 1962) at the time.
4. Speech, July 26, 1961.
5. *Cuba Socialista*, September 1961.
6. Cited in Huberman and Sweezy, p. 144.
7. Ibid., p. 146.

1: Rough School for Beginners

1. Alfredo Guevara to author, Havana, February 7, 1973. Guevara was president of the Cuban National Film Institute (ICAIC) from its foundation in 1960 until December 1976, when he became a high official of the newly created Ministry of Culture.
2. I heard Fidel refer to himself humorously as an "F-1," the term used in Cuba to denote the first-generation offspring of the cross between Holstein (often of foreign origin) and Cuban Brahma cattle. (Batabanó, Cuba, July 17, 1968.)
3. Cited in Robert Merle, *Premier combat de Fidel Castro*, (Paris, 1965), p. 341.
4. *Guajiro* is a typical Cuban word for farmer.
5. Hugh Thomas, *Cuba or the Pursuit of Freedom* (London, 1971), says on page 803 that Castro was born on August 13, 1926. Nevertheless, on page 1616 Castro is listed as having been born in 1927. In August 1976, Leonid Brezhnev congratulated Castro on his fiftieth birthday, and Castro acknowledged the greeting. By doing so he seemingly accepted 1926 as his birth

year. However, I specifically asked Ramón Castro about Fidel's birthdate (Picadura Valley, December 12, 1972), and he said it was 1927.

6. "Fidel y los Cristianos" in a supplement to *Pastoral Popular* (Santiago de Chile, November 1971). The pamphlet carries an interchange between Chilean priests and Fidel Castro.

7. Ibid.

8. Castellanos became defense attorney for a group that participated in the attack on the Moncada Barracks under Fidel in July 1953.

9. Since the revolutionary victory, Ichaústegui has held a series of important posts. He was ambassador to Chile during Salvador Allende's regime.

10. Mario Salabarría, linked to the Movimiento Socialista Revolucionario, was secret-police chief; Fabio Ruís of the Güiteras Revolutionary Action Group was Havana police chief; Emilio Tro of the Unión Insurrección Revolucionaria was the head of the National Police Academy.

11. This explains why Batista fled into exile upon Grau's victory in 1944. Batista worked hand in glove with U.S. Special Envoy Summer Wells in suppressing the revolutionary upsurge in 1933. (See U.S. State Department, Foreign Relations of the United States, vol. 5, 1933, *The American Republics*.) Batista was the "power behind the throne" in Cuba until 1940, when he was elected president of Cuba (1940–1944).

12. Félix Olivera, Interview, Havana, February 28, 1973. Olivera was a police reporter in Havana during the decades prior to the victory of the Cuban Revolution. He is renowned among his peers for his encyclopedic knowledge of prerevolutionary politics.

13. For the most complete account of his life, see Luis Conte Agüero, *Eduardo Chibás, el Adalid de Cuba* (Mexico, 1955).

14. Ibid., p. 457.

15. As a co-worker of left-wing architect professor Ramiro Valdés Daussau in 1940, Manolo Castro had fought El Bonche, a group of delinquents who had terrorized the campus. When Valdés Daussau was allegedly murdered in August of that year, Manolo avenged his death by killing professor-politician Raúl Fernández Fiallo, believed to be a protector of El Bonche.

16. Alfredo Guevara.

17. *El Mundo*, January 17, 1947. Grau had pledged before the tomb of a Cuban independence hero several weeks before that he would not be a candidate for a second term. See *El Mundo*, December 8, 1946.

18. *Bohemia*, January 18, 1956.

19. Castro told this story to Gloria Gaitán de Valencia. See *América Libre* (Caracas), May 8, 1961. Carlos Rafael Rodríguez, a

Cuban Politburo member and a vice-president of the State Council, recalls Fidel telling the same story. (Interview, September 27, 1972, Havana.)

20. Masferrer quit the Communist party in 1944 and devoted the remainder of his days to fighting progressive causes and to enriching himself. Despite its name, his Socialist Revolutionary Movement (MSR) was a gangster organization. In 1952 Masferrer became a supporter of Cuban dictator Fulgencio Batista. His feared "Tigers" murdered Cuban revolutionaries. According to the *Miami Daily News* (November 1, 1975), Masferrer left Santiago de Cuba for Miami with $17 million, hours before Fidel Castro led his rebel army into the city on January 1, 1959. When Masferrer was blown to bits in a dynamite explosion in Miami the same newspaper wrote that he "died as he lived—by violence."

21. I've been told that the UIR was at first considered by some to be "the purest of the revolutionary-action groups." Emilio Tro, its founder, who had been in the U.S. army during World War II, was considered politically progressive, and his organization attracted some idealists. It soon began degenerating into a typical self-seeking *pistolero* group.

22. Jesús Diegues, a leader of the UIR during the late forties. Cited in Bonachea and Valdés, *Revolutionary Struggle 1947–1959, volume 1 of the Selected Works of Fidel Castro* (Cambridge, Mass., 1972), p. 20n.

23. Fidel Castro, in Concepción, Chile (speech), December 10, 1971.

24. Conte Agüero, *Chibás . . .* , p. 506.

25. Ibid., p. 507.

26. The name of Cuba's Young Communist League was, in fact, Young Socialists (Juventud Socialista). I take the liberty of using the term Young Communists throughout the book.

27. Alfredo Guevara was a member of the Young Communists, but this was not supposed to be public knowledge.

28. This speech is not mentioned in Bonachea and Valdés's collection of Castro's writings and speeches. In fact, this is the first time it has been quoted in any contemporary study, as far as I can tell.

29. Mella is a leading hero of the Cuban revolutionaries, who see their history as a single thread running from independence heroes like José Martí through to revolutionaries like Mella, to Fidel.

30. Valdés Daussa had close ties with the Communists. Peligrín Torras, now a Vice Minister of the Cuban Foreign Ministry told me he was one of the C.P.'s contacts with the crusading professor in 1939 and 1940.

31. *Información*, July 17, 1947. Other newspapers carried shorter quotes or paraphrases. The "two false leaders" to whom he

refers are Fulgencio Batista (president, 1940–44) and his successor, Ramón Grau San Martín.

32. Julio Ortega Frier, the Dominican ambassador in Washington, knew that an invasion was being planned in Cuba. (See *Información*, July 27, 1947.)
33. Trujillo ruled from 1930 until he was gunned down on May 30, 1961.
34. José Martí (1853–95), the "apostle of Cuban independence," in his essay "Nuestra América." Martí was the principal organizer of the last phase of Cuba's war for independence against Spain. A prolific writer, he left a rich literary and ideological heritage. Already in 1889, he warned Latin America of the dangers of U.S. imperialism in a series of articles for *La Nación* of Buenos Aires.
35. *Bohemia*, October 5, 1947.
36. J. L. Wangüermert, *Carteles*, October 7, 1947.
37. Alfredo Guevara, interview.
38. *El Mundo*, September 30, 1947.
39. Tro, founder of the UIR and commander of the Police Academy, was visiting the home of the police chief, Morín Dopico, in Marianao. Salabarría and his men arrived to issue a warrant for Tro's arrest. When Tro refused to come out, Salabarría's men opened fire on the house. After a two-hour battle, Tro, unarmed, left the house with the pregnant wife of Morín Dopico. A newsreel shows them both being shot down by Salabarría's men on the sidewalk.
40. *El Mundo*, September 16, 1947.
41. See *Bohemia*, September 28, 1947, for a vivid account of the event.
42. *Carteles*, October 5, 1947. U.S. Customs announced that fighter planes and more than three tons of rockets and guns had been shipped from the United States to the plotters. See *El Mundo*, October 1, 1947.
43. *Información*, October 1, 1947.
44. *El Mundo*, October 1, 1947.
45. Ibid. Also *Información* of same date.

2: Under Clubs and Bullets

1. *Bohemia*, October 19, 1947.
2. Carlos Martínez Junco.
3. *El Mundo*, October 1, 1947.
4. *Bohemia*, October 19, 1947.
5. Ibid.
6. Ibid.
7. *Diario de la Marina*, January 14, 1959. Castro was quoted as making this statement a few days after the revolutionary victory. "The Sierra Maestra" refers to his two-year guerrilla war in the

Sierra Maestra mountains. He is, of course, exaggerating, but the point he makes is that at the university he was an inexperienced *individual* who confronted gangster elements, whereas in the Sierra he was the leader of an army and a mass movement.

8. Luis Más Martín to author, January 17, 1973. Flavio Bravo confirmed this to author on July 29, 1974. Fidel Castro also told the author (March 20, 1975) that he had fraternal contacts with Communists at the university.

9. *Marxist-Leninist* denotes the entire content of Marxist thought and practice as developed by Lenin and is considered to include the theory and practice of making a socialist and Communist revolution.

10. Fidel Castro (speech in Chile), December 19, 1971.

11. Marx and Engels, *Manifesto of the Communist Party.* From Samuel Moore translation (1888), published in Moscow in 1953.

12. For a classic study of Cuban society during Castro's early university days see: Lowry Nelson, *Rural Cuba* (Minneapolis, 1950).

13. Marx and Engels, *Manifesto of the Communist Party,* op. cit.

14. Ibid.

15. Alfredo Guevara to author.

16. *El Mundo,* October 8, 1947.

17. Communist leader Francisco (Paquito) Rosales was elected mayor of Manzanillo in 1940 and later congressman from the same district. He was assassinated by Batista henchmen in February 1958.

18. *El Mundo,* November 4, 1947.

19. Ibid.

20. *Bohemia,* November 16, 1947.

21. *Información,* November 6, 1947. The statement was signed by Jesús Diegues and other UIR leaders. This is definite proof that Hugh Thomas (*Cuba or Pursuit . . . ,* op. cit., p. 812) is wrong in suggesting that Castro was in this period a member of the UIR.

22. *Bohemia,* November 16, 1947, p. 47f.

23. Ibid. Also *Información,* November 6, 1947.

24. *El Mundo* and *Información,* November 7, 1947, carried reports on the speech. Most of the text was taken from *Información.*

25. The "millionth" was a demand based on article 52 of the 1940 Cuban constitution: "The monthly salary of an elementary-school teacher should be no less than a millionth part of the national budget."

26. Article 280 of the 1940 constitution stipulated that a national bank of Cuba should be established. It was not implemented until President Prio took office in 1948.

27. The establishment of a financial-watchdog court (Tribunal de Cuentas) was stipulated under article 266 of the 1940 constitution. It was finally set up under Grau's successor, Prio.

28. Because of continued shortages, price controls remained in effect

on meat and other essential items following World War II. Black-market operations became a lucrative source of income for politicians, businessmen, and police officials.

29. See footnote 38.
30. *El Mundo,* November 7, 1947.
31. Loynaz del Castillo, an old independence-war general, was given the bell on November 8, and he immediately handed it over to Grau. Grau wanted to keep the historic bell in Havana, but Manzanillo protested successfully with a forty-eight-hour general strike, and the bell was returned. See *El Mundo,* November 8, 11, and 12, 1947.
32. Menéndez was a congressman from 1940 to 1942 and again from 1946 until his murder on January 28, 1948. He began his activities as a sugar-cane cutter and later worked in a sugar mill. He joined the Communist party in 1931, was a founder of the National Federation of Sugar Workers, and became president of the militant union in 1943. He is celebrated as a hero in revolutionary Cuba.
33. In early 1947, Eusebio Mujal and other Authentic-party labor leaders visited Miami to meet with leaders of the American Federation of Labor to map out an anti-Communist strategy for Cuba. They returned and received government backing for a takeover of the labor movement.
34. *Información,* July 30, 1947.
35. *El Mundo,* October 16, 1947.
36. *Granma,* January 22, 1968.
37. As told by Manuel Quesada, a trade-union leader who was with Menéndez at the time of his murder. See *Juventud Rebelde,* January 24, 1970.
38. *Prensa Libre,* January 24, 1948. Cited also in *Granma,* January, 22, 1969.
39. Mario Kuchilán, *Fabulario—Retrato de una Época* (Havana, 1973), p. 9.
40. *Hoy,* February 13, 1947. Also personal interview with victim, Alfonso Seisdedos, Havana, January 15, 1973.
41. *Información,* February 13, 1948. Also, *Hoy* of same date. Both newspapers carry photos of Fidel.
42. Alfonso Seisdedos, interview.
43. *Información,* February 13, 1948. Also *Hoy* of same date.
44. *Información,* February 14, 1948.
45. Más Martín, interview, January 12, 1973.
46. *Antorcha* (University of Havana student publication), August 15, 1945.
47. *Alerta,* February 23, 1948. Also *Bohemia,* February 29, 1948. The other two students were Justo Fuentes and Pedro Mirassou.
48. *Tiempo en Cuba,* February 8, 1948.

49. *Información,* February 26, 1948.
50. Alfredo Guevara, interview.
51. *Información,* February 26, 1948. Also *Alerta* of same date.
52. Ibid. Castro showed the judge a copy of the February 8 issue of *Tiempo en Cuba* to prove that Masferrer wanted to turn public opinion against him.
53. Alfredo Guevara, interview.
54. *Información,* March 21, 1948.
55. Ibid. Also *Hoy* of same date.
56. Ibid.
57. Hugh Thomas, *Cuba or Pursuit . . .* , p. 812.

3: 'Twixt the Tropics of Cancer and Capricorn

1. The Falkland Islands, off Argentina's southeast coast, were generally recognized as Argentine territory until the British occupied them in 1833. Since then, periodically, Argentina has unsuccessfully brought up the issue of its sovereignty over the tiny islands.
2. Alfredo Guevara.
3. Luis Más Martín to author, May 29, 1975.
4. Ibid.
5. Cited in *Bohemia,* March 17, 1957, p. 62f.
6. *Pensamiento Crítico,* Havana, August 1969, p. 85.
7. Alfredo Guevara.
8. Ibid.
9. *El Tiempo,* Bogotá, April 12, 1961. Cited by Thomas, p. 816n.
10. *Communist Threat to the U.S.A. through the Caribbean,* Hearings of Internal Security Subcommittee, U.S. Senate (Washington, D.C., 1962), p. 724f.
11. Pauley was founder of Cubana Airlines and the Havana Trolley Company.
12. Alfredo Guevara.
13. Jules Dubois, *Fidel Castro* (Buenos Aires, 1959), p. 20ff.
14. Manuel Piniero to author, June 30, 1975. Major Piniero fought in Castro's guerrilla army. For many years after the revolutionary victory he was vice-minister of the Ministry of the Interior and more recently head of the department of the Americas of the central committee of Cuba's Communist party.
15. See *Bohemia,* April 25, 1948, Supplement, p. 8f. Castro's own story of the *bogotazo* is ostensibly given in Carlos Franqui, *Journal de la révolution cubaine* (Paris, 1976).
16. Ibid.
17. The charter of the OAS was approved in Bogotá. Following the triumph of the Cuban Revolution, the OAS expelled Cuba and sanctioned an economic embargo against her. Castro has expressed

his disdain for the organization dozens of times. He has gloated over its crisis and has called it "a putrefied cadaver" (July 26, 1974).

18. *El Mundo,* May 25, 1948.
19. Fidel Castro to author, July 29, 1974.
20. Ibid.
21. Luis Conte Agüero, *Fidel Castro—Vida y Obra* (Havana, 1959), p. 30.
22. *El Mundo,* May 25, 1948. Also *Diario de Cuba,* Santiago de Cuba, May 25, 1948.
23. Conte Agüero, *Fidel Castro . . . ,* p. 30.
24. The scene is shown in the full-length Cuban documentary *Viva la República.* Director, Pastor Vega.
25. Fidel Castro to author, July 29, 1974.
26. In 1946, Chibás fought "Fico" Fernández (see *Bohemia,* June 30, 1946). Later he invited him to join the Orthodox party. Years later from jail, Castro wrote in a letter, dated June 12, 1954: "Those big landowners, millionaires, and exploiters of farmers—what were they doing in a party whose first duty is social justice?" (See Conte Agüero, *Cartas del Presidio,* Havana, 1959.)
27. Conte Agüero, *Chibás . . . ,* p. 565.
28. Felix Olivera, interview.
29. *Prensa Libre,* Havana, March 31, 1948.
30. Hugh Thomas, p. 817.
31. Baudilio Castellanos, *La Historia Me Absolverá* (Documento Especialmente Marxista, Havana, July 18, 1962). Castellanos was defense lawyer at the Moncada trial. Más Martín told me Castro's interest in Marxism increased after the Bogotá experience.
32. Fidel Castro (speech in Chile). December 10, 1971.
33. Nidia Sarabia to author, Havana, January 31, 1973. Sarabia works on a special history commission under central-committee member Celia Sánchez, secretary of the council of state, that is compiling information on Fidel Castro and the Cuban Revolution.
34. Hugh Thomas, p. 818f.
35. Flavio Bravo to author, June 28, 1975. Bravo was national chairman of the Young Communists (Juventud Socialista). Luis Más Martín, the YC Havana chairman at the time, confirms Castro's regular fraternal contacts with the Communists.
36. Carlos Rafael Rodríguez to author, September 27, 1972. Rodríguez is a vice-president of the council of state and a member of the CP political bureau. He was a leader of Cuba's prerevolutionary Communist party (PSP).
37. Fidel Castro (speech in Chile), December 10, 1971. Castro's most complete analysis of his own political development was

given on the televised "Universidad Popular," December 1961.
38. Cited in Agüero, *Fidel Castro* . . . , p. 32f.
39. *Hoy,* Havana, September 2, 1948.
40. *Prensa Libre,* Havana, September 9, 1948.
41. *Hoy,* September 11, 1948. There is a photo of Fidel on p. 6.
42. Ibid.
43. *Bohemia,* September 19, 1948.
44. Más Martín to author.
45. *Bohemia,* January 30, 1949.
46. *Bohemia,* April 10, 1949.
47. *Alerta,* Havana, March 12, 1949.
48. Alfredo Guevara to author.
49. *Bohemia,* March 20, 1949. Guevara remembers saying, "You have no right to say that, as long as the imperialist government of the United States continues its occupation of Guantánamo Naval Base" (personal interview).
50. *Información,* March 13, 1949.
51. In Cuban documentary film *Viva la República.*
52. *Bohemia,* February 15, 1959. The article is written by Rene Bentancourt, leader of the University Committee for the Struggle against Racial Discrimination in 1949 and later a leader of black fraternal associations. The article is accompanied by a photograph showing Castro in 1949 with other members of the committee.
53. Hugh Thomas, p. 822.
54. Félix Olivera to author, February 28, 1973. Jesús Reyes, a black who had been financial secretary of the Havana Orthodox Youth, remembers Castro as one of the most outspoken critics of racism within the party.
55. Fidel to author, July 29, 1974.
56. *Libro de Actas de Exámenes,* Facultad de Derecho, Universidad de La Habana, Año 1948–49. These records are to be found in the Cuban National Archives.
57. Aspiazo-Castro-Resende. Doctor of Laws was the title given graduates from the University of Havana law school.
58. Fidel married Mirtha Díaz-Balart on October 12, 1948. They were officially divorced in 1955.
59. *Prensa Libre,* Havana, September 17, 1948.
60. *Prensa Libre,* Havana, September 18, 1948.
61. "Fidel Castro, Frente a Todos," *Bohemia,* January 8, 1956. Translation from Bonachea and Valdés, p. 297.

4: J'accuse

1. Bonachea and Valdés, p. 136.
2. On April 13, 1949, Chibás replied to an appeal from the PSP

general secretary Blas Roca by declaring that he would never be an ally of the Communists. (See Conte Agüero, *Eduardo Chibás* . . . , p. 565.)

3. Ibid., p. 718.
4. *Mella,* Havana, September 1950. Castro's signing this peace petition has never been noted in *any* previous study.
5. *Mella,* November 1950. This is the same month that Castro was arrested in Cienfuegos, a seaport in south central Cuba, for inciting to riot. The local student association had invited him to participate as a speaker in a protest against government persecution. He was arrested on November 12, spent hours in jail before being released on parole, and was tried on December 6. He defended himself and won the case. (See *Correspondencia,* Cienfuegos, November 13, 1950, for story of arrest. For a more complete account see article of Aldo Isidrón del Valle, *Granma,* July 17, 1975.
6. *SAETA,* March 1951. The Spanish word *saeta* means, variously, "dart," "hand of a watch," or the "magnetic needle of a compass."
7. Raúl Castro in an interview in Moscow with Igor Nemira of the Soviet Novosti agency. Nemira told me this in Havana, where he was Novosti correspondent.
8. *SAETA,* March 1951.
9. *SAETA,* January 1951.
10. Ibid.
11. *Alerta,* June 6, 1951.
12. Conte Agüero, *Eduardo Chibás* . . . , p. 761.
13. Fidel Castro to author, July 29, 1974.
14. *Alerta,* August 6, 1951.
15. Felix Olivera to author.
16. *Alerta,* August 16, 1951.
17. *Alerta,* August 17, 1951.
18. Ibid.
19. Felix Olivera.
20. From newspaper clipping of the era which carried neither the source nor the date.
21. Pedro Trigo in *Verde Olivo* (monthly magazine of the Cuban armed forces), July 26, 1964.
22. One of them was Gildo Fleitas, who produced the radio program "Vergüenza contra Dinero" (Pit Honor against Money), for which Castro often wrote editorials.
23. *Alerta,* January 28, 1952. Eduardo Chibás had written a similar exposé of Fulgencio Batista's property acquisitions (see *Bohemia,* May 8, 1949).
24. *Alerta,* January 28, 1952.
25. *Alerta,* February 5, 1952.
26. Más Martín.

27. Fidel Castro to author, July 29, 1974.
28. Ibid.
29. *El País,* Havana, March 6, 1952.
30. *Hoy,* February 20, 1952.
31. *Hoy,* November 6, 1951.
32. See *Hoy,* November 6, 1951. Also *Hoy,* November 21, 1951.
33. Fidel Castro to author, March 20, 1975.
34. *Alerta,* February 26, 1952.
35. Fidel Castro to author, March 20, 1975.
36. *Alerta,* February 20, 1952.
37. Ibid.
38. Ibid.
39. Ibid.
40. Fidel Castro to author, July 29, 1974.
41. Ibid.
42. Ibid.
43. Ibid.
44. Ibid.

5: Seed of Rebellion

1. Actually, the Cuban Military Intelligence Service (SIM) was already privy to the conspiracy in early February 1952. See top-secret report of SIM Captain Salvador Díaz, reprinted in E. Vignier and G. Alonso, *La Corrupción Política y Administrativa en Cuba 1944–1952* (Havana, 1973), p. 313ff.
2. Edmundo A. Chester, *Un Sargento Llamado Batista* (Havana, no date), chapter 28. The book is an apologia for Batista.
3. *Bohemia,* March 23, 1952.
4. Pedro Miret in *Verde Olivo,* July 29, 1962.
5. *Bohemia,* March 23, 1952.
6. *Hoy,* March 11, 1952. Hugh Thomas is obviously wrong in asserting that "for a few days Batista and the Communists held back in their attitudes towards each other." See Thomas, p. 793.
7. *Bohemia,* March 23, 1952.
8. *Moncada, Antecedentes y Preparativos* (Havana, 1973), p. 106. The pamphlet was published by the Cuban armed forces.
9. Ibid.
10. *Alerta* (Havana), March 17, 1952. As far as I know, this is the first time that this quotation has been used in any postrevolutionary writing on Cuba.
11. Mario Dalmau to author, April 19, 1967. Dalmau participated with Castro in the attack on the Moncada barracks on July 26, 1953.
12. *Moncada, Antecedentes . . . ,* p. 106.
13. *Alerta,* March 25, 1952. *Alerta* says that Castro presented his

petition to the Urgency Court (*tribunal de urgencia*). Castro, in his testimony of September 21, 1953, following the Moncada attack, says it was the court of constitutional guarantees.

14. *Granma*, special edition of July 26, 1966, carries the full text.
15. Julio Antonio Mella, founder of the Cuban FEU and the Communist party of Cuba (1903–29); Rafael Trejo, a student killed in a demonstration against the Machado dictatorship (1910–30); Antonio Güiteras, a revolutionary leader in the immediate post-Machado period who was gunned down at Batista's orders (1906–35).
16. Pedro Miret in *Verde Olivo*, July 29, 1962.
17. Fidel Castro (televised interview), December 1, 1961.
18. Marta Rojas in *Verde Olivo*, July 28, 1968.
19. Cited in *Bohemia*, July 6, 1973.
20. Jesús Montané to author, February 20, 1974. Montané was active in trade-union activities at General Motors. Abel Santamaría worked at a Pontiac agency on the same block. Montané is a veteran of both the Moncada attack and the *Granma* landing. He is now a member of the central committee of the Cuban Communist party.
21. *Bohemia*, July 13, 1973.
22. Ibid. Also *Granma*, June 29, 1973. A great many articles about the Moncada appeared in Cuba on the twentieth anniversary of the attack in 1973.
23. *Bohemia*, Ibid.
24. *Bohemia*, July 6, 1973.
25. *Bohemia*, July 13, 1973.
26. *Granma*, June 29, 1973.
27. *Granma*, July 13, 1970.
28. *Moncada, Antecedentes* . . .
29. Ibid. for full text.
30. Pedro Miret in *Verde Olivo*, July 28, 1964.
31. Melba Hernández in *Verde Olivo*, July 28, 1963. She was one of the two women who participated in the Moncada Barracks attack of July 26, 1953.
32. For a complete account see Teresa Iglesias, "El Asesinato de Rubén Batista," *Granma*, February 13, 1973.
33. Ibid.
34. Flavio Bravo to author, June 28, 1975. Bravo is now a vice-president of the Cuban State Council and a member of the central committee of the Cuban Communist party.
35. Melba Hernández to author, August 27, 1965. She writes about the bystanders' comment in *Verde Olivo*, July 28, 1963.
36. *Bohemia*, February 8, 1953. The inscription was a reference to Martí's words: "For Cuba who suffers, the first word," from his speech of November 26, 1891, in Tampa, Florida. See

José Martí, *Ideas Políticas y Sociales* (Havana, 1960), volume 2, p. 35.

37. See *Bohemia*, July 13, 1973. The trial was set for June 10, but five days before the date, and amnesty decree was issued applying to Castro's "crime" (Presidential Decree 885 of 1953).

38. The May Day meeting was held in the university stadium. Despite attempts at police intimidation, tens of thousands of workers showed up. The next morning, *Hoy* (May 2, 1953) carried jubilant headlines: **Energetic and Combative Attitude of the Masses in the Face of Threats and Confusionist Campaign. The Masses Applaud the Anti-Imperialist and Unifying Declarations of Student Orators.**

39. Hugh Thomas, p. 822.

40. See García Bárcena articles about the role of youth in the struggle in *Bohemia*, September 24, 1947; December 7, 1947; May 11, 1952; May 25, 1952.

41. *Alma Mater* (University of Havana student publication), June 10, 1951.

42. Fidel Castro, December 1, 1961.

43. *"Hace falta echar a andar un motor pequeño que ayude arrancar el motor grande."* See Raúl Castro's speech of July 26, 1961.

44. Jesús Montané to author.

45. From Castro's first appearance in court during the Moncada trial. See *Verde Olivo*, July 29, 1973.

46. Ibid.

47. Pedro Miret in *Verde Olivo*, July 29, 1962.

48. Fidel Castro, December 1, 1961.

49. Raúl Castro, July 26, 1961.

50. It was during one of Matthew's periodic visits to Cuba. We were both staying at the Hotel Nacional, and we spent some hours together in conversation.

51. Cited by Melba Hernández, *Granma*, June 29, 1973.

52. José Leva, unpublished work. Leva is a Havana worker turned historian who has meticulously pursued the history of virtually every person who participated in the Moncada attack. He offered me use of his data with total selflessness.

6: The Moncada

1. Fidel Castro (speech in Chile), December 10, 1971.

2. Juan Almeida in Carlos Franqui, *Libro de los Doce* (Havana, 1967), p. 17.

3. Pedro Miret, *Verde Olivo*, July 29, 1962.

4. This information was given to me by two Cuban-army officers who heard it from Castro during a meeting with him. Castro has also said publicly, "The basic nucleus of leaders of our

movement . . . found time to study Marx, Engels, and Lenin."
(Speech, July 26, 1973.)

5. Marta Rojas, *Le generación en el Juicio del Moncada* (Havana, 1974), p. 68. This is a sourcebook for details of the trial that followed the Moncada attack.

6. Fidel Castro, December 1, 1961.

7. Melba Hernández accompanied Haydée. After their discussion Santamaría talked to them about what they had learned. He also told them, "Your example will determine the incorporation of other women in the armed struggle." See interview with Melba Hernández in *Santiago* (University of Oriente), June 1973.

8. *Granma*, June 28, 1973. At that time the CP was called Partido Union Revolucionario.

9. *Granma*, July 6, 1973.

10. *Granma*, July 3, 1973.

11. Marta Rojas in *Granma*, January 27, 1973. In 1955, Nico worked closely with the Young Communists in seeking student unity at the University of Havana after his return from exile. (See statement by Raúl Valdéz Vivó, *Hoy*, March 25, 1964). Nico later left to join Fidel in México.

12. *Granma*, June 22, 1973.

13. *Granma*, July 11, 1973.

14. *Granma*, June 30, 1973.

15. Ibid.

16. Flavio Bravo to author, July 28, 1975. Also Más Martín to author.

17. Robert Merle, *Moncada, Premier combat* . . . p. 120ff. Merle's book is the most complete collection of interviews with survivors of the Moncada attack. Raúl Castro tells him how he came to join the Communist party (PSP) upon his return from eastern Europe shortly before the Moncada attack.

18. *Granma*, July 10, 1973.

19. *Granma*, July 12, 1973.

20. *Granma*, July 10 and 12, 1973.

21. *Granma*, July 12, 1973.

22. Ramiro Valdés to author, March 22, 1974. Valdéz, a veteran of the Moncada attack and the *Granma* landing, is a member of the Cuban CP's thirteen-person politiburo.

23. Ibid.

24. As told by Pedro Gutierrez, who worked at the factory and was a member of Trigo's Movement cell. See *Bohemia*, July 29, 1973.

25. At the trial Raúl was asked the object of the proposed revolution. He limited himself to mentioning the plight of the farmers, illiteracy, and corruption. For testimony see *Verde Olivo*, July 29, 1973.

26. Fidel Castro, July 26, 1973.

27. Haydée Santamaría, cited in *Concada, Antecedentes . . .* , p. 166,
28. Conte Agüero, *Cartas del Presidio* (Havana, 1959). The letter is dated May 2, 1955.
29. Más Martín to author. See p. 000.
30. Carlos Rafael Rodríguez to author, September 27, 1972. Rodríguez is a vice-president of the state council and a member of the political bureau of the central committee of the Cuban CP.
31. Ibid.
32. Raúl Castro, July 26, 1961.
33. For full text see *Raúl Gómez García* (Havana, 1971), p. 133ff. The manifesto is dated July 23, 1953.
34. Thomas, p. 829. Thomas is concerned with proving that Castro's ideas in 1953 were simply liberal, in an effort to refute Castro's own affirmation that he was essentially a Marxist at that time.
35. Armando Hart to author, January 9, 1975. Hart was a leader of the July 26 underground and is now a member of the politburo of the central committee of Cuba's CP and the Minister of Culture.
36. For an excellent appraisal of Martí's progressive outlook see *Casa de las Américas* (Havana), May–June 1975.
37. Conte Agüero, *Chibás . . .* , p. 506ff.
38. *Ahora* (Havana). October 24, 1934. Reprinted in *Pensamiento Crítico* (Havana), April 1970.
39. Letter written from prison. See Conte Agüero, *Cartas . . .* , p. 13.
40. Ibid.
41. Fidel Castro, December 1, 1961.
42. Más Martín to author.
43. Felipe Elosequi, "La Tumba de Mineros," *Bohemia*, October 24, 1954.
44. Pedro Aguilera in Moncada, *Antecedentes . . . .* , p. 239.
45. Ibid.
46. Ibid. A few days before the Moncada attack, Castro ordered Aguilera and Ortega to Havana. Ortega returned to Santiago de Cuba in the same car as Castro. On July 27, he was captured and assassinated. (See *Granma*, July 6, 1973.)
47. Leopoldo Horrego Estuch, *Juan Gualberto Gómez*, (Havana, 1954), p. 115.
48. *Granma*, July 29, 1973. Lester Rodríguez says he also knew of the attack plan. (See *Moncada*, Havana, 1973).
49. *Santiago* (University of Oriente), June 1973.
50. Leva, in his unpublished work, gives the following new information:

Number who left for Santiago de Cuba and Bayamo, plus those already there	162
Number who dropped out before arrival	4
Number who arrived in Bayamo for attack	25

Number who arrived in Santiago but were not picked
up as planned to go to Siboney (Emilio Albentosa)   1
Number who gathered at Siboney   132
Number who dropped out at Siboney
    Student group   4
    Havana cell   5
    Radioman   1
Number who went to the attack in Santiago on
July 26   122

51. *Moncada.*
52. Melba Hernández in *Santiago,* p. 93. Also see *Granma,* June 29, 1973.
53. Castillo Ramos in *Bohemia,* June 23, 1961.
54. José Leva.
55. The letter is reprinted in Marta Rojas, *La generación de centenario* . . . , p. 232.
56. Ibid.
57. "Because of the chauffeur's mistake, the combatants got on the road to Siboney instead of going to Caney as Fidel wanted . . .", *Moncada,* p. 141.
58. Leva.
59. Severino Rosell in *Veintiseis,* (Havana, 1970), p. 166. Severino was one of the small group that accompanied Fidel.
60. Ibid.
61. *Avance,* Havana, July 27, 1953.
62. Pedro Sarría in *Verde Olivo,* July 28, 1973. Also Revolución, July 26, 1962.
63. Sarría in *Verde Olivo,* Ibid. Thomas (p. 1122) claims that "Batista's soldiers openly said it was a disgrace to follow a white such as Castro against a *mestizo* such as Batista." Sarria's version showed that, rather, the soldiers felt *consternation,* not abhorrence, on seeing other blacks in such a compromising situation. The difference is important.

7: "History will Absolve Me"

1. Most of them had no connection with Castro's Movement and were later freed. Among those against whom charges were dropped was ex-President Prio.
2. Marta Rojas, *La generación* . . . , p. 66. The government was interested in involving Prio. Many questions were asked about the Montreal Pact, subscribed to by followers of Prio and a sector of the Orthodox Party.
3. Ibid., p. 150.
4. *Moncada,* p. 265.
5. In the final decision, seventy-five were absolved of guilt.
6. Rojas, p. 345.

7. Theodore Draper, *Castroism: Theory and Practice* (N.Y., 1965), p. 6.
8. Fidel Castro (in Prague), June 22, 1972.
9. The translation is from Bonachea and Valdés, *Revolutionary Struggle . . .* , p. 209. The book contains an excellent translation of "History Will Absolve Me."
10. Ibid.
11. Ibid., p. 185.
12. Ibid.
13. Ibid.
14. Ibid. For the five immediate revolutionary laws, see p. 185f.
15. Ibid., p. 185. "These laws would have been proclaimed immediately and were to be followed, once the battle had ended and after a minute study of their contents and scope, by another series of laws and measures, all fundamental."
16. Ibid., p. 187.
17. Ibid., p. 186.
18. Ibid., p. 189.
19. Ibid.
20. Ibid., p. 183f. He also mentions as "the people," teachers, young professionals, and "twenty thousand debt-ridden small merchants."
21. Ibid., p. 186.
22. Fidel Castro, July 26, 1973.
23. Fidel Castro (in Chile), November 18, 1971.
24. Fidel Castro, December 1, 1961.
25. Fidel Castro (in Prague), June 22, 1972.
26. Hugh Thomas, p. 822.
27. Ibid., p. 510.
28. Ibid., p. 1120.
29. It should be noted that in "History Will Absolve Me," Castro mentions Maceo's name several times as an example of Cuban patriotism and struggle. "They are generals who would not have been fit to drive the mules which carried the equipment for the army of Antonio Maceo." Also, "We were told that the titan Maceo had said that you do not beg freedom, but that you win it with the edge of the sword."
30. Reprinted in *Verde Olivo*, July 29, 1973.
31. As part of his strategy during most of the fifties, Castro normally avoided *direct* reference to the United States as a "threat." His choice of this reference in his testimony gives us an insight into his thinking on the matter.
32. Hugh Thomas, p. 1320.
33. He is now a member of the politburo of the central committee of the Cuban CP. He has shown himself a man of great talent as a leader and organizer.
34. Reprinted in *Verde Olivo*, July 29, 1973. Almeida testified on September 28, 1953.

35. José Antonio Portuondo, *El Pensamiento Vivo de Maceo*, (Havana, undated), p. 49. The quote comes from a proclamation written in Jamaica on September 5, 1879.
36. José Martí, *Obras Completas* (Havana, 1961), volume 23, p. 295.
37. The struggle against racism since the victory of the Cuban Revolution has been seen by Cubans as part of a broader struggle for social and economic progress. Without emphasizing the issue as such, racial discrimination has been fast disappearing in Cuba and is, of course, contrary to government policy. Castro made a strong attack on racial discrimination on March 25, 1959, and has touched on the issue innumerable times.
38. The inventory was sent to the president of the Urgency Court and is dated July, 29, 1953. For photocopy see Moncada, p. 217.
39. *Prensa Libre*, July 28, 1953.
40. Leva, interview with Bernardo Hernández, one of those who attended the national-assembly meeting.
41. They were Lázaro Peña, Antonio Pérez, José Cabrera, Bernardo Hernández, Juan Llosa, Armando Díaz, Rolando Hevia, Joaquín Ordoqui, and Juan Marinello (the president of the party).
42. García Gallo to author, February 23, 1967. Gallo, a Communist-party leader from Las Villas and a philosophy professor, was one of those who gave classes. A Las Villas physician, Dr. Guadalupe Cott, sent the men a volume of Martí's writings. Gallo now works at the CP central committee in Havana on questions of history, pedagogy, and philosophy.
43. As cited by Rojas, *Generación . . .* , p. 92.
44. *Daily Worker*, New York, August 5, 1953, carried the statement. The PSP newspaper, *Hoy*, in Cuba had been outlawed.
45. Carlos Rafael Rodríguez to author, September 27, 1972.
46. Peña was speaking to Yeye Restano, a Havana Communist activist. She told me about it on February 1, 1967. In December 1972, at a reception in Havana for visiting Chilean President Salvador Allende, I had the occasion to mention Restano's comment to Peña. "Yes, I remember," he said. "She wasn't the only one I said it to."
47. Twenty-eight of the Moncada participants were sent to the Isle of Pines on October 13, 1953. Fidel was sent there three days later. Haydée Santamaría and Melba Hernández were sent to the women's reformatory at Guanajay, near Havana.
48. Jesús Montané to author, March 28, 1974. Also see Abelardo Crespo's account in *Veintiseis*, p. 177. Crespo says that there were writings of Lenin and Marx's *Capital*. Montané and Crespo were among the Moncada prisoners. A letter from Castro (see Conte Agüero, *Cartas . . .* , p. 92) also lists some of the books he had On a visit to the former Isle of Pines prison on July 25, 1976, Fidel Castro told reporters of the Marxist books.

49. Jesús Montané to author, March 28, 1974.
50. Cited by Robert Merle, *Moncada, Premier Combat* . . . , p. 346.
51. The hymn was composed by one of the Moncada prisoners, Agustín Díaz Cartaya, a black. He was beaten by guards and thrown into solitary. Data from Israel Tápanes, another Moncada prisoner, in an unpublished speech delivered on July 13, 1973, and heard by author.
52. Letter from Castro dated June 19, 1954. See Conte Agüero, *Cartas* . . . , p. 34.
53. Conte Agüero, *Cartas* . . . , p. 52. Letter from Castro is dated July 31, 1954.
54. For a complete account of this operation see *Juventud Rebelde*, July 20, 1971. Fidel Castro described how to reporters at the Isle of Pines prison, now a museum, on July 15, 1976.
55. *Bohemia*, October 31, 1954.
56. Letter from Castro dated October 25, 1954. See Conte Agüero, *Cartas* . . . , p. 63.
57. The two works are studies of the *coup d'état* in December 1851 by Louis Bonaparte, the nephew of Napoleon I.
58. Letter from Castro dated April 14, 1954. See Merle, p. 344.
59. Merle, p. 344. Marx himself criticized Hugo's analysis: "He sees in [the *coup d'état* of Louis Bonaparte] only the violent act of a single individual" (from Marx's preface to the second edition of *The Eighteenth Brumaire* . . .).
60. Letter written by Castro dated April 14,, 1954. See Merle, p. 348.
61. Castro to author, Havana, June 20, 1975. I asked him the question at a reception for Eric Williams, the prime minister of Trinidad-Tobago.
62. Ibid. When Castro quoted this passage from Martí's letter to Manuel Mercado, I had already used it on the title page of the draft of my book, inasmuch as I was convinced that Castro, a profound student of Martí since his youth, had been influenced by this passage. Naturally, I was gratified to hear him cite it from memory and say that he had been guided by it.
63. Hernández and Haydée Santamaría had been released from prison on February 20, 1954.
64. The original reads, "*Mucha mano izquierda y sonrisa con todo el mundo.*"
65. Conte Agüero, *Cartas* . . . , p . 37f. I have used the Bonachea and Valdés translation, in *Revolutionary Struggle* . . . , p. 231.

8: Amnesty and Exile

1. Letter dated August 14, 1954. See Conte Agüero, *Cartas* . . . , p. 60.
2. Conte Agüero, *Cartas* . . . , p. 61.

3. Ibid., p. 60.
4. Ibid., p. 61.
5. Ibid.
6. Merle, p. 344.
7. Conte Agüero, *Cartas* . . . , p. 60.
8. There was strong pressure in Cuba for a general amnesty for political prisoners. The amnesty decree was a concrete way in which Batista could show that constitutional guarantees had been restored, as he had promised. He chose May 8, Mothers' Day, to issue the decree, a transparent attempt to benefit from the emotional appeal of that celebration. A week before, "A Committee of Mothers" had asked Batista to issue the decree. See *Prensa Libra*, May 3, 1955.
9. Letter dated March 1955. See Conte Agüero, *Cartas* . . .
10. Conte Argüero, *Cartas* . . .
11. Fidel, dressed in a gray suit, his only one, and a sports shirt, was embraced by his three sisters, Lidia, Emma, and Juana, and his two comrades-in-arms Melba and Haydée. The emotional atmosphere was intense, and one account said that Fidel cried for a moment. See *Bohemia*, May 22, 1955.
12. *Información*, May 17, 1955. *Prensa Libre* of the same day has Lieutenant Pérez saying, "Thank you. We are all Cubans." Lieutenant Sarría led the squad that captured Castro. Captain Tamayo was the physician who saved the lives of three *Moncadistas* by refusing to give them up to Moncada authorities.
13. Cited in Conte Agüero, *Fidel Castro* . . . , p. 231. Two days before Castro was released a group of Orthodox Youth leaders presented a petition to the supreme court charging that the government had plans to kill Castro.
14. *Bohemia*, May 22, 1955. Interview with Agustín Alles Soberón. Translation from Bonachea and Valdéz, p. 239 f.
15. Cited in Conte Agüero, *Fidel Castro* . . . , p. 231.
16. Ibid., p. 237.
17. V. I. Lenin, *Revolutionary Adventurism*, written in August 1902. The translation is from a Spanish version published by Progress Books, Moscow.
18. *Prensa Libre*, May 17, 1955.
19. Marta Rojas in *Granma*, July 26, 1966.
20. *Movimiento 26 de Julio*, abbreviated M-26-7. ". . . Its leadership is collective and secret." (See Manifesto 1 of the July 26 Movement in Bonachea and Valdéz, p. 269.
21. *Prensa Libre*, May 17, 1955.
22. Conte Agüero, *Fidel Castro* . . . , p. 241.
23. *Prensa Libre*, May 20 and 22, 1955.
24. *Prensa Libre*, May 22, 1955.
25. *Prensa Libre*, May 25, 1955.

26. Ibid. Also *El Mundo* of same day. For translation see Bonachea and Valdés, p. 243.
27. "Mientes, Chaviano," in *Bohemia*, May 29, 1955.
28. *Información*, May 29, 1955.
29. *Prensa Libre*, May 29, 1955.
30. "*Manos Asesinos*" (Murderer's Hands), *La Calle*, June 7, 1955. Batista made his statement on June 4th. See Bonachea and Valdés, p. 252.
31. Letter dated April 17, 1954. See Conte Agüero, *Cartas . . .* , p. 37.
32. Cited in Conte Agüero, *Fidel Castro . . .* , p. 261f. The date is not given, but it would probably be from *La Calle*, mid-June 1955. Unfortunately, copies of old newspapers are in a tragic condition in Cuba's public libraries, with whole issues and separate articles missing. Microfilming old newspapers has hardly begun.
33. Conte Agüero, *Fidel Castro . . .* , p. 261f.
34. Agostini was gunned down in a courtyard where police said they found, next to his body, a doctor's satchel containing two hand grenades, a pistol, and ammunition clips. See *La Calle*, June 11, 1955.
35. Ibid. Translation from Bonachea and Valdés, p. 253.
36. *Prensa Libre*, June 16, 1955.
37. *Prensa Libre*, June 17, 1955. Masferrer was a senator and head of the Union Radical party in Oriente province. In less than two decades he had traveled the route from Communist to archconservative. He became an ally of Batista, and the "Tigers of Masferrer" operated with impunity in Oriente province, sowing terror among peasants and workers.
38. Luis Orlando Rodríguez. Since the revolutionary victory he has held important posts in the Cuban foreign service. Castro had called on the people to support the *La Calle* financially. *La Calle*, June 8, 1955.
39. *Prensa Libre*, June 18, 1955.
40. Ibid.
41. *Información*, June 18, 1955.
42. The right of asylum in foreign embassies and safe conduct out of the country is widely recognized in Latin American countries.
43. What probably kept him from appearing at the station was the belief that he would be arrested or assaulted if he showed up. The columnist Mendo in *Prensa Libre* wrote, "After what has happened it seems to me he was right in not appearing." See *Prensa Libre*, June 19, 1955.
44. Armando Hart, Faustino Pérez, and Juan Manuel Márquez, among others. Márquez came in the *Granma* as second in command. Pérez and Hart both became leaders of the M-26-7 underground.
45. *Prensa Libre*, June 7, 1955.
46. Castro recalls these offers in *Bohemia*, January 8, 1956.

47. *Prensa Libre*, July 1, 1955. Other signatories were Juan Manuel Márquez, Pastor Nuñez, Eduardo Corona, and Orlando Castro.
48. Letter to Executive Committee of M-26-7 in Cuba from Castro in Mexico, August 2, 1955. See Conte Agüero, *Fidel Castro . . .*, p. 280.
49. Pedro Miret and Lester Rodríguez, both *Moncadistas*, were sent to Oriente. María Antonia Figueroa, the financier of M-26-7 in Santiago de Cuba, introduced them to País.
50. Arturo Duque de Estrada to author, June 30, 1970, in Santiago de Cuba. Duque de Estrada worked closely with Frank País. The cable announcing Fidel's departure on the *Granma* from Mexico was addressed to him. At the time of the interview he was head of the historical commission of the CP in Oriente.
51. Carlos Rafael Rodríguez to author, September 27, 1972.
52. *Información*, July 6, 1955, carries a partial text. The text was reprinted in *Hoy*, December 2, 1962. Translation from Bonachea and Valdés, p. 257.
53. Letter to Melba Hernández from Mexico, dated July 24, 1955. Cited in Conte Agüero, *Fidel Castro . . .* , p. 274.
54. Conte Agüero, *Fidel Castro . . .* , p. 274. Castro requested that his appearance at the Ateneo Español be given "as little publicity as possible."
55. Theodore Draper seems to have believed that there was only one declaration, and he therefore confuses the two. See Draper, *Castroism: Theory and Practice*, p. 9f. Thomas (p. 66), following Draper, attributes to the *Manifesto* a quote that, in fact, comes from the *Message to the Congress of Orthodox Militants*.
56. Letter to Melba Hernández, July 24, 1955.
57. Letter from Mexico dated August 2, 1955. Cited in Conte Agüero, *Fidel Castro . . .*
58. Ibid.
59. When the call signed by Fidel Castro and other Orthodox militants went out for the grass-roots congress, there was resistance on the part of the Orthodox leadership. Later, in an effort at better control of the growing revolt in the party, Raúl Chibás, president of the Orthodoxy, gave his benediction to the gathering.
60. The translation is from Bonachea and Valdés, p. 271. I took the liberty of changing their *Ortodoxo* to Orthodox to maintain consistency of use.
61. *Chambelonas*, like *congas*, refers to the frenetic dancing through the streets behind a typical Cuban band organized in the service of a political candidate or party. It was, in the Roman sense, "circus" for the people, a popular distraction without any political content. *Chambelonas* were organized by the Liberal party in Cuba. Bonachea and Valdés, p. 264, are wrong in translating *chambelonas* into *sinecures* in this passage.

62. Translation from Bonachea and Valdés, p. 263.
63. Ibid., p. 265.
64. From part 2, "Proletarians and Communists." The translation used is that which Samuel Moore did in 1888. The edition was published in Moscow in 1953. See p. 72.
65. Fidel Castro, November 18, 1971.
66. Bonachea and Valdés, p. 266.
67. Marx and Engels, *Communist Manifesto*, p. 72.
68. This vision of Fidel's, which seemed romantic in 1955, is becoming a reality in Cuba. There are now more than one hundred thousand *becados* (fully supported "scholarship" students) in modern "schools in the countryside."
69. *Communist Manifesto*, p. 80.

9: ". . . Or We Will Be Martyrs"

1. Colonel Jacobo Arbenz became president of Guatemala in 1950. He led a progressive, nationalist-minded regime that gave land to 120,000 farm families and began to control the excesses of the United Fruit Company. In June 1954 the CIA masterminded the overthrow of his popular government.
2. Che Guevara in *Bohemia*, October 20, 1967. The article was originally published in *O Cruzeiro* (Rio de Janeiro) in 1959.
3. Andrés Suárez, *Cuba–Castroism and Communism* (Mass., 1967), p. 39.
4. In December 1974 (Havana).
5. Hilda Gadea, *Memoirs of "Che" Guevara* (New York, 1972), p. 19. Gadea, Che's first wife, was a Peruvian and a member of APRA when she met Che. She died of cancer in Havana in 1974.
6. Ibid. Hilda and I periodically conversed about Che long before she wrote her book.
7. Mirna Torres to author, November 27, 1967. Mirna was an activist of the Alianza and kept a schoolgirl's diary in which are anecdotes about Che in Guatemala. Hilda Gadea used material from the diary for her book about Che.
8. Dr. Edelberto Torres to author (Havana), January 8, 1968. He told the same story in a letter to his son-in-law dated October 25, 1967, which Gadea quotes in her book. He is the author of *La Dramática Vida de Rubén Darío* (Mexico, 1957).
9. Mirna Torres to author. Mirna challenges her friend Hilda Gadea's assertion that Che refused a job with the Guatemalan government after being informed that he would first have to join the Guatemalan Communist party. Mirna says that many non-Communist foreigners worked for the Arbenz government, including Hilda herself, who worked for the Instituto de Fomento de Producción. Another story says Che could have worked as a

physician at the national department of statistics if he joined the *official* party, but he turned this down on principle. (See *Verde Olivo*, Havana, October 22, 1967.)

10. White, Utah-born, studied to be a Mormon clergyman. He became a Marxist, worked for a New Deal agency in the F. D. Roosevelt administration, taught philosophy, and ran a chicken farm. He went to Guatemala to participate in a process he had hoped would transform itself into a socialist revolution.

11. White told me this story in Hilda Gadea's presence in Havana on November 18, 1967. White died in 1972, and I now possess the only existing copy of his unpublished book. White also recalled an afternoon in Guatemala when he and Che were feeling depressed with the turn of events in the country. Che was waxing nostalgic. He talked about his vagabond trip through Latin American and then blurted out, "Let's get a little boat and go to the Soviet Union."

12. Fidel Castro, November 28, 1971 (in Chile).

13. They visited New York City; Union City, New Jersey; Bridgeport, Connecticut; and Miami, Tampa, and Key West, Florida.

14. Fidel spoke on November 1, 1955. He quotes this passage in a *Bohemia* article (January 8, 1956). Translation from Bonachea and Valdés, p. 283.

15. The Manifesto is dated Nassau, December 10, 1955.

16. Bonachea and Valdés, p. 287–92.

17. *Bohemia*, December 4, 1955. The column was authored by Ichaso. It is probably the first time the word *Fidelismo* is used to describe Castro's Movement.

18. Miguel Hernández "La patria No Es de Fidel," *Bohemia*, December 18, 1955.

19. Fidel Castro, "¡Frente a Todos!" (Against Everyone), *Bohemia*, January 8, 1956.

20. Translation from Bonachea and Valdés, p. 300f.

21. *Alerta*, Havana, January 3, 1956.

22. Letter dated August 26, 1956. It appeared in *Bohemia*, September 2, 1956.

23. Fidel Castro, "El Movimiento 26 de Julio," *Bohemia*, April 1, 1956. Translation from Bonachea and Valdés, p. 313.

24. Bonachea and Valdés, p. 314.

25. Ibid., p. 318f.

26. Departamento Federal de Seguridad.

27. Fidel Castro, "¡Basta Ya de Mentiras!" (Enough Lies!), *Bohemia*, July 15, 1956.

28. Article 28 of the General Law of Population of the United States of Mexico.

29. *Excelsior* (Mexico City), June 26, 1956.

30. *Excelsior* (Mexico City), June 27, 1956.

31. Cuban-born Bayo published in Barcelona in 1937 *La Guerra*

Será da los Guerrilleros (The War Will Be That of the Guerrillas). He personally led a guerrilla operation in Mallorca. (See Alberto Bayo, *Mi Desembarco en Mallorca* (Guadalajara, Mexico, 1944).

32. *La Prensa* (Mexico City), June 27, 1956. Thomas, p. 887, is wrong in naming Bayo as one of those originally arrested.

33. Luis Dam, "El Grupo 26 de Julio en la Carcel," *Bohemia*, July 8, 1956.

34. Hugh Thomas, p. 887, makes such a claim.

35. "¡Basta Ya de Mentiras!" translation from Bonachea and Valdés, p. 320.

36. Fidel Castro has paid special homage to both. On October 3, 1965, he spoke of the *greatness* of Blas Roca. On March 13, 1974, he delivered the grave-side address at Peña's burial and said, "He consecrated his whole life for the cause of the poor and exploited."

37. Blas Roca to author (Havana), May 15, 1974.

38. *Prensa Libre* (Havana), June 19 and July 14, 1955.

39. Batista at this time supported the celebration of a constitutional convention, unquestionably a progressive step, and the Communists were following their international policy of a united front against fascism.

40. Federal Judge Miguel Lavalle Fuentes ruled in favor of Castro's men and criticized the excesses of the DSF.

41. Carlos Rafael Rodríguez to author, September 27, 1972.

42. Ibid. Blas Roca also mentioned the CP's criteria to me on May 15, 1974. Roca had been secretary general of the PSP until 1961. When I spoke to him he was heading the work of drawing up Cuba's new constitution. In December 1976 he became president of the Cuban National Assembly.

43. Carlos Rafael Rodríguez to author, September 27, 1972.

44. Ibid.

45. Lester Rodríguez, *Hoy*, December 1, 1973.

46. Carlos Rafael Rodríguez to author, September 27, 1972.

47. Flavio Bravo to author, July 29, 1974, and April 7, 1975.

48. Letter from Frank País to "Alejandro" (Fidel Castro) dated Santiago de Cuba, July 7, 1957. Published in *Pensamiento Crítico* (Havana), June 1969, p. 252. Fidel in a letter to María Antonia Figueroa, secretary of finances for the M-26-7 in Oriente province, wrote: "I am able to confirm all that you told me about Frank's magnificent quality as organizer, his courage and capabilities." (Dated Mexico City, August 8, 1956.)

49. Herbert Matthews, *Fidel Castro*, (New York, 1969), p. 90.

50. Thomas, p. 868.

51. Enzo Infante to author in Havana, September 15, 1972. Enzo went to teacher's college with País, joined his revolutionary group in 1954, and was head of an attack squad during the November

30, 1956, uprising in Santiago de Cuba. Infante challenges Thomas's suggestion (p. 897) that País's followers in Santiago were primarily from the middle class. Most of them were workers or struggling teachers like himself, he insists.

52. Ibid.
53. Letter from Frank País to Elia Frometa dated July 28, 1953. Republished in *Granma*, July 30, 1973.
54. *Diario de Cuba* (Santiago de Cuba), August 18, 1953.
55. Farmers in Realengo 18, originally squatters, organized a "government" and army to defend their land against private encroachment that was supported by the rural guard. In September 1934, five thousand farmers held off the army with shotguns and machetes. There was strong Communist influence within the area. See Pablo de la Torriente Brau, *Realengo 18* (Havana, 1935). Brau later died in the Spanish Civil War.
56. *Mercury* (University of Oriente), June 1954. In the same month, País was taken before a university disciplinary committee for incidents growing out of his protest against the overthrow of the Arbenz government in Guatemala.
57. Ladeslao G. Carbajal *Paquito Rosales*, (Havana 1966), p. 24f.
58. Lester Rodríguez. Enzo Infante, one of País's collaborators, also told me of these meetings.
59. Juan Taquechel to author, January 2, 1973.
60. Ladeslao Carbajal to author, December 29, 1972, and Juan Taquechel to author, January 2, 1973. Carbajal was general secretary of the PSP in Oriente province. Taquechel was a trade-union leader and a member of the PSP provincial committee. In 1976 Carbajal was Cuban ambassador to China.
61. *Oriente* (Santiago de Cuba), November 29, 1956.
62. The call was signed by Estenio Mediaceja, Sergio Valiente, and Edunio Hernández, members of the PSP in Santiago de Cuba.
63. Carlos Rafael Rodrígues to author, September 27, 1972.
64. *Obras Agotadas.*
65. For information on the military aspects of the uprising see *Libro Segundo Instrucción Política FAR* (Havana 1959). The book was written by the political committee of the Cuban armed forces. For an account by participants in the uprising see *Revolución* (Havana), November 29, 1962, magazine section *(rotograbado).*

10: Battling on Native Soil

1. *Ernesto Che Guevara, Escritos y Discursos* (Havana, 1972), II/9. Originally published in *O Cruzeiro* (Rio de Janeiro), June 19, 1959.
2. For the best description of the landing see Faustino Pérez's account in *La Sierra y el Llano* (Havana, 1969).

3. *Granma,* December 3, 1973.
4. *Guevara Escritos . . . ,* 11/10. By this time Francis McCarthy (United Press) had reported that Fidel Castro had been killed at Niquero. See *Tiempo,* Havana, December 4, 1956.
5. Fidel Castro (speech), July 26, 1975. Fidel has also mentioned twelve as the number of original survivors. Significantly, Carlos-Manuel Céspedes, the "father of Cuban independence," was the leader of a group of twelve men who survived at the beginning of Cuba's war against Spain in 1868.
6. Universo Sánchez, one of the original band, in *Libro de los Doce* (Havana, 1967), p. 66. Edited by Carlos Franqui. Also Raúl Castro, May 13, 1960 (speech).
7. Peasant or farmer.
8. For accounts of how Pérez and García helped, see Universo Sánchez and Calixto García's account in *Revolución* (November 27, 1963). Calixto García was also one of the original band.
9. Major. Castro wanted to differentiate his army from those of Latin America where the "strongmen" were inevitably "Generals" and "Colonels."
10. Literally, *plains.* The July 26 Movement in the *llano* meant in the area outside the Sierras, in both the cities and the countryside.
11. Herbert Matthews, *Fidel Castro* (New York, 1970), p. 116. She joined the M-26-7 in 1954 and wanted to go to Mexico to join the *Granma* expedition but was dissuaded by Frank País and Haydée Santamaría. She took part in several battles and is one of the heroes of the guerrilla war.
12. *Guevara Escritos,* p. 14.
13. Ibid., p. 30f.
14. Ibid., p. 33.
15. Ibid., p. 33.
16. He found after the work was done that there was no procedure for payment, and he was afraid he might be thought as having accepted a gift. He finally ended up giving the dentist a carton of cigarettes.
17. Major Jesús Montané told me (February 20, 1974): "We know that Mr. Matthews does not agree with many things we do, but we consider him our friend." Matthews' death in 1977 rated an article in *Granma.*
18. *Guevara Escritos,* p. 191.
19. Ibid., p. 56.
20. Che Guevara, *Proyecciones Sociales del Ejército Rebelde.* This was a speech given before Nuestro Tiempo Society in Havana on January 27, 1959. It was reprinted in *Humanismo* (Havana), January–April 1959.
21. *Bohemia,* March 19, 1957. Also Herbert Matthews, *Fidel Castro,* p. 107f.

22. *Bohemia,* Ibid.
23. Matthews, p. 108.
24. Ibid.
25. *Guevara Escritos,* p. 55. From Guevara's "Pasajes de la Guerra Revolucionaria."
26. The Matthews article gave the impression that Castro had a formidable force. Raúl Castro used ruses to trick Matthews into exaggerating the number of men. (See *Libro de los Doce,* p. 111.) Matthews denies having even noticed the ruses. (Matthews, *Fidel Castro,* p. 109).
27. *El Campesino,* March 1957.
28. The Communists believed it was necessary to organize an upsurge of activity on the part of the Cuban people, especially the working class, that would culminate in a general strike like the one that brought down the Machado dictatorship in 1933.
29. Matthews quotes this in *The Cuban Story* (New York, 1961), which has a complete account of his interview with Castro. The letter is dated March 17, 1957, and is found in the Columbia University library.
30. On March 13, 1957, the Student Revolutionary Directorate, led by José Antonio Echeverría, organized an unsuccessful attack on the presidential palace in Havana.
31. Guevara, *Proyecciones . . .*
32. *Las Sierras de Oriente* (Havana, 1963). This report on the class composition of the Sierra population of Oriente, published by the National Commission of Schools of Revolutionary Instruction, is based on a two-month study by cadres in Oriente Province of Revolutionary Instruction Schools.
33. Ibid.
34. For a history of these struggles see Antero Regalado, *Las Luchas Campesinas en Cuba* (Havana, 1973).
35. Even in the highest and most isolated part of the Sierra Maestra, called *Guamá* by the *campesinos* of the area, the farmers united to defend their land, which they usually held without title from lumber and mining interests. When outsiders came to survey the land and its resources, the farmers would organize themselves into an army to resist encroachment.
36. I have conversed long hours with Antero Regalado, Facundo Martínez, and José "Pepe" Ramírez, all veteran Communists who organized and participated in hundreds of *campesino* struggles in the decades before the Revolution. I was impressed with the work of the Communists in the rural areas of Cuba, work almost totally ignored outside of Cuba.
37. The Soviet of Mabay was one of a number of areas near Cuban sugar mills where workers took physical control of the territory, ran up the red flag, and organized incipient workers' governments.
38. Francisco "Paquito" Rosales.

39. Carlos Rafael Rodríguez to author, September 27, 1972.
40. Ibid.
41. Ibid.
42. I learned from José Ramírez, head of Cuba's small farmers' association, that his full name is Conrado Enríquez.
43. *Guevara Escritos* . . . , p. 183–90. In the English version, *Reminiscences of the Cuban Revolutionary War* (New York, 1968), see chapter entitled "The Heights of Conrado."
44. They arrived in guerrilla territory on April 23, 1957, accompanied by Celia Sánchez, Haydée Santamaría, and others. They accompanied Castro's column on a march to Pico Turquino, Cuba's highest mountain peak.
45. *Instrucción Política FAR*, libro segundo (Havana, 1969), p. 260f. This book is published by the Cuban armed forces (FAR).
46. Che Guevara, *Pasajes de la Guerra Revolucionaria*, Chapter "Se Gesta una Traición." See *Guevara Escritos* . . . , p. 129.
47. This was the month Frank País was shot down by police on a Santiago de Cuba street. Castro was moved to write: "The people of Cuba do not even suspect who Frank País was, what greatness and promise there was in him." País was twenty-three when he died.
48. *Guevara Escritos* . . . , p. 123f.
49. Ibid., p. 124.
50. Ibid., p. 126.
51. Bonachea and Valdés, p. 345.
52. Ibid., p. 348.
53. Ibid., p. 348.
54. As cited in Castro's letter to the Cuban Liberation Junta of December 14, 1957. See Bonachea and Valdés, p. 352f.
55. Rojas told of his visit to the Sierra on a television broadcast, February 16, 1959. See *Bohemia*, number 9, 1959, p. 90.
56. Peligrín Torras to author, January 18, 1967. Torras was a leader of the PSP. He is now a vice minister of foreign affairs.
57. *El Campesino*, January 1958. *El Campesino* was put out by the National Committee of the PSP. It was mimeographed and cost three cents.
58. Ibid.
59. Más Martín to author, January 12, 1973. A revolutionary committee, established in Luyano, included Communists, July 26 activists, and others. It issued a daily underground mimeographed newspaper in 1957 called *Noticias* (News).
60. *Granma*, November 8, 1966. They were Rogelio Perea, Machaco Almeijeras, and Pedro Gutiérrez.
61. *Revolución* (Havana), March 20, 1965.
62. *Guevara Escritos* . . . , p. 304. The note is dated January 6. 1958.
63. *Bohemia* (Havana), February 2, 1958. Translation in Bonachea and Valdés, p. 351.

64. Bonachea and Valdés, p. 352.
65. Ibid.
66. Ibid., p. 354.
67. Ibid., p. 355.
68. Ibid.
69. Ibid., p. 357.
70. Ibid., p. 354.
71. Fidel Castro, December 2, 1961 (television panel program).
72. Letter from prison, cited in Merle, p. 348.
73. Progressive Cuban historians believe that the dissolution of the Cuban liberation army after the victory over Spain, under pressure from the United States government, was a critical historical error. Castro could not have helped but be aware of the analogous situation facing him.
74. *Carta Semanal,* January 15, 1958. *Carta Semanal* was the official underground newspaper of the PSP.

11: My True Destiny

1. This, of course, was done in the Dominican Republic in 1965, when a popular revolt threatened the existence of an army-backed civilian triumvirate that had come to power after a military coup.
2. *Manifesto Number One of the July 26 Movement,* August 1955.
3. U.S. forces remained in Cuba for four years after the victory over Spain. The United States imposed the onerous Platt Amendment on the new republic, set up another American caretaker government in Cuba between 1906 and 1909, and threatened intervention (it was not necessary) when it feared a "Communist" revolution after the overthrow of the dictator Machado in 1933.
4. José Martí's letter to his friend Manuel Mercado, written on the field of battle May 18, 1895. See *Obras Completas,* Havana 1961, volume 25, p. 95.
5. *Bohemia,* May 18, 1973, for Spanish version. The letter was printed in English for the first time in *Granma Weekly Review,* Havana, August 27, 1967. See Bonachea and Valdés, p. 379. The note was dated June 5, 1958, and was not generally known about until 1967.
6. The *llano* had carried out many sensational actions. On a single night in December 1957, they set off one hundred bombs in Havana. They won publicity by kidnapping and then returning unharmed the famous Argentine race-car driver Fangio. M-26-7 action groups executed informers, blew up some public-service facilities, etc.
7. Pérez had been on the *Granma* expedition. After Alegría de Pio, he was one of the tiny group that escaped with Fidel Castro. Castro then sent him to the *llano* to inform his followers of the fate of the expedition. It was Pérez who contacted Herbert Mat-

thews for the famous interview. Pérez then became head of the July 26 Movement in Havana.

8. Pérez has said that Castro agreed to call the strike on the basis of his information. See *Pensamiento Crítico*, Havana, August 1969, p. 74.

9. For translation see Bonachea and Valdés, p. 373–79.

10. *Carta Semanal*, March 19, 1959.

11. The PSP followed the "August line." This refers to August 1933, when strikes and demonstrations forced the overthrow of the unpopular Machado government.

12. *Carta semanal*, March 19, 1959.

13. Carlos Rafael Rodríguez to author, September 27, 1972.

14. Cited in *Hoy*, Havana, April 9, 1964. This key document, so important to understanding Castro's viewpoint, is absent from Bonachea and Valdés, volume 1 of the *Selected Works of Fidel Castro*, which covers the year 1958.

15. Clodomira Ferrals was one of Castro's messengers. Like Lidia Doce, Che Guevara's messenger, she is a heroine of the guerrilla war. Both were from poor farm families in the Sierra Maestra. They were killed by Batista forces during a joint mission in the second half of 1958, and their bodies have never been located. They are known to Cubans only by their first names. See Che Guevara, "Lidia," in *Humanismo*, Havana, January–April 1961.

16. The claim that the directive arrived too late to implement is not convincing. At least ten days remained in which to include Communists as full participants in the preparatory stage.

17. *Carta Semanal*, April 1, 1958.

18. *Carta Semanal*, April 2, 1958.

19. For a complete description of the military aspects of the April 9 operation in Havana, see *Revolución*, Havana, April 9, 1964.

20. *Carta Semanal*, April 16, 1958. For a detailed account of the strike in Sagua la Grande (Las Villas province), where a prolonged armed struggle took place, see *Hoy*, Havana, April 9, 1963.

21. *Carta Semanal*, April 16, 1958.

22. *Guevara Escritos . . .* , volume 2, p. 249–56. "The Decisive Meeting" is a chapter in Guevara's *Reminiscences of the Cuban Revolutionary War*.

23. Ibid., p. 250.

24. Ibid.

25. Ibid.

26. Enzo Infante to author, May 6, 1965. Che mentions Infante (nom de guerre–Bruno) in his account of "The Decisive Meeting."

27. Guevara, "Proyecciones Sociales del Ejército Rebelde," *Humanismo*, Havana, January–April 1959, p. 349.

28. Ibid.

29. *Guevara Escritos* . . . , volume 2, p. 258.
30. Jules Dubois, *Fidel Castro: Rebel, Liberator, or Dictator* (Indianapolis, 1959), p. 263.
31. Bonachea and Valdés, p. 387.
32. Ibid., p. 388.
33. Ibid.
34. Ibid., p. 362.
35. Fidel Castro, December 1, 1961.
36. Carlos Rafael Rodríguez to author, September 27, 1972.
37. José Ramírez to author, August 5, 1972.
38. Ibid.
39. Among them were Romarico Cordero, a legend among *campesinos* of Oriente; Miguel Betancourt; Juan Frometa; Regelino Zaldiver; and Candito Betancourt.
40. Cited in *Granma*, September 24, 1974. The article is entitled: "On the Campesino Congress in Arms."
41. At this school a *History of Cuba* text was begun— "an early attempt at a Marxist interpretation without mentioning the word *Marxist*." (Carlos Díaz to author, January 5, 1953.) Díaz is now a professor of history at the University of Havana.
42. Title IV, section 1, article 24. One of the first acts of the revolutionary government (February 7, 1959) was to modify this section of the constitution.
43. *Guevara Escritos* . . . , volume 2, p. 353.
44. Merle, p. 344. The letter was dated March 1, 1954. It was cited earlier in this book. Castro was criticizing Hugo's *Napoleon, le Pétit*.
45. Carlos Rafael Rodríguez, *La Revolución Cubana y el Período de Transición*, University of Havana, 1966. These are mimeographed lectures by Rodríguez on which his name, as author, does not appear. (University of Havana Publications F-1810 and F-1815.)
46. January 17, 1973.
47 *Hoy*, September 11, 1948.
48. Más Martín had been imprisoned after the April 9 strike.

12: "Yes, It Is a Revolution!"

1. Camilo Cienfuegos (1932–59) was one of the last men accepted on the *Granma* expedition. He was among Castro's most dashing officers and, following victory, probably second only to Fidel in popularity. In 1959 he was sent to mediate political unrest in Camaguey province, where he ordered the arrest of Hubert Matos, the province's anti-Communist chief. The plane taking him back to Havana disappeared over the sea. Every year, on the day of his disappearance, Cubans go down to the shore and cast flowers into the sea.
2. Castro's orders were that he lead his troops to Pinar del Río,

Cuba's westernmost province, just as General Antonio Maceo had done in the war against Spain. Cienfuegos was later ordered to remain in Las Villas, and he was fighting there when Batista fled.

3. See their long reports in *Guevara Escritos* . . . , volume 2, pp. 275–83 and in *Camilo Cienfuegos, Heroe del Pueblo*, (Havana, pamphlet, no date), p. 7–17.

4. Carlos Rafael Rodríguez to author, September 27, 1972. He left the Sierra on August 18. Che Guevara accompanied him as far as it was safe to do so. Rodríguez thought he would end his mission at the end of August and still find Che there when he returned, but Che's column had already left.

5. Ibid. Camagüey lies between Oriente and Las Villas provinces.

6. *Guevara Escritos* . . . , volume 2, p. 281.

7. The Escambray Second Front began operations in November 1957. In February 1958 Castro sent them the following message: "We have given instructions to the July 26 Movement to give you all possible help." He invited them to join him in the Sierra if they failed to consolidate their front in the Escambray. (Cited in *Bohemia*, March 6, 1960.)

8. *Guevara Escritos* . . . , volume 2, p. 286.

9. Faure Chaumón, "Cuando el Che Llegó al Escambray," *Verde Olivo*, Havana, December 12, 1965. Chaumón was general secretary of the Revolutionary Directorate in 1958.

10. Ibid.

11. Ibid. Che's invasion force included known PSP members: Armando Acosta (now *commandante* and a member of the central committee of the Cuban CP), Angel Frias (who rose to the rank of *comandante*), Captain Pablo Revalta (captain and head of Che's school at Caballete in the Escambray), Wilfredo Cabrera. Subsequently other Communists were sent to join Che in the Escambray: Cidroc Ramos, Guillermo Arrastía Fundora, José Galbán del Río, Ignacio Pérez Rivas, Fausto Rodríguez, Iran Pratts, and others. Che's thousand-watt transmitter was built by Pratts in Havana and taken to the Escambray, where it was run by Pratts and Fausto Rodríguez.

12. Major William Gálvez in *Granma*, December 31, 1974, special supplement on Camilo Cienfuegos, p. 33. Gálvez was one of Cienfuegos' officers during the invasion.

13. Gabriel Pérez Tarrau, Camilo Cienfuegos, *Cronología de un Heroe* (Havana, 1968), p. 43.

14. Félix Torres to author, May 10, 1966. The interview took place in Camaguey. Before the Revolution Torres had been general secretary of the *campesino* federation of Las Villas and a member of the provincial bureau of the PSP.

15. Major William Gálvez, p. 36f.

16. Ibid., p. 41. Present were Félix Torres; Wilfredo Velazquez of the provincial committee of the PSP; Victor Paneque (*Coman-*

dante Diego), chief of action of the M-26-7 in Las Villas; and Captain Regino Machado, also of the M-26-7 group in Las Villas. Paneque and Machado later deserted the Revolution.

17. Major William Gálvez, p. 44. Nogueras was officially appointed by Cienfuegos on November 16.
18. Gabriel Pérez Tarrau, p. 52.
19. Ibid., p. 51.
20. It was held on December 21, with three thousand sugar workers present. One resolution passed by the conference removed all top labor leaders of the Sugar Workers Union from office and empowered the workers to elect new representatives in liberated territories.
21. Carlos Rafael Rodrígues, *La Revolución Cubana . . .* , p. 31.
22. The following anecdotes were told me by Raúl Gutiérrez Serrano, who had been owner of one of Havana's leading advertising agencies.
23. Luis Más Martín to author, April 13, 1974. On being released from jail, Más Martín arrived in the Sierra several months after the April 9, 1958, strike. He rose to the rank of captain in the revolutionary army.
24. Ibid.
25. Ibid.
26. *Instrucción Política FAR* (Revolutionary Armed Forces), Book 2 (Havana, 1969), p. 257. The battle began on November 20.
27. Carlos Rafael Rodríguez, *La Revolución Cubana . . .* , p. 32.
28. Ibid.
29. Fidel Castro (speech in Santiago de Cuba), January 2, 1959. For text see Cuadernos de Historia Habanera, number 66 (Havana, 1959). Issued by the office of the historian of the city of Havana.
30. Ibid, p. 81.
31. "Fidel en Radio Rebelde," *Granma,* March 8, 1973, special supplement, p. 29. For English version see Bonachea and Valdés.
32. Castro speech in Santiago, January 2, 1959. *Cuadernos . . .* , p. 84. The message was addressed to Colonel Rubido.
33. For strike call see Bonachea and Valdés, p. 448.
34. Castro speech in Santiago, January 2, 1959. *Cuadernos . . .* , p. 87. Castro said that Piedra "has been until today president of the supreme court of justice where there was no justice of any kind."
35. Ibid., p. 90.
36. Ibid., p. 76. '33 refers to the overthrow of the dictator Machado and his temporary replacement by a revolutionary government. '44 refers to the election of Grau San Martín as president of Cuba.
37. Ibid., p. 91.